STONE MOTHER

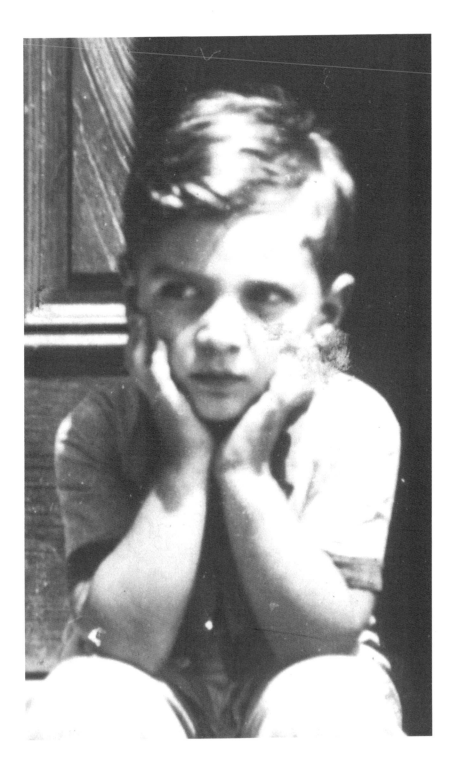

STONE MOTHER

A BROOKLYN LIFE

BARRY MENIKOFF

Cover art:
Louis Eilshemius, *Statue of Liberty,* c. 1913,
oil on fiberboard. Hirshhorn Museum and Sculpture Garden, Smithsonian Institution, Washington, DC.

Printed in the USA

ISBN: 978-1-63385-285-3
Library of Congress Control Number: 2018914210

Layout and Design by Jason Price

Published by
Word Association Publishers
205 Fifth Avenue
Tarentum, Pennsylvania 15084

www.wordassociation.com
1.800.827.7903

TO MY SISTER MIRIAM

for that far home that might have been

I sing of Brooklyn, city of myth, stone mother,
whose cobbled caress shaped me, for better or worse,
into the man I am today.

IRWIN SHAW

CONTENTS

PROLOGUE

And how should I begin? What do I remember? The evenings of silent thought summon memories out of sequence and of no consequence, as if a handful of jacks were suddenly dropped and splayed out on the sidewalk. There was a radio under the counter of my father's grocery on Belmont Avenue. In the afternoons and long evenings when I worked alone I would listen to William B. Williams, one of New York's great jockeys, who played everything from the 30s to the 50s, with Bing Crosby and Nat King Cole and Frank Sinatra holding center stage. A wit radiated over the air that I was always intent on capturing or picking up, a city smartness that I knew was sophistication, or something like, even though I could never have articulated it. There were fixtures on the dial like Abe Burrows and Henry Morgan whose cleverness I would try and absorb, but never consciously imitate. Yet looking back I see a deep desire to copy those voices, for they were beyond the streets of Brooklyn, siren songs from another city, one I knew I belonged to although it was clear across the river and far from where I lived.

Last night I saw *The Bandwagon* on a movie channel, and I recalled the first time I saw it in the theater, and how I took Fred Astaire's rendition of "By Myself" as my personal anthem *(I'll face the unknown / I'll build a world of my own / No one knows better than I myself / I'm by myself alone)*. How explain that? Why does a fourteen-year old boy identify with a song tinged with world weariness, performed by a master whose voice registered hope just below a high note and melancholy just above a low one? For I retained that song deep into the years when they matched Astaire's own, and I would sing it to myself, often after an affair gone awry, and it would provide comfort, as well as a spur to go on, accenting the hope of the song rather than the melancholy. For a young boy it seemed a smooth fit for his nascent life, as popular music would prove to be for years to come. I knew it from the radio, listening to the DJs that crowded the airwaves in New York City during the 50s, even morning hosts like Ted Brown and the Redhead *(Am I blue? / No I'm Brown)*. It would be years before I connected that clever signature with the Ethel Waters' classic, and then the song, like a madeleine, returned those early mornings before school, absorbing the comedy and play that was a part of live radio in the city. Music and banter was life to the boy born two days into a new year, one that saw the opening of the World's Fair just a borough away, a year of Hollywood's most acclaimed films *(Gone With the Wind, Stagecoach, The Wizard of Oz)*, and one that closed with the lightning attack on Poland.

BOOK ONE

1. STREET LIFE

CHRISTOPHER AVENUE. A street lying between Pitkin, just beyond the cavalcade of stores that made that place a promenade, and Belmont, one block past the pushcarts, a rundown street where my father's house was the largest on the block. We lived on the upper floor and my grandmother (*Bubbie*) and grandfather (*Zeyde*) lived below. I see my mother walking me to a nursery school nearby (no one knew the term *preschool*), down Belmont Avenue toward the train station, elevated at that point, and surrounded by what I think of as ruins but were probably nothing more than decrepit houses and broken sidewalks, for that station was one you wanted to avoid, and when I was older, and living alone with Bubbie, I mostly did. But my mother took the rumbling train from there to work—I never knew where she went or what she did—and on this day she dropped me off at the nursery, and it was there that I remember nothing more than getting sick from the food, not any of the teachers or any of the other children. I only see myself alone, in a cavernous space, and I cannot even remember my mother picking me up in the afternoon. I was three years old, four at the most, and it is the earliest memory I have.

It would be easy to link "By Myself" and "My First Memory," but that is the work of adult knowledge, where we superimpose on our recollections what we have learned over far too many years. Ideally, we should retrieve the early experience without the overlay, without the *idea* of abandonment, for what can a three or four year old make of being deposited in a dark and strange place? With the support of psychology we manufacture a meaning, but the inspiration should be Wordsworth rather than Freud, the sensory before the analytical. The nursery school survives as a joint visual and visceral image. No memories of other days, whether I was taken out of school or continued to be delivered to a warehouse without light. But those were war years, and the light went out at other times too, during the air raid sirens that shuttered the Venetian blinds and drew the curtains, while we waited in stillness for the wailing of the all clear. And I remember being in my father's car when a voice broke in over the radio and said that President Roosevelt had died, a pall covering the automobile like a shroud. But I knew the war was over when I was awakened in the darkness of the early morning by the shouting of Izzy, the local *shiker*, banging on street cans and crashing bottles on the sidewalks. While I knew he should be arrested, even at six years I sensed that this was a justifiable personal riot, and people were likely glad of the noise.

Nobody ever came to Christopher Avenue who did not live there. It was a street whose decrepitude marked its character. I have a photograph of myself on the wooden steps of some forgotten, boarded up storefront across from my house, with a pretty girl, *circa* five years old, her right arm wrapped around my shoulder. I vividly remember my sister taking the picture, prodding the girl because I was too shy to move my own arm.

Although her name survives, Elaine, I have no idea who she was. That side of the street was derelict, hence the wooden steps, but the picture has a special resonance beyond that of local color as it is the earliest sign of my closeness with girls, later women, a closeness that was either habit or trait, and one that was to dominate my life, providing some of my greatest pleasures, and no small share of pain. But here again the future is pressed upon a very old past. A plain photograph is imbued with all the inconclusive consequences of life's encounters, or put another way, those years of glorious and failed moments are compressed into a black and white snapshot, a palimpsest possibly, or merely a simple relic. The small girl holding the boy with her arm, secure in herself as she faces the camera boldly and directly. The boy, not unwilling yet coaxed into the scene, betrays a look of uncertainty, if not doubt, as to the nature of the shoot. *It's kind of wonderful, but what am I doing here?*

The picture is priceless, and draws me back to 162 Christopher, the largest home I lived in with my intact family until I was seven years old, and a world apart from the wooden steps and broken fronts across the street. It is a wonder as I think of it what my father was doing in a house out of all proportion to the rest of the street. Clearly a vestige from his years as the owner of the Zion Grocery Stores, but as my family was notorious for never speaking about anything of importance, and especially not to children, it was unlikely I would get an answer to any question about why we lived where we did. Frank (*Ephraim* was his pre-American name) was born in the year of the new century, came over from a *shtetl* in Russia-Poland in early 1921 with his sister Nettie (*Nechame*). His father followed in half a year, and two years later his mother brought over the remaining family, three brothers and one sister. Stories of the old country, so fascinating to a boy, were zipped up and consigned to a permanent state of oblivion. I'm left with two-three tales pertaining to my father, pulling them out of him in a quiet moment in the store, about the deep, quarter to half-dollar size indentations in his neck, scars from the rope strung over a tree that he hanged from until his father and a neighbor cut him down. Or about the time he slipped off a train moments before the Russians could impress him into their army. These fragments, barren of detail, are all that I have of my father's history in the Pale, nothing of his schooling, or his work, or the life of his family, just some scanty lines whose truth rests in those indelible marks on his neck that imprinted themselves on my mind ever since I was a small child.

The house on Christopher Avenue had one playroom, which must have been a place of delight for my two sisters, eleven and seven years older than me, but had little in it for myself. There were two adjoining rooms overlooking the street that made a living room, and it was there that I remember getting a brand new, fire-engine red wagon. It was very heavy, made of sturdy metal, and had a long and powerful handle that could easily pull a grown up. I could not have been more than six years old, and since we never celebrated Christmas it might have been a gift from Santa, as there seems no other explanation. I hold onto that wagon because it is the only present I remember getting as a child. When my father was working in the Brooklyn Navy Yard during the war he would occasionally bring something home, but it was never a toy and never anything a small boy would want. And yet it was exciting to see him, and to find something in his pocket, even if it was nothing more than a gleaming holder for toilet paper. I have the flimsiest of memories of my parents at this time, I suppose because I never remember their making a fuss over me, but more likely because it was on Christopher Avenue that my mother first fell ill, when I was six, and was in the hospital for several weeks. I spent the time downstairs in my grandparents' apartment, and came up to see her when she was recovering, in the spacious bedroom with its French provincial furniture, of which only a small night table survives in my nephew's home. All that ornate, hard furniture, much of which I kept when I was renting and going to college, but found impossible to hold onto when I left New York. Now I tamp down any longing for that unstylish dresser and bureau that my mother bought when it was all the rage, and she was well, but had little use for when she became ill again. It is heartbreaking to see her wedding picture, in 1927, the very heart of the jazz age, in a beautiful white dress, the loveliest of faces, and to see her twenty-one years later, at her daughter's wedding, in the dowdiest of outfits. Where did all that beauty go? Was it drained by my father's indifference? Suspended between her two illnesses? Exhausted by living just above her mother-in-law? The sweetest of women, she was no match for my formidable grandmother, who ever received obeisance from her sons, with little regard for their wives.

There was a small bakery on Belmont Avenue, near the corner of Christopher, where I got Kaiser rolls, and the occasional French cruller with white icing that I craved. My father's store took delivery of unwrapped breads, and I was used to rye and pumpernickel in round loaves, with the flour on the pumpernickel bottoms dusting off in your hands and onto the shelf. We sold *Silvercup* wrapped white bread, but nobody except the Blacks who lived in the neighborhood bought that, and I never understood how it could be eaten. My sense of bread—-of rolls and bagels and rye and pumpernickel—-was formed very early, and when I later moved away from New York I could never get used to what passed for bread in the markets. Near the bakery, often in the center of the road and leaving just enough room for a car to pass, an occasional portable cart would appear. It was a contraption straight out of a silent comedy, made of wood and strips of tin, and sold sweet potatoes wrapped in tissue-like papers with pictures of fruits. I used to wonder where all those used papers came from. There would be a small fire at the bottom of the cart that kept the food warm. I would eat the entire sweet potato, and I especially loved the skins.

The vendors were all of a piece, and looked a bit like tramps, they wore whatever was warm, as they were outside all day, but curiously they never seemed strange to me. They were the people who went with those carts, and it never occurred to me to be afraid of them. Possibly because Belmont Avenue, further down the street, from Stone to Rockaway, still had pushcarts, a holdover that carried you back to the earlier twentieth century. I used to go down those blocks, but even as a young boy I knew it was a picture from another world, although it was curb steps away from my own. There is a single photograph of the pushcarts, *c.* 1910, often reproduced in reference books, and except for the dress and general confusion of the scene, it was not much different from the street forty years later. The push-cart vendors looked much like those who sold sweet potatoes on their mobile carts, but the pushcarts themselves, a cornucopia of buttons and remnants and kitchen gadgets, were much larger and stationary, and were moved in and out of their spots flush against the curb at the start and end of the day. Years later, when I would go into the city during Christmas, just to walk around, an adolescent crossing over into a sparkling world of bells and colored paper and bustling shoppers, I would buy chestnuts from a small cart on the sidewalk in front of Macy's. And even now, when December comes round, and I hear Nat King Cole intone Mel Tormé's wistful opening line, I'm drawn back to Herald Square and the crowds bulging in and out of Macy's and Gimbels and Ohrbach's, and I like to imagine that those half-baked carts with their sweet potatoes were a subliminal part of the pleasure of those roasted nuts.

Within the densely packed blocks of my early home there was a striking variety of life, of people, and commerce, that seems extraordinary only in retrospect. From Blacks who lived in the worn tenements that fronted my father's store on Belmont Avenue, and in the newly built "projects" that raised a city overnight just a stone's throw from Christopher Avenue, to Puerto Ricans who were slowly making their migration north from "San Juan," as Chita Rivera would later immortalize it, and opening bodegas with exotic foodstuffs like rice and beans and plantains. There was a Chinese laundry on my street, past the apartment building next to our house, where you stepped down below sidewalk level into the store, and I was fascinated by the way the packages were flawlessly wrapped in brown paper, tied with white string, and then piled one on top of the other, in all their different sizes, and set against the window so they could be seen from outside. The meticulous care of that wrapping, together with the clean smell of the laundry, stays with me still. As for my people, a remainder of the early settlers of this part of Brooklyn, left behind by sons and daughters of my father's generation who made it out to Eastern Parkway and beyond, they were painters and florists and bartenders and candy store owners who populated the small apartments on all the side streets, along with the pushcart peddlers and Yeshiva teachers and displaced persons, this last another remnant who wound their way to a dying quarter.

If this mélange of peoples were crowded together cheek by jowl, however tensely and uneasily, in an odd way so too were the stores, as if commerce imitated life. Stone Avenue, which ran parallel to Christopher and perpendicular to Belmont, was a wide street, befitting its importance, with a yeshiva on the corner of Pitkin, a movie theater with a jutting marquee smack in the middle of the block, and a Hebrew school and synagogue where the pushcarts began. On one side of Stone, within eyeshot of the peddlers' market, and steps below Sutter Avenue, there was a men's store squeezed between the ordinary shops that looked completely out of place. *Ed Richilson's.* Even the writing was strange. I was familiar with Yiddish engraved on the windows of butcher shops, where *kosher* could be read in Hebrew lettering, but black-letter font was outside my experience. Not so men's stores, which were ubiquitous, as Pitkin Avenue was one long stretch of haberdasheries that I never tired of peering into. For those stores were big, usually with two great windows filled with suits and shirts and pants and belts, cufflinks and handkerchiefs and scarves and gloves. Behind that plate glass was a world apart, even if I had no idea quite what that meant, much less what to do if I took heart and walked past the open doors.

And while my nose was pressed against the glass it turned out that the largest store on the avenue, *Abe Stark's,* achieved notoriety separate from any dress distinction displayed in its windows. It was where Harry Gross, a "resplendently tailored" Brooklyn bookie, who ran a twenty million dollar a year gambling operation, sent his police grafters for free clothing. And so a store I had walked past innumerable times figured in a city-wide scandal that sent a mayor into exile, a police commissioner into retirement, and upended the entire New York City police department. As an eleven year old, I was enthralled by the story as it unfolded in the daily newspapers, and the single detail that stayed with me all these years was the offhand line that *Abe Stark's* was where the cops got their suits. I wondered at the time whether Abe Stark himself was part of the scheme, or whether he was faultless if Harry Gross paid for the clothes. But this was a legal puzzle beyond my limits, and the papers never wrote about it, and so I instead took pleasure in reading of the judge who presided over the trial, Samuel Leibowitz. He had been a great criminal lawyer and was incapable of being conned, since his "knowledge of the devious ways of the criminal was acquired from his clients at first-hand." That pulpy description would never pass muster today, but as a young boy I was thrilled that one of our own was so important, a genuine big shot (of course I knew nothing of his heroic role as lawyer for the "Scottsboro boys") and I liked to imagine that he rose to distinction from these same streets.

Ed Richilson's was nothing like *Abe Stark's*. And it was not just the small sculpted Gothic lettering as opposed to the latter's large and cursive neon script. The store was as modest in size as the other was expansive. There was a narrow walkway between the two windows, and the display carried clothes that were not anything like the gabardines and worsteds on Pitkin Avenue, and although I had no words for any of the suits, in any of the stores, my eyes told me that this was a doorway to

Aladdin's cave. It was an Ivy store on a hard-heeled street in interior Brooklyn where a tree never grew. Where did it come from? And who on earth shopped there? Nobody I saw in the streets wore clothes like that, and the men who dressed for *shul* and congregated outside on *shabbos* were uniformly drab and nondescript, a condition of their pocketbook as much as their *shtetl* taste. As I think about it, my uncle Max, the youngest of my father's siblings, would have been a likely customer. Max was the most Americanized of my uncles, very good-looking and quite dapper. I have a snapshot of him in his paratrooper uniform, cap jauntily tilted on his head, with a broad smile. He was driven to go overseas and fight Nazis, but an ear condition kept him from jumping, and he remained stateside for the duration of the war. Max was a commercial artist, that perhaps explains his style, and he had a wonderful collection of 78 jazz records that were left behind on Belmont Avenue after he married and left his mother's apartment. Those records were my introduction to Billie Holliday, accompanied by Teddy Wilson on piano, and Stan Kenton leading his orchestra at the Philharmonic. It was a private seminar held in the small living room above my father's store, and while I had no musical instruction I read the liner notes and listened religiously to the songs, imprinting the words on my mind, and for years, long before Billie Holliday was mainstreamed, I could silently sing along with her. I always felt as if Max had passed the records on to me, almost as an inheritance. Years later, when my daughter called her first son Max, with no thought of her great uncle, I took quiet pleasure in knowing that he carried the name of that brave and stoic man.

Standing on the sidewalk before the windows of *Ed Richilson's* shop, my gaze was fixed upon thick tweed coats and solid knit ties and penny loafers. And on a red-checked shirt, small

brick checks, that I could not take my eyes from. I had never seen a shirt like that before. Nor did I ever see anyone wearing one. It was not loud, but it was distinctive. And it was something I knew I wanted. But how to get it? I could not have been more than thirteen or fourteen, and I had very little experience buying clothes. Actually I had none at all. I bought a suit for my bar mitzvah, I can see myself trying it on, and agreeing to it, but I am utterly blank as to who was there. And that was the extent of my memory buying clothes. So there I am in front of a store staring at a shirt I felt a desperate need for. How would I even wear it? What with? And where to? All these questions were beyond me. All I know is that I pored my sight on that checked cloth and returned to the window several different times. I must have persuaded my father to let me buy it, and my guess is that it cannot have been more than fourteen dollars, a significant expenditure. When I had the money, I discovered that crossing the threshold proved more daunting than I expected, for I was stepping into another world, and one that was clearly not Jewish. I had to pretend to know what I was about or else reveal my ignorance, my lower class bearing, in front of people who knew about tweed coats and canvas belts and dressing in a manner that was nothing like Pitkin Avenue, the height of men's fashion, but indisputably Jewish. In some unfathomable way I was moving to separate myself from that identifying style, although I could not say what that even meant.

Intuitively I knew that *Ed Richilson's* was far away from Belmont Avenue, even though it was just yards from the pushcarts. How could a style so different, so *goyish*, be right there on Stone Avenue? And it must be obvious that the Blacks and Puerto Ricans were never identified in my mind with the world of *goyim*, for they were part of my landscape while the others were not. Except for Miss Martin, my first grade teacher, no people were visible to me as *goyim*. But this store struck me as that. Maybe I was wrong, and maybe it *was* a Jewish shop, but if so it fooled me. It was as if I had walked through the looking glass and entered wonderland. And finding myself in a strange place, and intensely self-conscious before the smooth salesman, my entire focus was on acting as if I knew what I was doing. So I asked for the shirt, but I failed to ask anything about size or sleeve length, or even about trying it on for fit. I cannot even remember whether I had enough money, or if I had to return with more. All I recall is making the buy, leaving the store, and feeling relieved, as if I had made off with some marked valuable and barely escaped notice. Yet I could not help thinking that the entire process was worth the price, worth more perhaps than the shirt itself. I had crossed a line and come back in one piece. There was no one to tell it to. It was an experience, like so many others, that I had simply to keep to myself. Many years after, wandering in Paris, I spied a checked chemise that was resting in a shop window, and paused, and for a long moment wondered if I should step inside.

Not far from *Ed Richilson's*, on the corner of Stone and Pitkin, and up the street from the synagogue, men would gather in groups on Saturday mornings, and possibly other days, solemnly standing and endlessly talking. What of? World crises? Israel and the Jews? Ordinary life seemed too mundane a topic for such a reverent assemblage. My sister remembers them too, and believes they were talking about jobs and unions, and that some men stood on boxes. That was an earlier time. I do not see any boxes. But it was a strange world of suits and coats and hats, all huddled in small pods, never raising their voices, yet always there, as if they were a seasonal element that knew no seasons, only the unending season of the Sabbath, or the gathering. To me it was mysterious and intriguing, all these men taking over a quarter of a city block, but at the same time it seemed closed and even parochial, although I would not have known that word nor understood its meaning. It struck me as old and out of place in the real world that *I* lived in, where I was always aware of the danger from the streets, of where I was walking, of how fast or how slow, how close to the curb or how far into the side of the street, a consciousness that never left me long after I left the city. But the men congregating on those mornings seemed oblivious to all that. They came together on the edge of the smartest haberdasheries in Brooklyn, yet they never looked as if they cared much about clothes. They were always decently if not respectfully dressed, but there was a dullness of color that fused in my mind with the drabness of their conversation, of which I knew nothing. My father, by contrast, who was never at these gatherings, and if they did concern unions and jobs he definitely would not have gone, took a punctilious care with his clothes—pants pressed, shirts worn clean and neat, shoes shined, and personal accessories like belts and wallets attended to. But I think now this may have been a family habit, a touch of the petit bourgeois. His brothers were like that as well. I never saw Irving in his grocery store when he did not look as neat in his way as my father; Charlie, a salesman for Sweet Life foods, dressed for travel and selling; and Max, a commercial artist, fitted himself as one who worked on Madison Avenue. One of my uncles by marriage stood out in my eyes because he looked distinctively different from the Menikoffs. He never seemed to be as concerned about his appearance, and for me this separated him. I liked him as an uncle, but I never felt he was part of the same "dress" world as they. And in some way, at that time, I thought just a little less of him for that.

Speak, memory, cried the great Russian, an epic invocation sheathed in lost estates and world capitals and multiple languages, ensuring a bountiful harvest of stylized tales, conveyed with baroque precision by a fabulist of the ever receding past. If the content evoked was far too grandiose for the son and grandson of shtetl immigrants, the exhortation itself was a talisman, spellbinding in its auditory and imaginative appeal. Speak, memory, yet how to tease out scattershot reminiscences separated in time and space, and made to cohere, marching them forward like soldiers in lockstep. For in reality they are impervious to that formal organization, constituting distinct experiences, discrete moments of self-reflection, whose importance is determined not by their chronological or logical order but by their remembering vitality. Reminiscences are like actors waiting in the wings, not even sure they are in the same play, with only the sketchiest of scripts, but prepared to deliver a performance they have waited for their entire lives, in the desperate hope that authenticity, like ripeness, will be all.

2. HEBREW TO HANDBALL

As I look back, it astonishes me how narrow was my world as a small boy. I had imagined blocks upon blocks of city streets as my bailiwick, from Stone Avenue east to Pennsylvania in the heart of East New York, south to the el that ran along Livonia, and west to Utica Avenue and Eastern Parkway in Crown Heights. The northernmost border was East New York Avenue, but for my purposes it was Glenmore Road, an unassuming street below, the site of a rich and storied public library. But all that was when I was older. When smaller I wandered over just a few streets, Christopher, Belmont, Stone, Pitkin, and Sutter Avenues, this last a thriving shopping area, with a delicatessen on the corner of Stone where I would regularly have hot dogs, forever holding the sauerkraut, and on the next corner a barber shop where I would be sent for a haircut. My father gave me the money, always silver, and then I was in the barber's hands. A heavy metal plank with a leather seat in the middle would be placed across the arms of the chair. That my hair was curly and thick and could be cut a certain way was completely outside the scope of my instructions. I have a picture of myself, *c.* two-three years old, sitting on a trunk, with high button shoes dangling half a foot above the floor, and rich full locks. No one ever remarked upon my hair except my sister, who compared it to Brillo, which I took as a sign to have it cut as close to the scalp as possible, though that was after some early adolescent days when I stood before a mirror endlessly trying to sculpt a wave on the top of my head.

But it never occurred to me then that any adult should have anything to say to me about my hair or my face or my dress. Whether I was a good-looking child, or merely ordinary, or what I might do to improve. And yet it cannot be that they were totally unaware of such physical concerns. My father was fastidious not just about dress but everything in his store, wrapping the loaves of cheese at the end of the day with wax paper in precise and even folds, arranging the cans on the shelves with the labels in exact alignment, folding his apron in half (he never put the top part over his neck) and tying it around his waist as carefully as a runner fixing his laces before a race. That was an aspect of my father's habits that I never stopped noticing from the time I was six or seven, when I first went with him to his store on Rutland Road, and played at stocking the shelves, trying hard to imitate his own neat practice. When I worked alone behind the counter and closed up at night, I covered the cheese as he did, folding the wax paper evenly and holding it tight as I secured it with a thick rubber band. Decades later, when I found myself working with the details of texts, I often wondered whether my obsessive focus on style was nothing more than the strange transfiguring of habits picked up as a boy.

Frank Menikoff had the talents of a good carpenter, and the hands for working with tools, which he did on a small scale in odd jobs around the store. It was a trade he wanted me to follow, believing that a carpenter's skill would always be in demand. It is curious how little regard he had for education, given that his own father had declared upon arrival in New York that he was a *teacher*, although what he would teach in America was a nice question. He taught *me* Hebrew before I read English, and I can still sense the fright that shivered through me every Friday afternoon when I would have to perform. I was seven years old. Zeyde would open up the glass bookcase in the small dining room where ledger size Hebrew volumes were shelved, turn to a page at random, or so I thought, and tell me to read. I was about to write that there were not even any vowel points in the texts, but that simply cannot be: it is not possible that he could have taught me without the dots and dashes beneath the letters. But he must have had some success, for he walked me over to the Hebrew school on the corner of Stone and Belmont, brought me to the rabbi, who gave me a reading test that completely escapes me, and left me with the indelible impression of a sadist, as he took my cheek between two thick fingers and twisted hard, smiling all the while. I was put in a class for second-graders, even though I was in the first grade in public school. I disliked that place because I was the youngest child there and I never understood anything. Hebrew was not a language but merely a vehicle for *shul*, something we needed to learn in order to pray, or *davnen*, which we could not do without reading quickly. It was always a wonder to me to stand in the pew, no higher than my father's waist, and watch the men as they swayed back and forth over their *sidurim*, all the while intoning like metronomes. With my limited ability I would try and read the Hebrew words, mouthing each one syllable by syllable, but after getting through a line or two the men would already be on the next page. It was a losing battle. In the end I would say a few words, glance surreptitiously at the page the man next to me was reading, and then move forward to stay abreast. I never mastered the skill of speed prayer, and on those rare occasions years later when I would go into a synagogue, usually Conservative because it felt more comfortable than the Reform temples, my shame would rise up anew when it came time to read the scripture.

Zeyde's success in moving me from that cramped space with the ledger books to Hebrew school must have encouraged him, for he wanted me to enter a yeshiva. On some intuitive level I did not want to separate myself from the world that way, although I would be hard pressed to say how I even perceived it as a separation. I simply refused to go. And to his credit he did not try to force me. To this day I cannot say what possessed me, for despite the Friday afternoon readings, and the compulsory Hebrew classes, I would never have uttered a contrary word to my grandfather. There was a stature about him, notwithstanding his short size and reserved manner. While Rose, his wife, would tend the cash register in the store, or lean out the window to catch the action on the street, or sit at a table and closely read the Yiddish newspaper (the Orthodox *Morgn Zhurnal* as opposed to the quasi-socialist *Forverts*), I never saw Harry Menikoff engaged in such commonplace activities. Yet he was the only one in the family who ever held a book in his hands apart from a *sidur*, even though I know that only from those Friday afternoon sessions. And as I think about it now, where did those cases with their ledger books come from? Clearly they were not brought from Poland but bought in America, when my father had stores and cash was flush. It is odd how my memories for all those years have been of want, and then I see in my mind's eye all that heavy furniture in the house on Christopher Avenue, and the remnants of good furniture in my grandparents' apartment on Belmont Avenue, and the thought that there was a time when they had money and bought stuff, like cars and clothes and furniture, strikes me as the strangest thing imaginable. It is as if I cannot fathom how my grandfather could have a glass bookcase filled with books while I never stepped inside a bookstore all the years I was growing up.

Yet as I write this, and think of Zeyde, I am struck by how much richer his life was than I ever envisioned as a child, when I thought he had nothing to do in this country. He led the services in our street synagogue whenever the rabbi was absent, was held in awe by the congregants, and always had a pew reserved for our family. But that profound respect could take a sudden twist toward veneration that was deeply troubling. About a year before she died, my mother came to Belmont Avenue late one morning for the sole purpose of having Zeyde touch her. In a scene that even then I associated with religious practices totally alien from Jewish belief, she fervently wanted his hands to transmit some spiritual power that she convinced herself he possessed. I was twelve years old. We were all packed into the small living room, my mother sitting on the couch, and my grandfather nearby. Zeyde was extremely uncomfortable, unwilling to perform an act such as we might see in a movie, because nobody would have any experience of the real thing. But my mother was imploring, beseeching a man whose humility was a counter against the very magic projected onto him. In the end his kindness overcame his resistance, and he made some gesture, some touch that satisfied my mother's supplication. All this while I was standing up, no more than several feet away, and unable to process what I was witnessing. I knew it was completely outside normal experience, that my grandfather's hands would have no effect on my mother's condition, yet the whole thing took place as if in another realm, one palpable and incomprehensible at the same time. I might have been in a dream except I knew I would not awaken out of it. What was most vivid, and stays with me still, was my mother's terror, and her willingness to jettison any custom, reach out for any balm that promised relief from suffering. It is sad to reflect upon, but true, that the spare memories I have of my mother in the last two years of her life are of a woman suffused with pain.

And then the next thing I knew we had gone from that house, and that broken down block, and those mean streets leading to the elevated station, and had moved to 1495 Lincoln Place, on the edge of Crown Heights, one block below Eastern Parkway. I imagined it *below* when in fact the compass pointed due north, but in my mind Eastern Parkway was the lodestar toward which everything was directed. In any case, the move for me was sudden and immediate, since nobody thought to tell me beforehand. As a seven year old, what input could I possibly offer? And what was I to object to? In spite of the size of the house I was born in I have no memory even of where I slept. Yet moving would take me away from PS 150, where I attended both kindergarten and first grade. The school is still standing, the open courtyard, broad and spacious, with two sets of wide steps leading up to it. Strikingly, the only physical structures in those neighborhoods that looked as if they were designed and built rather than raised and glued together were the Carnegie libraries and, in this case, the elementary school. Not that I would notice as a child, although I was aware of the libraries as places apart architecturally, even without knowing the word, once I started going there on my own.

But I loved going to grade school. It is a question what I liked about it. In some subconscious way I wanted to get out of the house and go somewhere that had nothing to do with my family, or maybe someplace where I would simply be noticed. Nobody walked me to school, but I remember always looking forward to it. I see myself lying on the floor in kindergarten during rest time, being told to shush and stay still, and seated in Miss Martin's class in first grade, a teacher who looked nothing like the women in the neighborhood. And she sounded different, a fact that sticks with me because she was always correcting our speech, in my case working to rid me of *tchree* and replace it with *tree*, an inverted version of Henry Higgins rummaging in the new world's Covent Garden. But the preoccupation with speech was not restricted to Irish teachers working with children of the interior. Miriam took me as a teenager to a speech therapist at Brooklyn College, hoping he might obliterate the dreaded *mockie* accent, one that sank her on her oral exam for the New York City public schools, as it earlier sank Irwin Shaw, who traced *his* failure to an ineradicable *Brooklyn* accent as opposed to any Yiddish-inflected speech.

Perhaps the prejudice that city schoolteachers should sound like Great Plains speakers had eased by then, but in any case the therapist remarked, in something of a cross between resignation and wisdom, that if he were to take me on he would have to include much of the city as well. The other thing about Miss Martin's class was bringing a dime in every Monday for the East New York Savings Bank account that we opened in school, a practice that now seems so antique as to be risible, but at the time had considerable value. I kept that bank account through college, never doubting that my loyalty would be reciprocated, and when I was in Wisconsin and needed a loan for graduate school, I turned to the East New York Savings Bank for help. Of course that was a bygone era, but the pride that went with a schoolboy bringing his passbook up to the teacher's desk in the morning, and having his ten cents recorded in ink, can still be called up, as well as the foolish wish of an older man that the original document might have been saved.

The move from Christopher Avenue to Lincoln Place could be seen in two opposing, even antithetical ways. On the one hand it was an escape from the dense compact of tenements and storefronts and pushcarts, of ceaseless movement and endless noise, to a narrow residential street of small apartments and quiet houses, tucked under a grand thoroughfare and just two blocks from a thriving commercial marketplace, Utica Avenue. What was not to like? I was too young to be conscious of the tension and fear of the growing Black population in the old neighborhood. That would come later, when I moved back, but I was intensely aware of the open streets as an almost limitless playground, and the great Lincoln Terrace Park, great to my eyes for it was the first park I encountered, was a short distance from my new home. As exciting as all this was for a small boy, it concealed the fact that the move was a catastrophic downward slide in my family's fortunes. Miriam tells me that before we came to Lincoln Place we spent a summer in Rockaway, my father running a store there that he quickly discarded. I have no memory of that. What we moved into was an apartment right behind a store, the entire cramped space a perfect railroad rectangle. I wondered why I could not picture my sister Ann there and then I realized that she had been sent to live with my other grandmother, Sarah Goldman, because there was not enough room for all of us. The entire family was forced out of a spacious dwelling and contracted into tighter and grimmer quarters. Ann simply disappeared; Miriam hated everything about the place; and the store was the barest shadow of the grocery on Rutland Road.

But I was obtuse to it all. I was not even aware until recently that the flat and store were rented, and I have no memory of the old woman who owned the site and lived above us. For someone entering the second grade in a school surrounded by streets of air and light, where I would run with my friends in later elementary years over the garage rooftops that edged the school grounds, or play Territory with knives on whatever patches of dirt we could find, Lincoln Place was Arcadia in concrete. Between the ages of seven and eleven, I lived on the streets, bounded by the elementary school and Lincoln Terrace Park on the northern and southern ends, and Utica and Ralph Avenues on the western and eastern sides. It is astonishing to me, as I think about it, how much fun I had then in the midst of such unhappiness. Miriam has told me how she suppressed everything about that time. My sister Ann will not speak of it at all. And despite living cribbed and cabined I have little sense of

my parents' lives, except for two moments that clearly suggest the terrible stress they were experiencing. My father, who could be blind to others' needs, to his wife's and later my own, was incongruously one of the kindest of men. Yet one time he chased me back to the end of the apartment, which was my parent's bedroom, and raised his arm above his head as if to strike me. He never did, and to this day I have no idea what act I committed, but I cannot forget the remorse I felt as I cowered and waited for the blow to fall. I am sure it was something awful, and it can only have had to do with my mother. I must never have gotten over the guilt for it to remain burrowed so deeply under cover for so long.

The other moment was when my mother told me there was nothing to eat for dinner. I was nine or ten. What she said seemed preposterous to me, even at that age, since the kitchen was the first room behind the grocery. We were not in some far away country whose name was called out when you did not finish the food on your plate. Yet she was serious, and distraught, and turned aside my offer to get a can of tuna fish from the store. I am sure it was an act of despair, a cry against the scantiness of their resources that was frustrating her ability to prepare a proper meal. But I was her youngest child, her baby really, and in the end she could not stay defiant at my expense. She boiled some potatoes, mashed them, and brought out a carton of sour cream from the refrigerator. I never forgot that meal. The table was flush against the wall, about two or three feet from the door to the store. I was sitting at one end, with my back to the door, and my mother was standing close by, watching me eat. Even now, when I think of that poor woman, I sometimes wish she knew how much I loved those potatoes.

Odd how that cramped space in the middle of an undistinguished street filled up with memories out of all proportion to its size. There was a small wood radio in the living room in the form of a gabled house, its two sloping roofs painted bright red, the base white, with two brown knobs for dials. Crafted by a tall, Black handyman named Joe who did occasional jobs for my father, that radio was the center of my life, carrying fifteen minutes of Abe Burrows and a half hour each of "Mr. Ace and Jane" and Henry Morgan. There were the serials, "Mr. Chameleon," "The Shadow," "Lux Radio Theater," and "The FBI in Peace and War," sponsored by Lava Soap, with its thumping introduction spelling out the initials in stentorian tones—L A V A L A V A. I knew that the black, brick-like soap was a rough cleanser for hard men, like auto mechanics and plumbers, although I could not figure out why it should be the sponsor for FBI agents, and I sometimes used it when my hands were dirty, or when I thought they were. I had no patience for "Baby Snooks," and thought it ridiculous that someone as old as Fanny Brice would be playing a child, a detail that must have been passed on to me, as I knew nothing about her or her status as a Jewish icon.

But one show I never missed, if I could help it, was Jack Benny's on Sunday evening. While Burrows' drollery and Goodman Ace's light wit were appealing, and Henry Morgan's anarchic humor made him a cult figure for all of us who grew up with Mad comics, it is less obvious what Jack Benny's attraction entailed. I loved the characters and their voices: Eddie Anderson as Rochester, "Oh, Boss," a signature that would lose a sitcom its slot today; Dennis Day, an Irish tenor with a too sweet repertoire; Don Wilson, a booming pitchman for what would become an anathema, Lucky Strike cigarettes; and Phil Harris, all Southern jive and risqué banter. And then there was Benny himself, a familiar, knowing voice, rising, falling, ever pausing, someone who gave his cast a wide berth yet was in full command of the entire production. Even then I knew that his constructed portrait—-penny pinching, off-tune fiddler, permanently thirty-nine, forever "feuding" with Fred Allen——was part of the show's masquerade, a broad joke that everybody agreed to keep quiet about so as not to spoil the fun. That Sunday night program offered bite size situation comedy before the phrase had any currency, and it is surprising to ponder how deeply stored those images were, for years later, when describing a comic dilemma in Kidnapped (the peril to your life or the danger to your purse), I found myself inwardly smiling as I obliquely alluded to Jack Benny's unforgettable response——"I'm thinking it over."

But for a nine year old the radio was more than serials and comedy: it was the voice of baseball. And for me it was the voice of Mel Allen and the New York Yankees. I remember listening to the game that Hank Bauer opened in——he hit well and got on base a couple of times——and ever after he was sealed in my mind as someone I was connected to. He never had the celebrity of Mantle, Berra and Ford, or the notoriety of Billy Martin, but my having heard the broadcast of his debut game made him special. And the story of his years as a combat Marine only polished the picture of one tough Yankee. It is strange how one fastens on a ballplayer, or a team, the reasons beyond what you can understand or are even aware of. In those days, with three ball clubs in the city, there was no shortage of stars to go around, and the clichéd arguments over the best centerfielder, or shortstop, or second baseman, were part of every boy's daily harangue. If you lived in Brooklyn you did not advertise your allegiance to the Yankees casually, even to your friends, and certainly not to strangers. Yet my attachment to a team from an unknown place with a name like a joke had the simplest of explanations. My uncle Irving, married to my father's sister, was originally from the Bronx and a fanatic fan. One day he decided to go to the Stadium and take me along. It was my first baseball game. The Yankees were playing the Cleveland Indians in a very tight pennant race. Of all this I knew nothing. I was just excited to *make the long trip on the subway and to be in the stadium. At one point, whether early or late I cannot remember, the Indians' player-manager, Lou Boudreau, was up at the plate. Boudreau had the most unorthodox batting stance imaginable: he stood as if facing the pitcher directly, and crouched as if he were squatting. I could not figure out how he could even hit the ball. I do not know who was pitching, but the next thing I knew Boudreau had smashed a drive to left field, covered by Johnny Lindell, that was a clear triple or an inside the park homer. And then, as if out of nowhere, an aging center fielder appeared on that great green expanse, put up his glove, and caught the ball. I can imagine going to a season's worth of games, waiting for one or two spectacular plays, and never seeing anything as beautiful as that catch.*

That was the only time I saw Joe DiMaggio.

After, when I went to ball games by myself, I would go to Ebbets Field, since traveling to the Stadium was out of the question. But I never went that much, and I never became a Dodgers fan, even in that fabled season in 1951 with their tie-breaking game against the New York Giants, as I was standing in the cramped backroom of my father's store, hoping that nobody would come in, and listening to the play-by-play, along with every pulsing body in the city, when the crack of Bobby Thomson's bat ended their gasping hope for a pennant. Anybody who heard that shot would always remember exactly where he stood at the time, just like the announcer who went wild before the ball cleared the stands. When the Dodgers finally left Brooklyn for Los Angeles I was already in college, and baseball had begun its recession into my small past, and even the Yankees, who were still in their glory days, no longer enthralled me. I often wondered, when I got older, where all that enthusiasm went, how it happened that a boy who scored the games and memorized the averages and idolized Jimmy Cannon suddenly turned indifferent to the explosion of teams and races and stratospheric statistics. *I followed Sandy Koufax a bit, probably because he was so commanding an athlete and decidedly Jewish, but I would not bet on which factor carried more weight. In a way, except for the superstars of other teams—the Fellers and Kiners and Musials—I was remarkably parochial in my baseball culture, endlessly juggling the players between three boroughs and otherwise ignorant, perhaps even indifferent to the dozen other cities that fielded teams.*

As I write this, I am struck by the great gap between what we knew then, what we were able *to know, and what we know now. With a couple of keyboard clicks a nine year old today can find out all the Jewish players in every conceivable sport. It is surprising how much casual chatter turned on who was famous and Jewish. It is as if we were legitimated by our identification with important people, although nobody would have said that. Yet on some visceral level we all knew. Our knowledge was akin to secret information, passed along from person to person, my brother-in-law telling me about watching Hank Greenburg at batting practice, somebody remarking apropos of a beer display that Bess Meyerson was Miss Rheingold before she became Miss America, everybody in the neighborhood aware of Max Zaslofsky, who played for the Knicks and went to high school in East New York. And then there was Danny Kaye. I could recite the childish verses to his junior high song—*
149 is the school for me / Drives away all adversity / Steady and true / We'll be to you / Loyal to old 149—*even though I never went there nor even knew where it was. Famous beyond measure, I memorized and mimicked his rendition of "Dinah," with its elongated e throughout, and tried to do the same with his patter songs, but for those I managed no more than a handful of lines. If that effort seems absurdly misplaced——my tin ear opposed to his perfect pitch——it was driven, or reinforced, by the inside knowledge that Danny Kaye was kicked out of Thomas Jefferson (my* school) *for*

cutting up in class. Where did that come from? It had no identifi-
able source. It was another piece of folk knowledge, like the gossip
about quotas for Jews at Columbia and the Ivy League, stories that
sounded serious but had no real meaning since no more than one
or two of us ever went to Columbia, and for sure nobody went to
Yale or Princeton. So what did these legends amount to? Why did
they hang on? They were part of the learning of the street, a reserve
of undocumented truth that we grew up with and took for granted.
If it turned out, when we were grown, that these stories were true,
that did nothing to alter the reality of how we received them, as
articles of faith, emblematic vignettes in the lives of our people. And
ambition, or dreams if a softer word is preferred, thrives on myth.

I loved sports, but I was small and inept at basketball,
the default activity in the city, since every corner playground
scrunched into the street came with an attached hoop and
backboard. As for baseball, it was at Lincoln Terrace Park that
I first saw a ball field open to the public. We never played on
that field, and I doubt we ever thought about it. Clearly the
green was reserved for official teams, but none of the boys on
Lincoln Place and the near streets were involved in anything as
organized as an activity. Mostly we ran through the sidewalks
and gutters playing whatever thrown together games we came
up with, like Ring-a-Levio, using car fenders as prisoners' bases,
and Johnny on a Pony, which had an element of roughhouse
danger about it but was never sustained for very long. I had to
suck up the taunts that were directed at me during this jousting,
namely "four eyes," since I wore glasses as early as age seven,
and "walking encyclopedia," the occasion for which eludes me
completely. Yet I remember getting a wonderful leather baseball
glove that I oiled religiously, and slammed a ball endlessly into
the pocket in order to break it in. It was certainly a sign of how

much the game meant to me then. Because I was short I pictured myself at second base, and I dimly see a signature on the glove of George "Snuffy" Stirnweiss, onetime second baseman for the Yankees. Of course this was all in my imagining, for I was on no team that assigned me a position, and could do nothing with the glove except catch a ball. And where would I do this? And who with? A hardball was out of the question and may even have been prohibited at the park. So there I was with my beautiful glove, all prepped but nowhere to go. I wish I knew how I got that glove, for it meant so much to me, and I wish too that I knew what happened to it, for it was the only sports gear I received as a boy.

But if the prospect of playing serious ball on a green was more illusion than reality, there was another kind of ball that was always with me—the versatile, many-faceted spaldeen. That small, high-bouncing, pink globe has, with the passage of time, entered the realm of folklore, and the very name "spaldeen" conjures images of city streets and city games that have been mythologized beyond their borders. Memory fails at how and where I learned to catch, but I became so proficient with this quintessential street prop that even today I surprise myself when I find those old skills intact. I played my share of boxball, a version of table tennis *sans* table or paddle, on two sidewalk squares with the groove between as an imaginary net, and Chinese handball, an easy game for fooling around, played against any building on the street, as long as the windows were at least half-a-story high, and the sidewalk squares were in alignment. The streets were not wide enough for stickball, as there was no way you could swing a piece of wood as long as a broom handle without causing some kind of damage, and as for punchball, it demanded a steadier and more controlled fist than I was able to muster. But the proximity of Lincoln Place to the Park gave me the chance to excel at one *spaldeen* game that I loved— handball. Perhaps "excel" is not the right word. I never played in tournaments, did not even know if there were tournaments, yet I would go to the park with my ball, play in pickup games, and handle myself creditably. Handball gave me a confidence that no other sport did, for my size did not work against me, in fact it may even have helped me, as I was nimble and fast on the court. A part of me would like to estimate how many games I played on those four concrete courts at Lincoln Terrace Park, but that would be fruitless. More to the point is the purpose and determination with which I marched up Rochester Avenue and crossed Eastern Parkway and dropped down the hill to those courts, started throwing the ball against the concrete wall, hitting it with the open palm of my right hand, and waited for anyone around to play with. In those days the Park was safe, or so it felt, and the only thing that darkened the day was the onset of dusk, when there was no longer light enough to see by, and even a pink ball got lost in the air.

Elementary school and Jewish school made up the other part of my life in Crown Heights. Although I was unhappy about leaving PS 150 on Christopher Avenue, my distress was eased by the assurance that I would be skipping a grade in the new school because of my reading ability, although why that would have any meaning for a six or seven year old is beyond me. Even more to the point, I have no idea where that notion of skipping a grade comes from or why it sticks so hard in my head. While my memories of Zeyde teaching me Hebrew are palpable, I do not know when or how I learned to read English. I was never read to as a child, and in my memory there were no children's books in my house. That was not the case for my sister, who cherishes the books our mother bought for her when she was very young. She loved *Heidi,* and was captivated by the illustrations of Arthur Rackham and N. C Wyeth, who inspired her talent for drawing and design. Mama also secured a collection of classical records by clipping coupons from one of the New York dailies, a gambit I recognize because I remember her faithfully going to the movies on weekday evenings in order to collect dishes, when the theaters gave them out as a way of drawing people in on an off night.

But if Miriam had books, she has no memory of Mama reading to her, so we were both left to fend for ourselves, and the only conclusion we can draw is that we learned to read in school and became adepts. Yet when I hear how involved our mother was with Miriam as a child, I can only regret that it was not the same for me. Yet that is not quite true, for you can neither miss nor regret that which you never had. What saddens me is the recognition of how little time our mother had for the pleasures of being a mother, or how little time she had for any pleasure. Miriam was sixteen when Mama got sick, and I was five, and Mama never fully recovered from that first illness. So she was unwell all those years at 1495 Lincoln Place, when I was going to school, playing handball in the park, following the Yankees on the radio, and running through the streets like a *vilde khaye*, or wild animal, as Bubbie would say. How could I see or imagine my mother's life? I was nothing but a boy reveling in the freedom to roam the world outside the walls of that tightened railroad apartment, and that nearly empty store, with very little to constrain me. In an odd way I was lucky, for had I the smallest understanding or the merest perception of what my mother was going through, then those halcyon days would have been even briefer than their fabled few.

A hotchpotch of memories that challenge meaning but cherish being, flotsam floating deep in the chambers of the mind, sufficient unto themselves, as if to say survival is enough, simply the remains of the day, or a life. On the corner of Belmont and Stone stood a great red cylindrical fire alarm box, with a round pedestal you could stand on while holding your arms around the post, and as I swung on this stationary playpiece, my feet on its narrow ridge, I instinctively gripped the handle of the alarm to keep from falling, somehow disengaging the guard, and the next thing I heard were the ear-piercing peals of a fire alarm screaming through the street. Even at that early age I knew that it was taboo to pull a false alarm. I could not separate in my head who might find me, the firemen or the policemen, but in any case I ran terrified to my grandmother's apartment, straight into her bedroom, which had a large vanity that stood kitty-corner before two adjoining walls, and I squeezed myself behind the vanity somehow, pulled my legs up to my chest, and prayed that nobody would find me. Another memory touched on comic books, which I loved, Captain Marvel especially, and the Classics Illustrated series. One day I was browsing through the selection in a candy store on St John's Place, one block up from our apartment, and there was a new book that I wanted. To this day the name of the colored comic eludes me, but the intensity of my desire does not. I am clueless as to how I stole it, although I see myself turning the rack that displayed the treasure, my eyes moving surreptitiously from the owner to the graphic, and I remember walking home quickly with my stash, accompanied by irregular twinges of conscience. I cannot say whether I enjoyed the book, for the next thing I knew my mother had discovered my caper and made me return it alone. I had to go back to the store, address the owner and tell him what I had done. She did not give me a dime to buy the book. Mortification is not a word I knew, but the shame stayed with me long after. Yet it is only now that I think of the incident in terms of my mother rather than myself, for it is the one moment I have of her teaching me a lesson, a small one to be sure, but dear for all that.

3. I'VE GOT NO STRINGS

WHILE I WAS COMFORTABLE at the Christopher Avenue elementary school, I was even more so at PS 191 on Park Place, three long blocks north of my home. But there was one problem that followed me through early school: I was something of a talker, and my mouth was constantly getting me into trouble. Although there is a certain farcical quality to disputing this now, as a boy the issue was beyond my knowing. I will not plead the rigidity of teachers and their hidebound habits, but I have no idea what I did that warranted branding as a troublemaker. Yet in the fifth grade I had a teacher who issued demerits for misbehavior. I received more than my share, and my mother was called to school to meet with the teacher. Strangely, he did not dislike me, nor I him, and I vaguely sensed that he wanted to talk with my mother about my abilities as a student. Odder still, while I resented her coming to school because of the physical hardship it imposed on her, I harbored a secret satisfaction at being singled out among my classmates. And there was one upside to this particular class. It was the first one where I consciously flirted with one of the girls. She sat in front of me—the desks fastened to the floor, with the tops opening up to hold supplies—and I played with her brown hair, and very quietly sang some of the words to "Nature Boy," then all the rage. I marvel now at my obliviousness to my perpetual off-key manner, which never kept me from breaking into song, until many years after, when I would go to a piano bar in Honolulu where everybody sang, and the maestro would often nod to me for some tune, but I always refused. At that point I was far too self-conscious of my musical failing. In any case, I asked the girl to go the movies, we did, and that may be the last I remember of my early flirtation.

Our teacher was also head of audio-visual equipment, which meant he ran the movie projector. And *Pinocchio*, which had been reissued about three years earlier, was being shown to the upper grades. Since he was in charge of running the film, we sat through three showings. What I remember most was Jiminy Cricket, the enchanting song that won an Oscar, "When You Wish Upon a Star," and the tumultuous rushing water, with Pinocchio's boat being tossed about like something made of balsa wood. But what stayed with me more than the movie was the sense of privilege I felt at being dismissed from regular class and sitting through a loop of screenings. It was my first experience in elementary school of any sort of ranking, where a teacher's skill or position set one class apart from another, and you were granted a special privilege, even if it was one you were not especially interested in. That was an accidental if rudimentary recognition that all things were not equal, hardly a lesson that anyone coming from the interior of Brooklyn needed to learn. You faced it the moment you stepped out into the street, and the farther you walked, and the more you were exposed to, only hardened the lesson: everybody is different, and given natural ability it is only striving that counts. The child in the darkened classroom, distracted from *Pinocchio* by the second and third showing, mused on the idea of being in that room on a special pass, one that gave him the freedom to linger on, when everybody else was a visitor for the moment. Years later, in Florence, I bought a wonderful wooden Pinocchio doll for my namesake girl, who was a little smaller than the boy when he watched the animation. She has it still.

What seems surprising about random memories is how they can be so intact and yet incomprehensible at the same time. Mr. Goldensohn was the teacher for the sixth grade. He was tall, of that I am certain, although what tall meant to an undersized ten or eleven year old would be hard to say. I have no memory of learning poetry, nor did I see him fling a class assignment into the garbage before the students' eyes, as other classmates recounted of their experiences, but thre was one startling incident. I was at my desk in the front row, he was writing on the board, his back to the class, when suddenly he wheeled around as if on a pitcher's mound and fired an eraser directly at me. He hit the sweet spot in the middle of that immovable wooden fixture. I imagine that I was talking—what else could have set him off?—but the ferocity of the pitch astonished me, and I sat there mute. Not that I would have dared say anything after that assault, which I suspect surprised him almost as much. But it was over as quickly as it began, with no words of apology or explanation. I picked up the chalked eraser and returned it to the narrow shelf that ran along the blackboard. Of course the boy with the mouth was at fault. And the man in the suit had the prerogative. Yet it is curious how matters of power and position play out even in an elementary school classroom, where the relations between teacher and students, and among classmates, are continuously threaded and ripped apart, much like Penelope's weaving.

If Mr. Goldensohn had a hair-trigger temper, he encouraged one craft activity that suited me wonderfully—working with leather. He allowed us to make small items, mainly key chains and coin purses and wallets. The size restriction was determined by the limited supply of leather, but even more by the belief that because we were novices it would be smarter to conserve rather than waste material. For some reason I was given permission to make a briefcase, with enough leather to dwarf a dozen coin purses. I relished working with a large piece of hide, aware I was making something unique. I wish I could detail the process, or the tools I worked with, but the best I can offer is that I stitched a zipper all along the top, and the case was large enough to fit a legal size notebook. The capstone of the project was when Mr. Goldensohn took me out of the classroom to go to the principal's office, briefcase in tow, to show off the finished work first-hand. We ran into her in the hallway instead, a smile, a plaudit or two, and so much for the long work of craft construction. In a strange way the feeling was much like what I came to know later, an amalgam of satisfaction, recognition, and a nagging disappointment. I held onto the briefcase, and used it, for as long as I could, but it disappeared along with the few other things from those early years that meant something to me. Still the experience left me with an abiding love for cowhide, and I could never after resist a kiosk or store that specialized in leatherwork, whether in New Mexico or anywhere in Italy.

And then there was the Mendele Folk Shul, as it was known, although it was not a synagogue but a school. My mother enrolled me when I was nine, as I have vivid memories of hawking stamps for Israel on the wide, open sidewalk outside the Utica Avenue subway station. It was during the war right after independence. The school was located at 259 Utica Avenue, a block away from our apartment, with the station half a block further. While I knew we were supporting the state of Israel, we were more conscious of helping Jews in trouble. Money was needed to buy arms, and Jews from as far away as Brooklyn were enlisted, although it would be laughable to imagine how little I knew of where Israel was in relation to New York City. But the school tasked us with aiding the war effort, and I did not object, mainly because I liked the place. It was a dramatic contrast with the Talmud Torah, where you were trained as a performing seal, while here you were expected to understand what you were taught.

For those who knew, there was a rich tradition behind the folk school movement. Zionism was one stone of its foundation, Jewish history and culture another, and Yiddish language a third. In retrospect, they probably erred in not promoting Hebrew as the proclaimed language of Israel. But their eye was fixed competitively on the local Talmud Torah, whose only interest was Biblical Hebrew, while they were determined to hold on to the voice of the remnant of the Shoah. Of all this I knew nothing. But I enjoyed learning Yiddish because it made sense and seemed practical. I could pick up the *Morgn Zhurnal* and read a page. I even remember once attending a Yiddish play with my grandmother on Eastern Parkway, up in the balcony, sitting forward and straining to understand, aware of the physical place, my own presence, and wondering all the while what my grandmother was doing there. I was oddly proud of what I thought of as my facility, even though I was nowhere near fluent, and could read more easily than I could speak. Many years after, when even the bits of language that I retained had atrophied, I sent a card to my father and did my best to inscribe it in Yiddish. Although we had almost no communication at that point, my sister told me much later that he was impressed that I wrote to him in his language, possibly the only thing he ever praised me for. Of course this was long ago, and a sea change in language learning has since taken place. Yet I looked forward to that school, except that I studiously avoided calling it "Hebrew school." And whatever slim knowledge of Jewish history I possess comes from those early classes one floor up and a door or two away from a sedate Manufacturers Trust Company bank building.

The event that culminated my time at the Mendele Folk Shul was a theatrical one. I played the role of Mordechai in a Purim play that was an elaborate production for a streetside school. There were full costumes, lines to be memorized, and a fair amount of rehearsal time. The upshot was that I won an award for best performance, a large, beautifully illustrated Haggadah. I cherished that prize long after, not for its utility, it could never be a working text for a seder, but because it was the first book that I ever received for myself. Although no member of my family attended the Purim pageant, one or two years later I was at Rolling Hills day camp in Searingtown, Long Island, courtesy of Miriam and her husband Harry, who were counselors there, and I was selected to play Tom Sawyer in the camp's summer finale. That performance so impressed them, especially Harry, who would periodically bring it up, that it was as if they had discovered some juvenile Marlon Brando in their midst. Miriam pressed me to apply to The High School of Performing Arts. Maybe if they did not live on the Island, and were around to badger me, I might have. But what did I know? Go to school in Manhattan when all my friends were going to Crown Heights or East New York? Do something so far outside the range of my clipped and narrow street experience? Unimaginable. By such absurdities are our lives arranged. When I think of it I am always amazed at how much more sophisticated Miriam was about education and the possibilities for life than I was. She wanted to go away to college. Recruiters had come to high school seeking girls as potential students for nursing school, the tuition to be underwritten by the Navy. I doubt that she was eager to be a nurse, Jewish girls did not become nurses, except for my cousin Evelyn, yet the opportunity to get out of a closed if not grim home could hardly be turned down. But for her parents it was as if she were asking to leave for *another world*, whose strangeness can only be conveyed by the Yiddish term—*yenevelt*. There was no discussion. *What discussion? It was just no.* When my turn came, there was no one around to not discuss anything with.

When I think back on the Mendele Folk Shul, I sometimes wonder how my mother knew of it, even though the school was barely a block away, and its politics far closer to my mother's family than my father's. She was the only one who cared enough to find a place for me. When I say I *wonder* it is not doubt but rather a side effect of blankness, for I have no picture of my mother ever going out and doing anything as ordinary as shopping, and certainly not with me. And yet she must have, for I remember going to the Horn & Hardart near Union Square. How could a small boy forget those great white marble counters, the cashier flipping nickels like falling dominoes, the sound almost as exciting as going up to the glistening compartments lined against the wall, slotting in the coins and waiting a moment to open the door, and then drawing out a chicken pot pie, which years later I would give to my own children for dinner after their swim practice. I can only believe I was there with my mother, for she had gone to Washington Irving High School nearby, and S. Klein, that monstrous emporium of bargains, was smack in the center of the square. There are a few memories of being on the bus and train with her, and the first, as if I were there now, when my mother told me to say I was five if the conductor questioned me because she was not going to pay my fare. As it happened, he asked how old I was, and I believe I was seven but I said five, and he shook his head in disbelief. I was angry and embarrassed. Why could she not pay for me instead of shaming me into being littler than I was? I was small but not a baby, and I resented being treated as one. And yet when I think of it now, and still remember how red I was, I think too of how hard it must have been for her to play such a charade. What could the fare have been? It was probably not more than a nickel, a dime at the most. Writing this now even the words—*nickel, dime*—sound like the relics they are, unable to conjure up what a woman went through to keep herself and her child together with any dignity. All I see is the boy's red face. I cannot see the mother's anguish.

Every story is selective, and the greatest art coldly and strictly so—"Oh, if I knew how to omit I would ask no other knowledge." But life is not a story until it is told, and before the telling it is nothing but a jumble of incidents bound in a tangle, with no simple way to pull apart the coiled and knotted threads. Enter linear time, with its tenacious grip on our memories, sorting them into platoons of meaning with indifferent yet ruthless efficiency. And so a life's tale begins, forced to deliver itself intact and in order. Artists like Proust and Joyce et al. take it upon themselves to pluck memory from where they will, before and after, in consciousness or out, and offer up a story that begins anywhere and ends nowhere. But they are free fictionists, endowed by their muse and indulged by their audience. The memoirist has not the same license: confined and contracted, he wrestles memory in due course, and nods all the while to the god of latitude.

4. THE OLD MUSIC BOX

My sister Miriam was a presence in my life at 1495 Lincoln Place, although I find it almost impossible to conjure up a physical image of her there. A young boy who spent his time roaming the streets when outside grade school could hardly be bothered with a woman who was already in Brooklyn College and dating a war veteran. Yet there were traces of her in my life even before Lincoln Place, as there was a phonograph in the basement of Christopher Avenue, and I remember rummaging around for records and playing "Mam'selle" over and over, either the Art Lund or Dick Haymes version. I could not have been more than seven, and it is strange how Mack Gordon's bittersweet lyric stayed with me, as I certainly cannot have understood it at the time (*And yet I know too well / Someday we'll say goodbye / Then violins will cry / And so will I, Mam'selle*). When I was older, bidding goodbye to a girl whom I had met in the summer, it was natural, almost cinematic, to sing a late thirties standard that was revived by Patti Page (*I know that I'll / Be contented with / Yesterday's memory, / Knowing you think of me*

/ *Once in a while*). At that age it made sense to self-consciously use popular songs to lament a love gone off-track. It was a city boy's rendering of Werther's sorrows. But looking back I find myself fastening on that ordinary phonograph on a discarded table under the house, a picture forming in my mind of a small café and a foreign scene, brought to life by two-three words. It may have been the start of my love affair with popular music, or simply the signal for a succession of songs layered through the years, each replacing the other with its own fresh memories, and all taken together making a harmony or a dissonance of a heart's life.

As for my sister's boy friend, Harry Kazenoff, I first became aware of him on Lincoln Place. He was six feet tall, slender, with striking good looks. He could not have been in the house minutes when I told him that he must have been older than my father because he had more gray hair. Any man in that situation, his eye on a woman and confronted with her nine year old brother, would find some way of playing down the remark. Harry responded with a light laugh, comfortable, engaging, and without a trace of unease or embarrassment. That was the first time I met the man whom I would grow to love as a brother. And in those early days of their courtship I never felt like an encumbrance. Miriam saw marriage as a way out of that tight apartment behind the grocery store, and it is a small if meaningless irony that her new address was still Lincoln Place, albeit 797, a second story flat in a brownstone further west. It was a young couple's perfect first apartment, on a block of stone houses with bow windows, shaded by trees. Miriam decorated the kitchen by painting the walls with birds, a touch that so impressed me I never ceased to marvel at it when I went over, since I never could trace the simplest line of a figure. She drew clever sketches of her college friends, and one had a distraught woman, a tear or two falling on her cheek, with the caption "I'm Just a Prisoner of Love." I can see myself pestering my sister, wanting to see the pictures, which fascinated me, having no idea what they meant, and yet pulled in by the caricature and slight raciness of the sketching.

It was odd to have an older sister who could make magic like these drawings, and yet not know anything about her life, as she was not at the front of my mind. I have only the vague sense that she was in college, and even less of what it

signified. When I asked her about the caption to the sketch she told me it was a song that the girl went around singing. Much later I learned the words—*Alone from night to night you'll find me / Too weak to break the chains that bind me / I need no shackles to remind me / I'm just a prisoner of love*—it had been a hit for Perry Como when the women were in college, and then the drawing and the song merged so that a boy's memory of the one was overlaid with an adult's understanding of both, either tainting the original memory or amplifying it. In another empty irony to my sister's marriage, she could not wait to rid herself of a blatantly Jewish name like *Menikoff* and succeeded only in collaring *Kazenoff* as a replacement, which may speak to nothing more than the ubiquity of the emigrant community in Lynn, Massachusetts as well as Brooklyn. If the second generation lived further afield than the first, they remained largely within the circle, even though their ambitions diverged sharply from their parents. My sister went to college against our father's wishes. As for what she studied, women did not go into gallery or museum work, which would have suited her, and certainly not poor ones from Brooklyn.

Was I a forced presence in Harry and Miriam's young married life? I am inclined to say *probably,* but that would only be in retrospect. They spent the summer after their marriage in Belle Harbor, in an attic room in an old Victorian house with a porch, very near the beach, one of the loveliest parts of the Rockaway peninsula. I passed a weekend with them there, in that large room, and wondering why I was there. I knew enough to know that they were a married couple and I was thrust into their small space, making it even closer. But I also knew I was being sent away to give my mother some relief, as well as offering me a weekend away from the city. I wonder now how I got there. I likely went alone, for by ten I was used to traveling by bus and subway, and I can imagine taking a train from Utica Avenue to the New Lots station, the last on the IRT line, and a bus from there to Rockaway. Livonia Avenue stays in my mind because it was shrouded in semi-darkness by the el, the kind of street noir filmmakers loved. It was also the odd site of *Fortunoff's*, a shopping mecca for women whose name was as familiar as *Abraham & Straus*. It was also where my father took me on a few occasions to a seedy movie house that showed three films. I doubt I was more than six. It was the only thing he did outside of work. We drove to the movies, parked somewhere on the street, entered a dismal place for the next three hours, and then rose out into the dim daylight and returned home, with no stop on the way back. There was always a Western on the bill, and my memories of Randolph Scott, that complete cowboy, are forever linked with that movie house, since he was never in a film that would be shown at the *Loew's Pitkin*, our grand palace, or even at the *Stone* around the corner from me. I cherished that cheap picture place because of the time with my father, since it was passed in darkness and silence, and yet I remember his presence, and the gladness I felt in being with him, and watching the Westerns with eager excitement, as they were the only movies I could follow, and the ones that in my mind gave him the most satisfaction.

The weekend in Belle Harbor should be juxtaposed with two or three weeks that I spent two years later in Far Rockaway at my aunt Minnie's summer bungalow, as those were the only times I went to the beach before I became a teenager and could go by myself. My memory of making the visit is blank, I cannot visualize where we slept, and can only guess that it strained the small bungalow. Yet I was consciousness of being *taken in,* as if in my cousins' eyes I was bandied about from one kinswoman to the next. That aside, who would argue with time at the beach? The summer was 1951, and Tony Bennett's break-out hit, "Because of You," was playing on an endless loop in the bungalows and on the portable radios on the outside tables where foursomes collected to play pinochle and canasta. There is a sweet picture of Eileen and me, almost an innocent version of American Gothic, she with bangs, a summer dress, saddle shoes, myself in a white tee shirt, khaki pants, brown shoes, our arms nearly hidden around each other's waists, and in the background, clapboard three story houses, while flush behind us a table of card players, with one man hanging a cigarette between his lips. Remove the subjects and it could be a scene from a pulp beach novel. Such was Far Rockaway, cheap in July.

But everything about my time there has been blanked out by one indelible incident. A group of us were playing running bases on the beach. I was catching and my cousin Art, ten days younger than me but several inches taller, was running. Instead of sliding ahead of the catch into soft, deep sand he jammed straight into my right foot, pushing the second toe completely over the third. As he remembers it: "I can see myself sliding into you and the scream you let out was enough to tell me that damage was done." At first, looking at it, you would have thought all you needed to do was lift the toe and move it back to its natural position. But it was so firmly clamped over the third toe that there was no way to dislodge it. The toes formed a diagonal cross that was locked together as if by a spring bolt. I cannot remember how I got to the hospital, as my aunt had no car, but I can see myself struggling up to a table in a makeshift emergency room, while a nurse was trying to calm me. I had a dislocated toe. The doctor was going to manually reset it. Lying on my back with the nurse at my side, he proceeded to force my second toe off the third, as if he were pushing a powerfully resistant object. The pain was fierce, but they apparently believed the procedure would be quick and easy, and all would be well.

At this distance, I cannot say how long they tried to maneuver my toe in place, and I had no option but to try and keep my outcries down to some moderate level. I had some experience with bearing pain stoically, from the quack dentist I was sent to in Williamsburg, whose palliative for drilling was to advise tightening your grip on the arms of the chair. At last, when they felt they could no longer inflict their advanced technique on me, they gave up and admitted me to the hospital. I do not know who was with me, perhaps my aunt was there, and I was sent to a bed in the children's ward. This was the height of indignity, or rather what I resented the most. I felt too old to be in a children's ward, but apparently I was neither old enough nor ill enough for the adult wing. So I had to bide my time, and indignation, in a bed I thought fit for a nursery. It was the next day when they returned, allowing me some recovery from the initial treatment, and this time they were more prepared, or they were simply coming up to the plate for a second time, having previously struck out. There was a nurse to hold me down, that was as much comfort as I could get, and the doctor who was again going to manipulate my toe. This time they worked right on my bed, no need for any special room, as there was no one else there. Clearly it was not much of a hospital, and if I were not so indignant at the idea of being in a children's ward it would not have been an unendurable situation. In any case, the second time was a charm, the doctor succeeded in dislodging my toe and locking it back in its rightful position. Whether it would ever work again was a question I had in my head, but lacked the temerity to ask, and as I think of it, I cannot remember if there was anyone *to* ask. Art remembers nothing at all after the slide. All that beach time vanished into sea and sky. What remains is the trace of a trauma, and a blurred image of a bungalow courtyard in Far Rockaway, triggered like a sensory impulse if I should hear Tony Bennett begin that long ago invocation of love.

5. MERRY MUSIC WHILE WE'RE YOUNG

MIRIAM LOVED THE THEATER, and she was my
entrée to the world of Broadway, to stage lights and live performers and jamming throngs that rustled the closed interiors
of old, worn buildings with names like nothing from real life—
Morosco, Lyceum, Cort, St James. It was a world I would slip
into by myself as a teenager, a ticket to the second balcony for
a dollar and seventy-five cents, for which price you could see
Deborah Kerr or Burl Ives or John Rait or Julie Harris. But all
that came later. First there was a children's theater production
of *Rumpelstiltskin* that Miriam took me to when I was about
eight years old. I have no idea where it was, but the place was
more like an auditorium than a theater, for the seating did not
rise towards the back, and I see myself, small as I was, twisting
and turning to get a better look at the stage. I remember little
of the show, but I have a clear picture of the girl at her spinning
wheel, the gnome-like Rumpelstiltskin entering from offstage,
leaving and returning in the final scene to claim his prize, and

when she names him he goes ballistic and starts jumping up and down, until he disappeared. What remains vivid is the live performance, seeing people moving and talking on a raised platform before your eyes, knowing they are real, that you could reach out and touch them if you were close enough, yet they are acting a part in a play, and are there to entertain you. If I knew nothing of what spinning straw into gold meant, and less of the story, I was still held in my seat by that bounding actor who dared the girl to guess his name, and if only for that scene and the setting I never forgot my first play.

In the next couple of years I saw two shows that are as vivid now as they were when my eyes were wide. *Where's Charley* had a plot that was simply unfathomable to a nine year old, but the antics on the stage were engrossing, the actors running around every which way, and the music impossible to forget. I can remember a complicated duet, *Someday they'll have horseless carriages,* and a succession of lines about all the new things in the brave new age, and then the kicker, *meanwhile, darling make a miracle and marry me."* But what enthralled me was an interval after the first act, the curtain drawn across the stage, and Ray Bolger out in front, dancing and singing with casual ease: *Once . . in Love. . . with Amy. . . Always. . . in love. . .with Amy.* I can see myself high in the balcony, straining forward in my seat, and watching entranced as that magic man hoofed his way across the stage, with nothing but a closed curtain behind him, crooning Frank Loesser's lyric, and holding the entire theater spellbound. Years later, when I was working in a hotel in New Jersey, I met an Amy, a lovely, smart woman whose beaked nose enhanced her beauty, and we became friends, and then she showed up in Madison, and long years after that on a bus in Cambridge, and I could never see her but what I would hear the words to her song, and once again see that wonderful gypsy soft-shoeing across the boards.

And then I saw *Guys and Dolls.* I was now old enough to follow most of the show, and it helped that the plot was more streamlined and less farcical than one that took for its book a late Victorian comedy. We also had better seats. I do not know when we saw the show, which opened in very late 1950, but Harry must have sprung for dynamite tickets because I was able to see everything happening up close and without strain. The opening, with Stubby Kaye as Nicely-Nicely Johnson, ambling back and forth across the stage while talking-singing *I got the horse right here / The name is Paul Revere* is as clear to me now as it was then. I knew that I could not follow the song, and the refrains puzzled me *(Can do, can do; Likes mud, likes mud)* because the words were simple but I could not fit them with the narrative, which got complicated and was delivered in a jargon whose vocabulary was familiar but whose sense was beyond me. Still it did not matter. Because the music was so rhythmic and the movement on stage so engaging it never occurred to me to worry about whether I understood it. But that was certainly not the case with the songs of Miss Adelaide and Nathan Detroit, which reverberated with me for being so *New Yorkese,* Vivian Blaine with her exaggerated lament, *a person can develop a cold,* and Sam Levene with his repeated *So sue me, sue me,* an expression, with its Yiddish intonation, that anyone from the city would immediately recognize. But however classic the show has become, nothing can diminish the memory of the one number that remains forever alive—Isabel Bigley, a.k.a. Sarah Brown, swinging on a gate in a make believe Cuba, drunk on cocktails but deliriously thrilled by her new-found lover: *Ask me how do I feel, little me with my quiet upbringing, / Well, sir, all I can say, is if I were a gate I'd be swinging.* And swing she did, holding on to the gate and swaying back and forth, all the while belting out those madcap yet ringing lyrics of love. Many years later, in a class in Honolulu, I read Damon Runyon's stories for the first time, and Sarah Brown, that Salvation Army Pygmalion, transformed herself once again from the lines in the book to the lineaments of that tall, dark-haired beauty who was Isabel Bigley.

It can only be a happy coincidence that the two shows I went to before I turned twelve were by one of Broadway's greatest music men. I knew nothing of that. Nor that George Balanchine was the man behind the dance design for *Where's Charley.* Or that George S. Kaufman directed and Jo Mielziner stage designed *Guys and Dolls.* As for the actors, I knew none of them. These would be names I learned of in my teens, when I would visit Miriam and Harry on Long Island and scroll through the Arts section of the *New York Times* on Sundays, a newspaper that was never in any of the apartments I lived in, yet always in their home. The difference between their lives and the one I knew in Brooklyn was striking. Even before they moved to the Island I would go to their flat on 797 Lincoln Place, with the decorated walls, and if I stayed late they would be listening to Barry Gray, the first late night talk show I remember in the city. Barry talked about books and authors, interviewed New York celebrities who were up after midnight, and he was himself a compressed cylinder of opinions and convictions. I was too young to understand the debates, although I was vaguely aware that some of his talk veered off-color, but I enjoyed being in a household, however small, where the radio aired ideas, and the people listening lived a life that extended beyond the narrow streets I was still confined by.

Although they lived close to my house, inside the walls they were miles away, tuned into a glistening island that broadcast live from what I imagined as exciting restaurants and night-clubs. They also left behind small habits that I never realized I still retained. I remember going to their house for dinner when they lived in Levittown, that massive postwar amalgam of land reclamation and class invention, and eating a satisfying meal of what I thought were lamb chops only to learn it was pork. And I threw a fit. How dare my sister serve me pig? You would have thought I had grown up in a Lubavitcher home and was betrayed from within. If I had paused for a moment, I might have admitted that I ate BLT sandwiches outside the house any time I had the chance. But somehow pork chops were too bla-tant a transgression to turn away from: on Christopher Avenue or Lincoln Place it would never do. But Miriam no longer lived there. She had crossed over to a new world of Cape Cod roof-lines and sized lawns and measured roads and supermarkets with cellophane wrapped meats, and on and on. What was I so irate about? That she had not told me ahead of time? I was too young and far too dull for such a fine principle. That I had breached some vestigial taboo that I held onto out of all reason? As I look at it now, in some way, and against my knowledge, the moorings that tied me to all that made up "Brooklyn" were slowly loosening, as if a straitjacket were being unlaced, and my response to that unhinging was an ever fiercer clinging to those cables, like barnacles fastened to a dying ship.

All our memories are unique, and yet we want them confirmed by others. If not it becomes nothing more than our singular experi-ence, a subjective trace that we pass along for the doubtful delight of others, all the while knowing that they may indulge us in their listening, even in their nodding, but there is nothing confirmable about the experience. Yes, I saw Guys and Dolls, *I might even have a saved* Playbill, *an artifact of memory. Yet we want some-thing more than documentary affirmation. For memories are not material, they are floating thoughts, and images, feelings that may even be sensations, and cannot be caught beyond the words that wrap them. So the wording must be careful, even exact, in order to sustain the recovered content, and make it felt. For* felt *is what the memory intends to convey, if it aspires to anything beyond nostalgia. For the memoirist the more immediate issue is securing sufficient affirmation to make the word-recorded memory a re-creation rather than an imagining. Miriam drew a blank on* Rumpelstiltskin. *She remembered* Where's Charley *and* Guys and Dolls. *But she forgot me. It goes without saying that everybody has different memories, yet it is still a surprise when you learn that something sharp and vivid to you is empty to another. You want to shout, 'How can you not remember? I was there!' But in a way I was not there, for the memory that I retain is mine alone and exists in a world apart. She remembers something else, but has no memory of me. For her the show was the thing. If it were not for my sister I would never have been there, yet for her I never was. And so here we are, the two of us, wondering how the other cannot possibly know, or whether it matters at all.*

6. OTHER BLOCKS, OTHER HOMES

ANOTHER STREET. Another house. My maternal grandmother lived at 503 Kosciusko Street in the heart of Bedford-Stuyvesant. The lame joke went like this: A horse is lying dead on the street. A cop arrives and tells the horse's owner to move the animal one block to Dekalb Avenue. *'Why?' 'Because I can't spell Kosciusko.'* It was a bit of a challenge, even as you got used to the name, but there was something oddly attractive about it to a boy, precisely because it *was* difficult, even strange sounding compared to Christopher and Belmont, although the latter, plain enough to say, held a subliminally appealing note, if it would be years before I connected it with the mythic home of the very beautiful Portia. Apparently there is more to a street name, even to an eleven or twelve year old boy, than can be gleaned from the sign on a post. *Kosciusko* was not only foreign but it was in an alien part of the borough, pulling me into streets that rose straight up from revolutionary war history, like Greene and Lafayette and Lexington, not to mention presidential history, like Madison and Monroe and Jefferson. It is hard to convey how strange another section of the city can seem when the names are unfamiliar and the streets all go places that you are completely ignorant of. And the houses were as different as the nomenclature, their sculpted facades so distinct from the ordinariness of Brownsville, and could not be missed even by a boy who knew nothing of building. They had stone stairs, wrought iron railings, bay windows, even postage stamp plots at the front with small plantings dug into the dirt.

My grandmother's block was all residential, not the mix of houses and stores I was used to, except for the oddity of a stable across the street, where a man would regularly emerge on a cart drawn by a horse, and depart for his daily activities. I have no idea what he did, or where he went, but the image of a ramshackle wooden cart clop clopping along a city street might be an invention of magic realism, except for a photograph of my younger cousin Steven, sitting on a pony in the middle of the street, with me standing near the pony's head. I was ten or eleven to his four or five, and I was looking out for the boy, who was something of a prodigy, which in our world meant he was especially smart, as evidenced by his near complete recital of the jingles to television advertisements. The photograph was taken in front of the stable, and the picture of the pony, together with that tired animal lugging a dilapidated wagon along Kosciusko Street, reminds me of the attraction I have always had for horses. It began with the mounted policemen in the city, who sat astride the gorgeous and beautifully groomed animals, and whenever I saw one of them I would stand and stare, afraid to get too close, yet always wishing I could be atop, although never caring about being a policeman. It was unlikely you would learn to ride a horse in Brooklyn, and certainly not if you grew up in the interior, but far in the future I did get up on a horse, and if I never became adept enough to gallop long, nor fearless enough to groom the horse's rear hooves, I still relished my time riding, whether in Taos or Victoria, Altadena or Waimanalo, and only wished they had been longer.

My mother's mother, Sarah Goldman née Aronoff, was known in our family as *Little Bubbie,* to keep her separate from my father's mother who went by the name *Big Bubbie.* Oddly enough there was virtually no difference in size between the two women, both were small, probably not above five feet three inches, and yet one was *Little* and the other *Big.* It caught me with a smile to learn recently that my cousin Laura, whose mother was my father's sister, called her other grandmother Little Bubbie as well. But without dwelling on the nature of Rose Menikoff's outsize personality, Sarah Goldman lived what struck a boy as a completely different life. My memories of her are of the sparest, as I did not go there often when I was young, but the house, which I later came to live in, I knew well. Sarah, like my paternal grandfather and grandmother, came from a large family, five sisters and one brother, and it is a marvel how quickly those large immigrant families shrunk in one generation, none of their children having more than three offspring, and the majority two. Mayshke, the baby brother, is the only one of the siblings I met, a man I might easily have passed on the streets near the pushcarts but never anyone I ordinarily sat next to at a kitchen table. He would show up at the house on Kosciusko Street, always looking as if he had been in jail for vagrancy. A singular recollection comes from the granddaughter of one of the Aronoff sisters: "When I was really little, Mayshke came to our house wearing old, torn and dirty clothes and Grandma asked him not to come again if he didn't look neat and clean. I think that was the only time I ever saw him."

Sarah Goldman was not so fastidious since she herself exhibited little interest in cleaning, and the single photograph I have, an odd shot, shows her standing outdoors, no backdrop, a *shmutsik* white apron on, the kind you might see in a butcher shop or grocery store after a hard day's work. I am unsure whether the oddity is the apron with its dirt or that she is wearing one in the first place. But Mayshke had a place in her home. I can see him playing cards by himself, and I would sit near him, trying to figure out how all the clothes got mashed together, and whether the smell that emanated was from the garments or the person. Yet despite the tramp-like appearance there was a gentleness to the man that was intuited even by a boy knowing nothing whatever about him—like where he came from or what he did or why he suddenly showed up with cans of olive oil, which I later learned he brought as a palliative after hearing of my mother's illness. He must have been fond of his sisters, or felt at home with them, and others besides my grandmother clearly reciprocated. One of these was Becky Tashman, who along with her husband Pesach lived on a farm in Colchester, Connecticut, one site of Baron Hirsch's great project for resettling Jews from Russia throughout North America. Miriam, who has strong memories of the farm, heard Baron Hirsch's name spoken on more than one occasion. In any case, Becky needed a horse for the farm and told Mayshke about it. Where, or how, he managed to acquire an animal is lost in the stars. But he did find a horse, and walked it all the way from Brooklyn to Connecticut, more than one hundred twenty miles. He slept in fields along the way, and, a committed vegetarian, managed to find something to eat for the three-day trek. Since traffic was a bit thinner in the nineteen-thirties, and Mayshke lived in Williamsburg, I like to think that he started out across the Bridge, but for the rest of the route I leave it for the reader to chart. The story is family lore, but who could make it up? When he reached Colchester, the horse in tow, Becky and Pesach asked why he walked the animal instead of riding him. "The horse was tired," said Mayshke, ever the oddly endearing itinerant in rags.

But the differences in lifestyle at Kosciusko Street were apparent in small ways even though I was never fully aware of their meaning. Sarah was a widow, a word I never heard: I simply did not have a grandfather in that place. I was curious about what happened to my non-existent grandfather, but true to that generation's habits nobody volunteered information. I learned much later from Miriam that Little Bubbie's first husband, *Goldman*, the father of Sam, Morris and my mother, died in the influenza epidemic, while her second husband, *Mandel*, the father of Irene, my adored aunt, hanged himself when his newborn was just a baby. I remember that I tried to reconcile in my head Irene's last name with my grandmother's, that she was her daughter, my mother's half-sister, yet I had a hard time making it all fit because Irene was young and vital while my grandmother was old. I could not get the picture to make sense. To my eyes K Street was way out, geographically, architecturally and culturally, words a boy would never have known yet whose meaning he could fully apprehend. It was different from Belmont Avenue and Lincoln Place, where life fit into a fabricated mold, cracked to be sure, but a mold for all that. And there was nothing remotely regular about that house on the unspellable street. For starters, Little Bubbie was dirt-poor, Miriam remembers an incident when Irene was hungry and she was given bread and mustard to eat. Perhaps it was a folk remedy and the mustard worked to cut the pangs of hunger. More likely the detail would fit in a novel by Erskine Caldwell. Sarah Goldman had strong principles about charity: she refused to deal with Jewish social agencies because of their intrusive questions. *Who needs them?* She depended upon her sons for support, which was a bit like betting on a long shot since neither of them was much of a moneymaker. I never went to her house and had a meal. Who knew a Jewish grandmother who did not cook? But the lack of money may not have been the sole reason: she did not see the point of spending all that time on an activity that would finish quickly and leave nothing to show for it.

By way of contrast, Rose Menikoff was legendary for her cooking, and there is not a cousin who will not break into elegiac song over *Pesach* seders, which she still prepared until Zeyde died. These dinners required tables to be connected from the dining room to the end of the living room and were a highlight of our lives. For a boy, the great test was to eat Big Bubbie's horseradish, which was always white and reserved for the adults. If we ate it with the fish it was a sign that we were growing up, and no longer hanging around for the four questions, which already seemed a kid's game to a nine or ten year old. Later, when I was living alone with her, she hardly ever cooked, except when her youngest son Max would come over on Friday evenings with his new wife, and she sent me out to the live chicken market for a freshly killed fowl, where I saw the women plucking the feathers of their birds over gas flames, then she would prepare a simple meal, which I relished, especially if I could have an egg in the chicken soup. Apart from that she largely gave it up, as there was nobody anymore to cook for. On a rare occasion I could cajole her into making a sponge cake, for I loved watching her crack the eggs and separate the yolks from the whites into the half-shells that she held in each hand, as if she were performing on stage, and in the end she would create a cake that was the opposite of flat and even, marked from one end of the pan to the other by deep furrows, with an irregular surface, and that tasted like god's creation.

Once, in Spain, I saw a cake that had the dark yellow color of my grandmother's, and I bought it, hoping it would bring back that off-sweet confection, but it had neither the texture nor the taste. As for my other grandmother, perhaps she was just too poor for too long to have ever seen the utility of spending time over a stove. But these habits, or skills, are also matters of temperament. Sarah Goldman had limited patience. She had worked in the garment industry in her early days—Miriam used the word *sweatshop* but I doubt it as a referent—and I can still see the Singer treadle sewing machine in the house, which I had always thought was my mother's only to learn that my mother could not sew. One time Miriam brought her some fabric for a blouse she was making in a class at school. The teacher had given strict directions on how to align the pieces, etc, and my obedient sister took the assignment to our grandmother, who dismissed the teacher's instructions as taking too much time. So Little Bubbie collected the pieces, sewed them together willy-nilly, and the result was a blouse fit for a tatterdemalion. That was the last time Miriam asked for help. But it is odd how that Singer machine stays with me. I remember sitting on a chair in front and rocking the treadle, rotating the hand wheel, and wishing I could see my mother sewing. I never did.

Perhaps nothing crystallized the difference between Kosciusko Street and Belmont Avenue / Lincoln Place more dramatically than politics. And yet politics was never spoken about in either place, at least not in my presence. For the Menikoff family, where nobody ever mentioned current events, the political mentality was a kind of petit bourgeois conservatism, without the French expression. It was a world of first generation Russian immigrants who concerned themselves with their businesses, occasionally their families, and a world shadowed by an Orthodox tradition: services on the high holy days, observance of major holidays like Passover, and ritual burials. In a way, except for Zeyde, Orthodoxy was a thin shield that kept the social and cultural world of America at bay. The *Morgn Zhurnal,* and in the early Fifties its merger with *Der Tog,* was the perfect paper: it could be depended upon not to disturb the reader with questions about social inequities or dubious labor practices. The vacancy of politics in my home is reflected in my utter ignorance as to who my father voted for in any election, whether mayor or governor or president, or if he indeed did vote. He was a small businessman, and I mean *small,* since I only knew him after the Zion stores were liquidated. As I think of it now, I try to fathom his experience, dropping from the ownership of flourishing markets to a caretaker of street groceries that barely covered their rent. And yet as I knew him I never was aware of any fall from on high, except for the grocery on Lincoln Place, which had to be the low point of his life.

The second brother, Irving, had small groceries that he ran for years in the Flatbush area. Charlie, the third brother, was more advanced: he had been a salesman for Sweet Life, so he had a career as a wholesaler and was widely traveled before he opened a large market on Montague Street in Brooklyn Heights. My father spoke little, and Irving made Harpo Marx sound loquacious. But Charlie was a talker, and he delivered a dramatic performance to me alone one early evening, seated at the head of the dining room table, myself not eighteen inches away, about his plans for his son Allan to go to Harvard. I cannot say whether I was more astonished that he thought of something so far beyond the sight of my world, or that he had the money to pull it off, or that he was convinced Allan was smart enough to get admitted in the first place. But what struck me most as I listened to him was how *American* his ambitions were, in a family where the consciousness of class, at least so far as American culture was concerned, seemed non-existent. The only attention to class was directed at the Hasidim, whose Yiddish pronunciation we mocked—for *butter* they said *pitter* instead of *puter* (poo'ter)—along with their *peyes* and their impossibly ugly dress. But they lived mostly in Williamsburg and we had little traffic with them. In a way they were lower down the pecking order, socially speaking, and so they were easy targets for ridicule. Who knew that in years to come, with a little help from Chaim Potok, they would become the face of Orthodoxy to Gentiles, and their exoticism would even carry a certain cachet. But within the narrow range of our world my uncle Charlie's dream for his son had a touch of Gatsbyesque grandeur to it, completely beyond the imagination of my father, and for sure of uncle Irving as well. As for the youngest brother, Max, artist and jazz buff, I can imagine the proud smile that crinkled his eyes as he drove his only son Jerry up to Harvard from a small town on Long Island, but then Jerry was gifted, and the dream well within reach.

For the Goldmans, politics was the very stuff of the place, and switching between households was like moving from night to day. From this vantage point decades later, the Goldmans were committed radicals, but for a boy who moved between the houses, it was a discovery ferreted out in surprising ways. I knew a little of my mother's leanings because the experimental *PM* newspaper, and its successor *The Daily Compass,* were regular purchases, and my father never read an English language paper. I learned later of the brilliant corps of writers and artists who contributed to *PM* in its glory days during the war, but even as a nine year old I was quick enough to know that these sheets were outliers in American journalism, championing causes far in advance of the times. I was too young to have any real understanding of politics, but I knew that Mama supported Henry

Wallace in the 1948 presidential election, which even then I realized was a declaration that you were different, because normal people would choose between Dewey and Truman. When I asked her what HST stood for, letters I kept seeing in bold capitals, she replied with something of a sneer, "He Stinks Terrible." If I doubted my memory, I could no more have invented that phrase than I could decipher the writing on the wall. It is an oddity how a few inadvertent words can lie encased for decades in a neuron or two, only to be released in an inconsequential act of composition, and become revelatory of truths that are harder to unearth from larger but less tangible recollections.

Mama also supported Vito Marcantonio, who ran for mayor when I was ten years old. I remember being taken with his name, which had a lilting cadence, and seeing the American Labor Party stickers throughout the streets, as he was as popular in the poorer sections of Brooklyn as he was in his district in East Harlem. I was aware that he was a marginal figure, although neither word nor idea had any meaning for me, but I thought it futile to support people who had no chance of winning. Of course I knew nothing of his heroic efforts on behalf of immigrants and workers and Puerto Ricans and Blacks. Yet I sensed well enough that he was outside the traditional political system, even though I was ignorant of just about everything that any of the people running for office stood for, and I did not know what the offices they were running for even meant. But I was conscious that the politics in Kosciusko Street were different. My mother's inclined only slightly, for she was primarily preoccupied with her domestic life, but her brother Morris, who worked as a clerk in a delicatessen, had strong union sympathies and supported many Communist causes. At that early time I had no idea what a "Communist" was, and no hard memory of the word itself.

My aunt Irene, the kindest of women, was a secretary for the American Peace Crusade, an organization that had Paul Robeson as a signatory and was a major target of the FBI, who considered it a "front" for the Communist Party. Agents from the Bureau followed her from the el station at Marcy Avenue to the house, where they accosted and questioned her. At the time I was unaware of all this. But as I rummaged through the shelves of a bookcase and saw pamphlets and brochures and small publications detailing stories about Korea and Negro rights that I never saw in the dailies, so closely printed as to be unappealing to the eye, which made it seem all the more important, I felt privy to a world of secret revelations that were too lethal to be published in ordinary newspapers. This was truly a world apart, and one branch of my family roiled around in that world. On the one hand there was a bit of excitement, akin to a thrill, at the thought that Irene was connected to something dangerous, maybe even sinister. And yet she was so sweet, and caring, that I had a hard time placing her in an underground world that seemed so hidden and removed from ordinary life. I saw myself with two families, one soberly predictable, the other unorthodox and chaotic, on the edge of poverty, and fastened to a politics just this side of legality.

How little we know of the people we are putting on the page. We know them as we encountered them at confined moments in our lives. In Charlie's case, I knew him when he came faithfully with his wife and two sons to visit his mother on weekends and holidays, and at other times alone to give her financial advice. Irving I saw rarely. And Max, whom I thought the world of, dropped out of my life after he moved to Long Island and settled into suburban living, I have a photograph of Irving with his brother Charlie and my uncle Morris Goldman, standing tall in a wide row, smiling, a broad sky in the background, bachelors in their late twenties and early thirties. *They were at the 1933 Chicago World's Fair. They brought back a hammered sterling bracelet with the logo of the Fair as a gift for the five-year old daughter of Frank, who remembers it still. They must have talked with each other, and laughed, and had times together that are completely beyond my ability to penetrate. And yet the men that I knew are not men I would have put in that photograph, separated as I knew them to be by their politics and experience, or what I thought was their politics and experience. The picture tells a story that I have no knowledge of, and possibly a truer one than what I am piecing together. But it is the fate of the memoir to twine itself around people whose dead lives are but wisps in the minds of the living, and whose truth or reality has long since disappeared.*

7. ACROSS THE RIVER

ON A WEEKDAY in early spring 1950 Sarah Goldman took the trolley from Bedford-Stuyvesant that went over the Williamsburg Bridge to visit her son Morris and his family on a slip of a block near Delancey Street. As I mark this detail, I marvel at how the process of recovering the past discloses the dead in a new form. It astonishes me that my grandmother could travel alone from Brooklyn to New York. Dead nearly sixty-five years, she suddenly has more nuance than she ever had for me in life, where her image was barely a two-dimensional sketch. In the act of writing I find myself unfolding a fuller story than the remembrance of the boy who was there, who knew nothing more than what he saw. How could he imagine Sarah Goldman's life in that teeming enclave across the river? My grandmother was a widow with four children: Sam and Harry, who were placed in an orphanage in the Bronx, and Blanche and Morris, who were put in day care while she went to work. My mother never talked about the nursery to me, I was not much beyond nursery age myself, and Miriam knew nothing of it. I had never heard of Harry, who ran away from the orphanage, or walked away from home, and whose entire story survives in his name alone.

So this is my private "Lower East Side" chronicle, one I knew nothing of before starting. But it takes little imagination to visualize my mother in the nursery. Or to see my uncle Sam in that orphanage, for there was an orphanage in Brownsville that my college roommate had been deposited in by his father. My grandmother remarried, some ten to fifteen years after her first husband's death. And then, shortly after the birth of a daughter in 1924, her second husband committed suicide. What must it have taken to go on after these experiences? Who was there to offer solace? And yet she went on, although all paid a price in blunted lives. My mother graduated from Washington Irving High School, in the same class as Claudette Colbert, as she relished telling me, for they were still living in Lower Manhattan (how much more mellifluous that sounds than "Lower East Side"). I have no inkling of how my grandmother managed to buy her house, but it was all she had, and if she was literally house poor, at least she had a roof over her head, and one that in due course would play a role in my life.

Sarah Goldman never made it back to Brooklyn. She was hit and killed by a small truck in her old neighborhood. I was standing in the living room, it was the middle of the morning, when I heard that Bubbie had been hit by a bus. They thought it was a bus. Nobody knew exactly, nor did anyone say anything to me. It is striking how invariable their behavior was. No matter how profound the incident, I was not to be talked to, and certainly not comforted, which was beyond their capacity. In fairness, they were not concealing tragedy, they lived in a world where death was received as a matter of course, and they had few protocols for talking about it. And a child, no matter that I was eleven years old, was not at the forefront of their consciousness. Sitting *shive* was a controlled way to manage death, but in Little Bubbie's case even that was out of the question. No one was going to sit at Kosciusko Street. Her two sons and their wives, my mother, one sister, and the ever-faithful Mayshke made up the funeral group. I knew no more about it at the time than I did the Greek alphabet. But I still see that room, the morning light as if suffused in a dismal haze, overhearing a bit of conversation about a "bus," and trying to process my grandmother's death by myself.

The summer after Little Bubbie died my mother told me I would be going to camp for two weeks. We were still at Lincoln Place and I was resistant to leaving the streets and the Park for something that had no meaning to me. I could not even visualize "camp," and knew no one who had ever gone. But I might as well have been a voiceless pulse for all the say I had. I am alternately perplexed and amazed at how little I mattered in everything that affected my life. Yet my parents, to give them their due, did not deliberately act to thwart their children's needs, they simply never noticed them. Their own decisions were made in an ad hoc fashion, opting for whatever seemed necessary at the moment. The needs of their children were not singled out for exclusion—they were imperceptible to people whose tightened circumstances consumed all their care. My father was a generous man in the only way he knew, often filling more than a few large bags of groceries for the family of Sam Goldman, who was regularly out of work. But on Lincoln Place, in the trough of his finances, he could hardly be expected to concern himself with me. My mother was better in this regard, but at the time how would I even know that? I was being summarily sent to Surprise Lake, which I had never heard of but quickly discovered was a charity camp. Later I learned of the storied history of the place, how Eddie Cantor was one of the original campers from the Lower East Side and a lifelong sponsor, and how its primary mission was to take poor boys out of the city and expose them to mountain greenery.

But there was a secondary goal, to fatten up boys who might have been undernourished, as in some souped-up version of Hansel and Gretel, and as odd as it sounds that is what I remember my mother telling me, that I was going to camp in order to put on weight. Of all the things that stay with me from childhood, that I should remember this as the rationale for summer camp might well be the most preposterous. I disliked the place, although I cannot say why, or even remember much of it at all. Nothing awful happened. I wanted to learn to swim, but that was not an option. Without a pool they were not going to chance a drowning in the lake. But one good thing lasted. Near the end of our second week we spent a day picking blueberries. It is curious because we delivered baskets of berries at the end and I remember thinking to myself that it seemed such a useless task, all that fruit that nobody could finish eating. The next day in the dining hall, a rough-looking structure with wooden tables lined up in rows in the center, what do we carry out from the kitchen but trays covered with blueberry pies. The cook, a woman whose visage I can dimly see, and the only person from that place who exhibited some kindness, although I cannot say why, made pies thick with the berries from all our pickings. I loved nothing as much as that pie, and to this day, on the odd chance that fresh blueberry pie is on the menu, I cannot eat it without thinking about the cabin filled with campers, and imagining the cook who gave me such pleasure as I finished out my time in Cold Spring, New York.

The bus brought me back to Manhattan, just as two weeks earlier it had taken me up to the country. My mother met me and we found the subway to return to Brooklyn. As hard as I try, and I sit here willing myself into reverie, I am unable to conjure up the image of my mother, what she was wearing, how she looked, but I remember being on the car as it was moving, and at some point realized we were not on the train going back to Lincoln Place. By age eleven I had traveled enough to know my way around the IRT, and the stations to Utica Avenue were in my head by rote. Where were we going? An anxiety coursed through me that I instinctively knew was about home, although I could not say it. I had just spent fourteen days in a thicket of brush, and all I now wanted was to get back to those comforting streets and handball courts. The succession of strange stations on a strange line compounded my fear. Unable to contain my confusion I confronted my mother. She told me that we had left Lincoln Place and moved to Kosciusko Street, and I could sense the turmoil, and even pain that she felt in telling me. As my emotions swirled between anger and misery, it suddenly dawned on me that I was sent to camp as a tactic to keep me away from home while they moved, a ruse to prevent my making a scene or having a fit, although I never threw tantrums. But here the simplest explanation is the best, and it was easier for them to move while I was away. Although at the time I made no connection with the earlier move from Christopher Avenue, now it seems as if it were a pattern. I may have been seven then, but the same practice prevailed: no knowledge, no trouble. And anyway, what could a boy do? Just cry and be a nuisance. After so many years you would imagine the emotion to have dissipated, and yet withal the anger is still sensible. But something that was cloudy at the time has now become crystalline, and I see as if anew how my mother felt the hurt but was unable to salve it, and so took the pain within, trying to console and protect her only son from his own agitation.

And then she bought me a puppy. I never had a pet before, and I am also convinced that my mother had no experience with household animals. Yet she took me to a pet store and told me I could pick out a puppy to take home. I think the shop was on Broadway, as I see the shadow of the el hovering over it, and I picked out a small, chocolate-coated dog that I took to immediately. I named him Cocoa, feeling smug at coming up with a perfect name, yet one not in the least obvious. I was thrilled with my new companion, and for a while put aside my complaints about being in an alien neighborhood. But my happiness was not meant to last. As I was getting more attached to Cocoa, it became clear that the puppy needed to be housebroken, of which I knew nothing, and my mother I fear as little. Training the puppy was more taxing than anticipated, and my mother was unwilling or unable to trudge up and down the two flights of stairs, plus the stone steps outside down to the street. If I had known, I would have taken Cocoa out and walked with him while he learned. I remember making this argument, but it was never a discussion, and a few soilings were all the excuse needed to nail the decision: the puppy had to go. I returned to the store with my mother, he gave the dog back, and I can still see myself on the bus after we left the shop, in tears, and inconsolable. For some reason I have kept Cocoa at the front of my mind all these years, and while the name now seems less original, it is as if the word itself guards not just the memory of the dog but the intensity of my desire, and all that I lost when we walked away from that store.

It is strange to ponder how the smallest incident acquires significance well beyond itself. Why do I hold onto this memory so tenaciously? I had the puppy no more than a week. I never had a dog of my own before or since. And yet the episode stays with me. I can see the dog, and almost taste the tears that coursed my cheeks on the bus. Yet now, as with other incidents, I see more than I remember, and what I see is my mother, who in her own fitful way was trying to bring joy into her son's life. Although she was born in Manhattan, and went through high school, and should have been a flapper, she was as culturally manacled as my father, who came from the old country. Maybe it was because I was just a boy, and after all what could you say to a boy? but she told me a few things in passing that either meant something to her, or that she momentarily remembered. And what is strangest is that I never forgot any of them, trivial as they were. That Gertrude Ederle was the first woman to swim the English Channel. That her favorite song was "Indian Love Call." And she sang some verses of "Dardenella," a popular song of 1920, that I committed to memory *(Oh sweet Dardanella / I love your harem eyes / I'm a lucky fellow / To capture such a prize)*. What to make of these bits? There is not enough to construct the barest reading of my mother's popular culture. She was fifteen when "Dardanella" was a hit, and she had two children when Nelson Eddy and Jeanette Macdonald were stars in *Rose-Marie*. That she was interested in Gertrude Ederle's feat and Claudette Colbert's success suggests that she was a woman of her time, yet she reverted in her life to a domestic regimen that was more appropriate to a generation that came off the boat rather than a graduate of a high school. It is as if my father's family overwhelmed her American life. Looked at another way, her childhood was fraught with enough trauma to do the job. I have neither the means nor the intention to write my mother's biography. Yet there is one unassailable fact of her life: after her first operation, when I was five or six, she was never well again. My time with her was so short that I seem to have carried these bits with me as if sewn into some hidden pocket—two-three verses to a silly popular song that today would be derided for its cultural insensitivity, and I doubt even "Indian Love Call" could get an airing without a disclaimer. But they are the only words that she transmitted in passing. They must have come about in some downtime, before *that* word ever existed, and I treasured them all the more for their rarity. But it is only now that I see how things unspoken may have been truer, and more revealing. Mama had no way to give me what a boy might have required, no resources of her own, and so she made what gestures she could to offer what she thought I might like. Maybe it was impelled by guilt, but I would hope not. I prefer to think of it as an effort to assuage a boy's sorrow, rather than an act of penitence, and in that way I hold no anger at her for taking Cocoa back. If anything, I feel sadness at being unable to let her know that I have come to see what she was doing, and how much I loved her for it.

8. *CLANG, CLANG, CLANG*

WHAT COMPLICATED the move to Kosciusko Street for me was that I was about to start junior high. My friends from elementary school would be moving a few blocks over to John Marshall, or 210, an institutional building that housed a world a bit less rough than it was made out, although in five years it became a zone of danger. But I was gone by then. For now, I did not want to leave my friends, and by going to 210 I would be staying in my old neighborhood, if only during the day. I suppose hanging on was simply a concession to my fierce attachment to what was mine, even if that was nothing more than streets and signs and storefronts, which in some uncanny way had a kind of life for me. And as I think of it, I did not even know what school was in the district for Kosciusko Street, so I never attended to that. I never changed my address, or even talked with my mother about it. In my sullen determination I acted as if I were still living in our old apartment. The more immediate problem was getting to class every day. The distance from school to my house was about two miles, not far behind the wheel of a car but considerable for legs in the city, and even more problematic because everyone went home for lunch. There was a trolley that ran along Nostrand Avenue, stretching all the way from Flatbush through Bedford-Stuyvesant, and that would be my transport.

I was used to riding buses, but this was another trip altogether. The cars were very old, and I was intrigued by the fact that they could be driven from either end. The conductor simply removed the handle that controlled the car from the vertical shaft, walked to the other end, and placed it on its twin steel bar. The other feature of the trolley that was exciting, if only to watch, was hopping on the outside of the car as it was moving, as there was a curved or sloping ledge big enough to put your feet on if they were turned in, holding tight to the cable that extended through the trolley pole to the electric wire overhead, and then jumping off again, usually after the trolley stopped. I never had the courage to grab a ride that way, and I was never sure exactly what was being held onto, for if it was the cable (I thought) what would keep you from getting electrocuted? But bigger boys, and more adventurous, did jump on the back, and I always wondered what they were like to be able to do that, if they imagined they were charmed, or just dared danger, for I could never get the thought out of my head for a moment of what might happen to me if I jumped on the back, and fell. It was a risk, like other physical risks, I would never take, and I admired, and even envied the boys who played life with such easy abandon.

The trolleys were gradually being replaced with electric buses, which ran on St Johns Place, and while they were newer, and looked modern, they still had twin poles that connected to electric wires overhead, and when the buses turned a corner one or another of the poles often slipped the lines, breaking the connection, and the driver had to get out and maneuver it back on, much like a small boy trying to get his Lionel train back on track after it overturned. It was common to see a new bus stalled in the middle of the road, the passengers waiting in the coach, while the driver patiently fitted the pole to the wire. Meanwhile, the trolley never broke down. It was like some giant artifact that came out of an old movie, impossible to clean from the outside, or so it seemed, yet show stopping if you were at the terminus of the line and saw the driver get up, cross the long carriage, all the while lifting and reversing the seats as he went along, put the handle on the opposite shaft and drive away. Years later, when I first rode the trams in San Francisco, which were steel cable cars and entirely different, I could not but think of the Brooklyn trolleys, and even had a wisp of feeling for the lumbering old cars, if only for their having played a bit part in my life.

But what was to be done about lunch? Dismissed from school for an hour, I had no place to go, and essentially wandered the streets until it was time to return to class. I had to eat, and it turned out that two places became sojourns during my midday wanderings. One was a small luncheonette on Buffalo Avenue, just below St Johns Place, if I am not mistaken, that became something of a refuge for me. The counter could not seat more than three people, the owners preparing sandwiches right behind it as if they were in their own kitchen, and there may have been three or four small tables. It was the kind of place that dotted any number of New York neighborhoods, and I never quite saw their like when I was in other American cities. The luncheonette, a coinage that dates from the twenties, was a limited operation, and I occasionally wondered how it supported itself. It did not function as an early morning coffee shop, and was open only a few hours in the afternoon, but the people may have owned the building, or lived behind or above the store, the kind of thinking that came automatically to someone whose entire life was spent in a small grocery, and who instinctively identified with people who owned and worked these places. Even today, when all those stores have long gone, displaced by upscale viand markets, I find myself gravitating to the individual odd shop, a shoemaker, say, whose place is a jumble of boxes and polishes and misplaced junk, yet who seems to be a master of his last, rather than go to a clean well lit store with all the redone shoes fitted up in order on the shelves. No doubt it is an absurd vestigial habit, but so much has that early texture of life seeped into the skin that you cannot separate it out from yourself, any more than you can separate yourself from it.

In any case, the luncheonette became a comfortable site, and the woman who made the sandwiches, whose name I have long forgotten but whose presence I can still make out, small, short brown hair, her compact body arcing over the spreads and breads and relishes, soon enough began to treat me as if I were a regular, albeit not a grown up regular. The people who ate there, or took food out, were adults. I was still a boy, and what was a boy doing by himself having lunch away from home all the time? Thinking about it now, I am grateful that she never interrogated me—*Why was I there? Where was my mother?*—but simply served me as a customer, if one she occasionally had to chastise when I did not order proper food, and just wanted an egg cream or a malted. But I loved whatever she made, and was partial to her egg salad sandwiches, on toasted bread, with lettuce and tomato and a pickle on the side, and I remember them as always being excellent. Of course I never really thought about the food, whether it was fresh or how it was prepared, and I realize now that little luncheonette spoiled me, for to this day I never assume that an egg salad sandwich ordered in a coffee shop outside a major city will be to my liking. But in Penn Station, say, a sandwich grabbed on the run will invariably be enjoyed, well worth the price, and no matter how long you have been gone from the city, when you pass through the lower level and see the offerings you know you are home, and that nowhere else can you find both the simplicity and the goodness of that egg salad to go. As for that eatery on a side street, I took a certain pleasure, or pride, at being able to walk in and order whatever I wanted, not being told I could not have this or I must have that, and it made me feel grown up, although at other times I remember wishing I did not have to go there again, and sit at the counter, or the small table, and eat lunch by myself. For I was by myself all those lunchtimes, my friends having gone home to meals prepared by their mothers, and I was passing the time until I returned to school. And I was also conscious of not staying in the store for the entire hour. A sandwich could be ordered and finished in less than twenty minutes, and what was I to do the rest of the time? The place was so small that I felt conspicuous, and even though the woman was friendly, and kind, I felt I was overstaying my welcome if I just sat there, long after finishing my food.

Where did I get the money for those lunches? It had to come from my mother, since I never saw my father in the morning, but what puzzles me is that I have no memory of her ever giving me money before school. I am certain that I never had a folding bill in my pocket, all I ever had were coins, and not many of those. And I used that change in the one other place I ate at regularly during lunchtimes, "the famous St Johns Place knishes," just off Utica Avenue, as it was advertised in the *Mendele Folk Shul* annual. St John's Place was a commercial street, and the optometrist who examined my eyes and made my glasses, Dr. Sidney M. Bauer, had his office not two doors from the knish store. I liked him, the care and gentleness with which he treated me, although I hated having to see him because I always needed new glasses, with thicker lenses, whenever I walked into his office, which in a twist I liked because it was attractive and quiet and understated, and gave off an aura of seriousness of purpose. I remember that the door did not open straight from the street, as most stores did, but at an angle, as if from the bottom leg of a triangle that cut a diagonal through the street. And hanging on the door was a wordless sign, a pair of expressionless eyes staring down and out at anyone about to enter the inner sanctum. Much later my sister told me that logo was an image of the huge eyes peering over the valley of ashes in *The Great Gatsby*. All this set Dr. Bauer's business apart from the others, and I always wanted to cross over from the outside, drawing in the smartness of the place, as if it were elsewhere, even though I got queasy whenever I opened the door.

In elementary school we would be given annual eye exams in class, and I would engage in the same doomed strategy to avoid getting a note from the teacher that said I needed to see the eye doctor. I would look at the chart, although I was too far away to memorize the letters, and listen to the students who went before me, trying to retain the order of the letters in my head so that when my turn came I would be able to "read" them correctly. It was an agony, because I never knew exactly when I would be called, and it was a toss up that I could keep the order straight, but I persisted with all my might because the thing I feared the most was getting that note, and imagining thick new glasses that would make my life miserable. It is poignant to look back now and retrieve the terror that overtook a boy of eight or nine at the prospect of looking like an almost blind person. At that time it was common to see older people in the streets wearing what we called "coke bottle" lenses. And I thought to myself, if I went on year after year getting thicker glasses, by the time I was a grown up I would look like those people, and when you looked closely at their lenses you could see they were edged all around with what looked like a glazed border, and the wider the border the thicker the lens, and the blinder the sight. The border on my lenses was still very narrow, but I was not even ten years old, and I could only imagine what it would be like when I was eighteen or nineteen. So my silent battle in the classroom with the teacher certainly seemed worth the struggle. But like so many other intense contests it was not a fight I could win. Fortunately, my eyes stabilized, and by the time I was in high school I no longer felt self-conscious about wearing glasses, although the trauma of those early days never went away completely, for when I first read Joyce's *Portrait* as a young man, I remember the closeness with which I followed the description of Stephen's short-sightedness.

Mama went with me to the knish store shortly after I started taking the trolley to school. She was worried about what I would do for lunch if it happened that one day I had no money. It seems odd to think that was a possibility, that I could leave the house empty handed, or that my mother had no change to give me. So she decided to make an arrangement with the owner of the store, that if I came in one afternoon and told him I had no money, he would let me have a knish, and she would make sure to pay him later, or else I would bring the money the next day. In brief, I had credit for knishes, although for how many exactly I cannot say. Why my mother thought that knishes were a proper lunch is a good question, but it may have been simpler to make a deal in a store that was a fast food takeout than in a luncheonette, and in any case a nutritional lunch was not a high priority. There was nothing else to eat there, although anyone who remembers the aroma of those soft buns as they came out of the oven would be more than satisfied with that immigrant delight for a meal. I am not sure why I turned away from kasha knishes, as I always enjoyed *kasha varnishkes*, but I only ate potato knishes. There was one other item in the store, something I have never seen since, yet I remember as clearly as if I were there now. A refrigerator standing along a wall, with glass doors, contained thick glasses filled, not quite to the top, with sour milk, a food-drink that looks like buttermilk or kefir, and that was common in Poland and Russia. It had a slightly tart taste, and I found it a delicious complement to the hot knish. I did not buy it often since I usually had just enough money for the main course, but when I did it was like a treat. There must have been times when I had nothing in my pocket, and am inclined to say I skipped eating rather than order a knish on credit. But I remember going into the luncheonette without money, and the woman saying that was fine, she would make me a sandwich and I could pay her tomorrow. For some reason I felt easier than in the knish store, which was always busy, traffic in and out without pause. The tables were exposed in an open space, people walking past them to the counter where they placed their orders, and if I sat at one of them I felt as if I were on display, and everyone who passed me knew I had nowhere to go. I could not stay in that store very long, and if eating a sandwich took twenty minutes, it was far quicker for a knish, even if I had a glass of sour milk. And so I went back to the street, and walked St John's Place, or Utica Avenue, I preferred the business streets that were filled with people, and had stores that could be looked into, until eventually I turned back on Rochester Avenue toward Park Place, to finish the afternoon at John Marshall.

9. SOUL AT REST

WHEN I THINK of the house on Kosciusko Street the most baffling thing is my inability to say who lived there. The apartment was a little larger than the one on Lincoln Place, but far too small for my mother and father, my sister Ann, my aunt Irene, and myself. All I can conjure are two bedrooms, and a dining room without doors that did double duty for sleeping, my allocated slot. After talking with Ann I learned that Irene did *not* live there, though she frequently visited, and brought with her a whiff of the wider world of Manhattan, even though I never knew exactly what she did, or where. The apartment was a small variation on a railroad grid: the kitchen, facing the back and overlooking a postage-sized dirt yard, ran straight into the dining room and that to the living room, which looked out on the street. Off the kitchen and living rooms were two small alcoves that jutted out like tiny feet on a stick figure, although you could get nothing in them beyond a single bed and maybe a small bureau squeezed between the wall and a corner of the mattress. As I write this I see, as I never had before, that the layout was almost an exact parallel to that on Belmont Avenue, except there the living room was at the opposite end, facing back rather than overlooking the street. It is the strangest discovery, two grandmothers, neither of whom had anything to do with the other, occupying counterpart apartments that were connected only by a shuttlecock of a boy, who knew of the women's silence, sensed their enmity, but never understood what it meant. It is curious how he carried within him this mute knowledge, and tried to hold together in his head these divided families, even though they themselves countenanced no connection, and were gratified by the absence of blood ties. But for the boy the two made one, or at least he persisted in that belief, and if he could not understand the meaning beneath the carping chatter of unchanging grievances, he still saw himself in the two of them, varying one over the other for smartness or savvy, but secretly glad to be a part of both.

I remember the front room on Kosciusko Street vividly, with its bay windows, because at the farthest end, away from the street, and flush against the wall, stood a desk with a heavy, standard typewriter in the center, and it was there that I learned my first technical skill. Irene gave me lessons that I followed faithfully, and I became quite adept, so that when I took a typing class in my last year in junior high, no more than two or three boys out of some twenty-five secretaries-in-the-making, I was near the top for speed and accuracy. Irene's instruction was as simple as it was spare: she gave me a booklet and told me to follow the directions *(asdf jkl; asdf jkl;)*. And I just banged away. I never thought of it, but I wonder now if in the intensity of my practice I was projecting onto the typewriter the musical training I would have loved but was altogether out of my grasp. I remember as a small boy listening to Miriam play the piano, and I would invariably fall asleep after awhile, and long after

I imagined a connection between listening to live music and being carried away to dreamland. Pondering it all, and acutely aware that I sat alone in front of that typewriter, in a corner of the room, robotically copying all the exercises, I wonder why I insisted for so long in saying that Irene taught me to type? I suppose it was an attachment to someone I loved, who took it upon herself to help me, even if that amounted to nothing more than telling me to read the booklet.

There were so few "things" that anyone in my family taught me directly, that when they pop up in this reconstruction I am taken aback. Clearly I learned, but I was not learning from my family. Looking back, that may have been an advantage, for I was not lectured to, and the kind of instruction that I imagine ran in families was thankfully absent from mine. Nobody was dishing out golden or silver rules, and so I was on my own, picking up whatever "rules" from wherever, and wherever was always outside, never at home. Miriam's childhood showed our mother's interest in music and books, but there was no way for her to sustain that with me. As my sister Ann said of those years, "Mama was sick all the time." It is curious, however much we know it, even try to forestall it, that we replicate our experience with our children, and years later, when I became a single parent, I instinctively followed the only practice I knew, and my children wound up living in a household *sans* silver and gold. I wish I could say it was a deliberate decision about bringing up baby, but in truth I had only one book, *Dr. Spock,* and all the rest was sailing with the wind.

A small clutch of memories of Kosciusko Street, random and insignificant, yet kept alive because they are all tied to Mama, for that was the one time I was together with her and old enough to be aware, although I still cannot remember how long I lived there, maybe seven or eight months, certainly not a year.

What remains of those remote months? Some few pictures fixed in my mind, like frames tossed from a movie screen, the film rolling but the fallen pictures silent, microdots locked into place and time, forever fastened onto Mama, who knew nothing of quotidian images, nor could ever imagine that those banalities would have an undying life as the stuff of memories. And one of the oddest was that of a new washing machine that stood like a solid sentry in the old kitchen. It was a Thor "Spinner Washer," one of the strangest appliances I ever saw, or perhaps it only seemed so in context, since the refrigerator and oven hardly suggested a modern home. It stood upright like a gleaming white colossus in a drab surrounding, its edges softened by curves as opposed to right angles, with its oddest feature a lever jutting out in the front that looked like a metallic rudder, and that you pressed down on and pushed to the left or right to engage the washer's cycles. I remember managing that lever for my mother, since it took some pressure to force it down, but I was glad to do it, for the machine was like a giant toy that I enjoyed "working" while at the same time I was inwardly pleased that there was something of today's world in the house, even though I vaguely sensed the impropriety of a washer squarely planted in the kitchen. The Thor was advertised at $199.50, a princely sum, and I can only suppose it was my father's gesture of help to ease my mother's burden.

Naturally there was no dryer, but there was a clothesline that ran from just outside the kitchen window to a pole at the very end of the backyard. I can see my mother leaning over the windowsill, hanging out the clothes, with wooden clothespins, either dark and worn, which meant they were old and weathered, or the color of bright wood, which meant they were new. I liked the clean clothespins because they were solid and strong, and always wanted to throw away the old ones. But I never did.

Nothing useful ever got thrown away then, and certain
for aesthetic reasons. I often wonder if my own proclivity
hanging on to old things, when I have no need of them, is t
as if by some invisible strand to a family who could never toss
cracked and discolored clothespin. My mother hung that laundry, working the pulley, out and in, and as a boy who had never
seen 1930s movies made up to look like city tenements, I still
thought to myself that the whole scene—middle-aged woman,
kitchen window, clothesline, dirt lot—was a little unreal. For in
truth this was going back to the past, and a regression from the
life my mother had known on Christopher Avenue. Although
everything about that address had become hazy in my mind,
I always had an inner realization that we came down in the
world, and I was aware, if not consciously, that my mother's fall
was the hardest of all.

*Yet there were a few spare incidents at Kosciusko Street that I
hold on to. There was a lilac bush in a corner of the backyard lot.
I knew nothing of flowers, never seeing them, or maybe never noticing them, but that bush in the back was inescapable, and what
I remember most about it was your telling me how much you loved
lilacs, and so ever after I thought of lilacs as my flower, although
I never bought them, but I held hard to the color, and years later,
when I first read Whitman's "Lilacs" poem I could not help thinking
of you, and you still come to mind whenever that poem is mentioned
in passing, and even if I should buy something of lavender, I think
of you. I also remember your making cheese blintzes in the kitchen,
putting a cloth down on the table, rolling the dough, and if there
was not enough room for all the cutouts you placed an extra cloth on
the seat of a wooden chair, and how I loved watching you do that.
And of course I remember your apple pies, although Miriam has
no memory of your baking, but I was there and even today I will
rarely order any other pie. I also remember the way you salted the*

'o prepare it for dinner, and I thought
t of work, and to what end I could not
ning the ritual. But one of the most lasting
, got me new roller skates, and told me to hide
ad not find out you had spent the money for them.
, like polished steel, with a great strong key to tighten
,s on my shoes, and I carried them to a side street that had a
,atholic school that took up nearly the entire block, because there
was less traffic, and I rode them over and over that pavement until
I could stay upright without falling, and years later I could go to
any indoor roller rink and skate with ease and confidence. And yet
sometimes I am not sure whether I cared more for the skates or for
you, wondering even now where and how you bought them. No one
else would have done that. No one else ever did.

On a late spring or early summer morning in 1951 I was
with my father at Belmont Avenue. Of that much I am certain.
He was taking Zeyde to see Dr. Pashman, our family doctor,
whose office was in an apartment building on Eastern Parkway. This was still a time when doctors made house calls, and I
knew Dr. Pashman because he came to see me on Christopher
Avenue after my tonsils were taken out, which I remembered
because as long as I was in bed I ate ice cream and jello. It is
a wonder, as I think about it, where these doctors came from.
There were certainly skilled physicians, like the eye doctor who
saved my father's sight after a coffee machine exploded in the
grocery store, and who saw my mother's tumor as soon as he
looked into her eyes, and immediately sent her to see a brain
surgeon. But the good ones seem to have been driven out by
those less able, in a kind of grim Gresham's Law of medicine.
Of the doctors who operated on my mother for ulcers, when
I was four or five, and whose grave mistakes were seared into
my sister's memory, I know nothing. Dr. Pashman was a small,

nondescript, man, with a personality that deepens the m[...]
of *bland,* except that he had a mustache that ran across hi[...]
per lip, which always reminded me of Thomas Dewey, althou[...]
he was not as nice looking as Dewey, and the governor himse[...]
was certainly no head-turner. I also remember wondering why
anyone after the war would want to sport such an unmistakable
sign under his nose. I suppose he wore it long before the war,
was oblivious to its meaning, and like many clung to his habits
against all reason.

But I knew something important and unsettling was going
on because we were taking Zeyde by car to see the doctor. I
had never gone to see a doctor in his office. Yet while I was
worried about my grandfather I was also excited at going into
one of those imposing buildings on Eastern Parkway, *my* world's
grandest street, passing through the doors into a large, circular
foyer, the light subdued but not dark, with couches and chairs
to sit on. I knew people lived in these buildings, but I knew no
one who did. Zeyde had trouble going to the bathroom: that is
the only information I received, if that. For I cannot say with
sureness whether I was told that much, or I am guessing that I
had to have been told: after all, I was twelve years old. I waited
outside in the lobby while my father went into the office with
Zeyde. I do not know how long I was there, certainly less than
an hour, and finally my father came out alone. He said no word
to me, and we walked hurriedly to the car. I kept trying to think
what Zeyde could be doing in the doctor's office, and I could
not get my head around any answer. I imagined that the doctor
performed some surgical procedure there, not knowing that
he was incapable of doing any kind of surgery, but why would
my father leave Zeyde in the office? I think now, how could I
not have questioned him, how could I have left that building
without making a fuss? And it comes to me that years of benign

ⁿded to, or asked to speak, a kind
itself to perfection that morning. It
alked too much for my own good, yet
.. That would change in a few years, as so
change in my life. But on that morning I never
. And I never saw Zeyde again.

had been transported to Beth Israel in Manhattan (the
ospital kept a kosher kitchen) where a prostate procedure was
performed, and he survived the surgery. But the postoperative
care was so misguided that he was confined to his bed on his
back and as a result contracted hypostatic pneumonia. Miriam
visited him on Belmont Avenue, where he was lying in bed,
his face turned away from the street and towards the dining
room, and he told her, with more resignation than anger, that
he was dying, that nobody liked it, but that it was something
that happens to everyone. I hear in those few words a stoic acceptance and quiet wisdom, as philosophical as it was religious,
and altogether fitting of the man. I do not know why I missed
the ritual service, an appalling absence, I was in Levittown that
summer, going to day camp, and it never entered anyone's mind
to tell me of Zeyde's death, though how my father failed to do
so baffles me. Nor was Miriam informed, and she too never saw
him at rest. But he had a wonderful sendoff. My grandmother
did not want to use a funeral parlor, so the bedroom on Belmont Avenue was rearranged and a large wooden box set up on
a table in the center of the room. Men from *shul* had prepared
the body, and my younger cousin Eileen, who was horrified
when she learned what was in the box, was hushed out of the
room, so unlike all those days when Zeyde took her with him to
shul and silenced with a word the men's criticism of a young girl
invading their holy space, keeping her close to him throughout
the morning service, while she played with the fringes on his

talles. After the mourners' prayers, Zeyde's coffin was carried down the single flight of stairs to the street, placed in a hearse that slowly made its way to several nearby *shuls*, with the rabbi at each one reciting prayers for the deceased. Eileen insists that she saw the coffin transported on a horse drawn wagon, clip-clopping its way along the streets, while her older brother remembers following a long, slow moving vehicle. Such is the inconstancy of memory, at once clear and opaque, fixed and mutable, our pilot to the past enmeshed in our shape-shifting mind. The solemn cortège included several people who lived in the tenements across the street, inquired about the activity, and joined the procession, either as a courtesy to my grandmother, whom they would have known, or out of respect for her husband. At last the hearse reached the Watkins Avenue *shul*, halted, the doors were opened, and Zeyde's prayer books placed inside the coffin, a final bow from that small temple to its honored sage.

It was not long after Zeyde's death that I was told I would be leaving Kosciusko Street and moving to Belmont Avenue. I cannot say how I received the news, for no matter my wishes, I was a bit like the tennis ball in the old John Webster play, with no say at all in the game. And as with all else, I was never asked how I felt, or what I thought. But one thing distinguished this transaction from everything that went before: I was given an explanation, and it had such simplicity that I never thought to question it. Since Zeyde was gone, somebody had to live with Bubbie, and I was selected. I remember thinking to myself, why was I chosen from everybody else in the family? Surely there were enough cousins to go around, and Art, my exact equal in age, lived just two blocks away. It seemed to me he was an excellent choice, and he could live with Bubbie and still be near his own family. But this all went round in my head, as the matter was not one for discussion. And if I had a wish, it would be that I could return to those days and those churning thoughts, and find out how I acquiesced in the rupture from my mother with such seeming ease. But as I think about it, I wonder if my mother's health was an unspoken factor, and my moving in with my grandmother served the dual purpose of providing her with help and easing my mother's burden. Of course there was logic to that argument, and certainly nobody was going to tell me that Mama was too sick to care for me herself, but to a boy of twelve none of this could be processed. I was not yet aware of just how bad my mother's condition was, and took at face value the need for someone to live with Bubbie. In some strange way I think I was ambivalent, at once secretly proud to be selected to sleep on Belmont Avenue, and serve as my grandmother's protector, yet at the same time resentful at being the family's pawn, and separated with not so much as a word from Mama.

10. BACK TO BROWNSVILLE

WITH MY MOVE back to Brownsville, after several years in Crown Heights, and a sojourn in Bedford-Stuyvesant, I found myself completely on my own. Although my grandmother had given birth to at least six children, and presided over countless Sunday afternoons and *Pesach Seders,* she was at this time older and measurably slower. Fortunately she never lost her wits, and could still exhibit the kind of sharpness that cowed most of her sons' wives in earlier days. One year, just before the high holidays, I was fifteen or sixteen, she was at the bottom of the stairs, holding the door open from the street, and called up to tell me that she had bought tickets for the services. Since I never went to *shul* on Saturdays, and religion was nowhere in my daily life, I saw no reason to spend two or three days in a place that by this time was nothing more than a remnant from my past. I told her I did not want to go. Gripping the open door, she looked up the dim stairwell, far too steep to see my eyes, and hurled a single, shrill rejoinder: *Goy!* I went to the services. The incident may be so vivid because it was the only discordance in all the years I lived with Bubbie. She was content to let me be, whether from tiredness, or age, or simply because she had raised too many children, fought one battle too many with in-laws or neighbors, and there was nobody left to protect or oversee. In a way, it was an arrangement that suited me, without my thinking too deeply on it. I had a place to live, yet with no obligations, and nobody to tell me what to do. I was independent long before I knew the word, and I took it for granted that I could go when and where I wanted, because I did not have to answer to anybody.

This was made easier because Bubbie, as I said earlier, had more or less stopped cooking, except on the odd occasion when I nudged her to make those golden French fries I could never get enough of, or the coffee cake that was like a babka with chocolate pieces sprinkled inside. I can still see all those baking tins coated black inside from countless years in the oven. I remember the times when she prepared something for me, because I loved the little help I could give her. She had a heavy, cast iron meat chopper that I attached to a wooden chair, tightening its clamp like a vise, and I would turn the iron handle with its wooden knob, which took some strength, as I pushed the meat in and watched with delight as it slithered through the disk and came out ground up and ready for cooking. The refrigerator in that tiny kitchen—and it is a wonder how those huge *seders* were ever prepared in that turnaround space—struck me even then as antique. It was a GE that looked like nothing more than an oblong box atop four legs, with a steel handle that lifted up to pull out and open the door. What made it seem so old to me, and drew my eyes all the time, was the round compressor sitting on top the white porcelain cabinet, which gave the model its name, *Monitor Top,* for the design was said to resemble the gun turret on a Civil War ship of the same name. There was usually shmaltz in a jar, as Bubbie still made boiled chicken, but even then I had an aversion to chicken fat, and rarely put it on my challah, although I loved eating the cold, leftover chicken from Friday night. I think it was the case that she wanted to do things for me, but the space between the desire and the act was simply too wide, and I wound up learning to do things for myself. Like ironing, and when I brought out the board, and heated up the iron, Bubbie commented that I would make some woman a fine husband. She delivered offhand remarks like that, which suggests she was not unaware of my situation, but was simply unable to engage directly with me. And she probably never knew how much I admired her, maybe even loved her, as she drank her tea, Russian-style, in a glass, putting two cubes of sugar in her mouth before sipping the hot brew, or as she brushed and braided her long hair that she washed with olive oil, an odd detail I never forgot, or sat at the cash register and toted up the grocery items in pencil on a brown paper bag, or daily pored over the small script of the Yiddish newspaper, while I wondered to myself why at this stage of her life she cared so much about what was going on in the world. But she always did. She never left the world until she did.

What is a memoir but a reconstruction? Or perhaps it is a construction in the process of its making, which is not exactly the same thing. You remember the past, or a part of it, and you record that memory faithfully, believing it a fair and accurate representation. But being excluded from the thoughts of others whose lives were stitched into that selfsame past, barred from their experience, makes it impossible to fully know them, and thus may entangle my story. Several years ago I was sitting with two older cousins in my sister's bright open kitchen on one of those lovely autumnal days on Long Island, gorgeous tall trees and an expansive lawn visible just outside, when one said, with such forcefulness that it could have been a stage delivery, If Bubbie were here now and I had a gun I would shoot her! *Whose grandmother had we been talking about? His? Or mine? My cousins and my sister have so hardened a picture of our grandmother that mine is but a minority report. And so even in a memoir, we occasionally wind up in the position of a novelist, trying to penetrate the people in our past with nothing more to work with than our insubstantial imagination. And that process, which may be more construction than reconstruction, becomes as bound to the book as the sensory experiences that are remembered with such immediacy, and gripped with such faith in their unshakable being.*

There is a compelling picture of my grandmother, *circa* 1930, taken at that great open space, Prospect Park, trees in the background, parked cars straight out of a vintage movie, and what seems the oddest touch, a man on horseback, erect in breeches and a white shirt, moving outside the border of the shot. But the foreground, covering nearly the whole of the photograph, has my grandmother seated with my cousin Laura and my sister Miriam, both about two, perched on her lap. She is in her early to mid fifties, hair still brown and cut short, but the look is striking, almost mesmerizing. The eyes are nearly closed, the right one barely visible, as she stares directly ahead, not at the camera but into the distance, as if she were searching for something, or someone, all the while exerting tight, physical control of the two girls, her only grandchildren at the time. The girls are adorable, but the face of the woman might make anyone pause, as you would before a lioness protecting its cubs. *Rasza* or *Rashi* Manikow née Salutsky, before becoming Rose in this country, was born in a section of Poland-Russia listed on the ship's manifest as *Dereczyn*, today known as *Derechin* and a part of Belarus. The place is noteworthy because it was the site of Jewish partisan resistance to the Nazis, and is so identified in a timeline in that granite museum that looks out at the harbor from Battery Park. This is a source of considerable pride in our family, and it is clear to me that Rasza Salutsky was as fierce a fighter as those of her kin who stayed behind and died years after she was settled in America.

She brought over two nephews after the war, Carl and Murray Salutsky, along with Murray's wife Sonya, all survivors of the Shoah. I came to know Murray because he would show up at the store on Belmont Avenue, never to any purpose that I could see, but there was just enough mystery to make him intriguing. Although my father and his family were from abroad, in actuality that meant little to me since it was a distant past and they never talked of it. But Murray was *now*, so new as to carry *abroad* and *foreign* and *Europe* in his very presence. He resembled my father in build, was much better looking than his brother Carl, with a mobile face and attractive dark hair, though thinning, that went straight back over his head. He always wore a coat and tie, which struck me as strange since I never knew him to be coming from an office, but it added a tone of seriousness to a man who was not like anybody else who walked into the store from off the street. Murray had tattooed numbers which he rolled up his sleeve to show me, and a wooden leg, which I never asked him about yet always wondered if it was a result of the "war," although I had no idea of the particularity of that term. The reason I looked forward to his visiting was because he would *talk* with me, and to my mind seemed incredibly educated, I remember an excited conversation about Dostoevsky, having myself read no more than *Crime and Punishment*, but it was so exhilarating to talk with someone in my family who read literature, and had a head full of ideas. I never knew what work he did, and I had a vague sense that being a refugee was no bed of roses.

But what I most remember are our long arguments about postwar Germany. I was a standout poster for teenage smugness, arguing smartly for treating Germany as a new country, that we not use the past to make present policy, and we should not think of contemporary Germans in the same way as those who were in the war. Even writing this makes me cringe, the parrot prose dinning in my ear, as I think of that sensitive, maybe even tormented man, whose hatred of Germany was so intense that at times I had the sense to realize we did better to stop talking, and on a rare occasion the thought occurred to me that I had no real understanding of what he had suffered. For although it was the Fifties, and I saw numerous people with tattoos on their forearms, in truth I was never aware of the reality of the death camps, and never heard the phrase, for they were always called "concentration camps," which to my literal mind meant that people were *concentrated* there, as in a prison. I had no picture in my head of the mass arrests of Jews in the cities of Europe, of the train deportations, the nakedness, the gassing and burning. I knew the number *six million*, yet had no deep comprehension as to what it meant. And of course it was impossible to visualize the figure, let alone try and connect it with the actual murder of people. I have no excuse for this ignorance, and am loath to blame it on my family, who never talked about anything before, so why should they start now? But it strikes me with shame, as I think of it, that my old grandmother, with her Yiddish newspaper, and her unflinching, almost tribal family loyalty, had a stronger grasp on reality and a harder knowledge of the world than I, a born and bred American, who thought it fun to argue with a man just back from hell.

Jack Fisher's *Little Oriental Restaurant* at 1546 Pitkin Avenue, a spaldeen's toss from the majestic *Loew's Pitkin*, the movie palace that anchored the western end of the long street, was neither little nor Asian. It was a white tablecloth, Romanian steakhouse on street level, while the upstairs was reserved for social functions, including engagements, weddings and anniversaries, what were commonly called *affairs.* The word was never used in the casual sense of *event,* but as a hard noun, *I have an affair to go to next Saturday.* There was a quaint obliviousness to the term's illicit meaning, and I remember wondering to myself if it might have been a peculiarly Jewish use of English, different from Yiddish inflected speech. But the *Little Oriental* was a durable Brownsville institution, where charities, merchant associations, and political groups conducted their business. Abe Stark, that ur-Brooklyn man whose grand haberdashery was a block up the street, was reputed to have been offered a deputy mayor's post at a dinner there. Clearly I knew zilch of all this. I never ate in the restaurant, which was unaffordable, and the quickness with which that statement tapped itself out suddenly made me ask myself, where *did* I eat? And I realized that I never ate in restaurants at all during those years (I do not count delicatessens and luncheonettes that I went to on my own). I have a dim memory of being in a Chinese restaurant when I was small, but other than that I have no recollection of going to a restaurant with grownups. Who would I have gone with? I cannot remember my mother ever taking me, and my father never had any time.

To say that eating out was not a cultural habit in my family would give an intellectual cast to a behavior that was more instinctual than reflective. In reality, the idea that a restaurant might be a pleasure, or a diversion from dailiness, never pierced the routine of their lives. Hard as I try, I cannot enter the minds of my parents about the most banal of daily activities. I can only surmise: my mother was ill, my father always at work, and anxiety over health and money preoccupied the two of them. All of the rest of life, how we spent our days and evenings, our plans for tomorrow, what we lived for, none of these were spelled out, all were displaced, if they ever existed, by narrower and grimmer concerns. And so a boy, any boy, had no choice but to take it as it was. And at twelve years old, living with my grandmother, I came to take the world as I found it. I never questioned whether it should be otherwise, or if it was fair or not. I never thought of myself as unlucky in any way. I was content with my situation, and relished the freedom to come and go at will. I believe that was more important to me than anything else. And it is not as if I wanted to do anything risky or subversive. From my perspective, the streets were perilous enough. Navigating them safely from point to point was all I needed of adventure. They were seductive as well as familiar, for there was always the prospect of ranging outside the comfort zone, which would take place in just a couple of years, in high school. But for the moment, my blank history of dining out had no effect on my conscious mind: I could not regret what I had never known.

My cousin Evelyn got married in Jack Fisher's open, second story space, with just enough people to fill the room. She was seven or eight years older than me, and married young. But what was far more exciting, the man she wed was not Jewish. Evelyn had two siblings, Laura and Marvin, their family almost an exact counterpart to mine. But their mother died a young woman, and their father remarried quickly, a mean woman with no interest or tolerance for his children. My grandmother once said that if a parent had to die it should be the father, because as long as the mother was alive the children will have a home. I am not sure what prompted that remark, but I never forgot it. Perhaps it struck me as old world wisdom, even though I was skeptical of country folklore. Another time, after some fraught conversation with a girl (I see myself huddled on a chair near a small table, cradling that black cast iron telephone against my ear), one I cannot believe my grandmother heard, let alone understood, she shook her head and said, as if to the air, that I was going to cause grief to women.

As I write this I suddenly realize that she never spoke directly to me but quietly aloud, as if no one were there, and that may be why these passing comments remain so stark in my memory. They were about *me*, and they were the only things she said that indicated she was aware of me as a person. She was devoted to her sons, and I was not her child. I lived with a woman who might be seen as a substitute for my mother, but who exhibited no affection. It sounds as if my grandmother was an unfeeling person, but that was not so. There was a stubborn streak in her nature—never forgive, never forget—that I see all too well in myself. But she was part of a generation who put no value on oral expression. In my grandmother's case I think the silence was borne by her experience in Poland, which had a far greater hold on her than any thought of satisfying the unformed needs of an American boy. Whenever I would ask about her life in the old country the response was always the same, *nisht shprakhn,* which loosely translates as "don't talk about it." As I think of it, survival was all, and that was the lesson she imparted more dramatically than any word of uplift she might have framed, although it would be droll to imagine my grandmother offering uplift. Zeyde had *shul* and his books, lived a life where the spiritual was manifest, and it leavened his relations with his grandchildren, who all cherish him in their memories. His wife elicited no such reverence. She interfered in others' lives, and those who bore the brunt of that meddling never forgot, and in their own way never forgave. I had it easy. She had no need to interfere with me, and was beyond the desire to do so. Yet now, oddly enough, I almost wish she *had* intruded a little more, not to direct my life, but simply to make it clearer, all these years later, that she did indeed care, if only in her fashion.

Naturally my grandparents did not go to Evelyn's wedding. Orthodoxy still held sway, and I am not sure anyone expected anything different. But my uncles and aunts and cousins were there, and for an eleven year old it was something to look forward to. For a large family there were surprisingly few events. My sister was married a year earlier, and no children were invited. Excluding children was a way of keeping the cost of the affair down, and though the amount seems ludicrous today, ten dollars a couple would have been the high end for Miriam's summer wedding. The other affair of note was Zeyde's and Bubbie's golden anniversary, a large and boisterous event recorded in an impressive album of black and white photographs. But it was Evelyn's wedding that made the greatest impression on me, though I remember nothing of the service, which was performed by a reformed cantor. Finding a rabbi in Brooklyn willing to celebrate a mixed marriage was akin to ordering a bagel at Howard Johnson's—on the face of it simple enough, but in reality dream on. Evelyn's event brought me face to face for the first time with outsiders who were different from the people I grew up with. Jack Macfadden, the groom, carried the name of a man who was famous, and even had a touch of notoriety about him. Bernarr Macfadden, proponent of fitness and healthy living, interviewed regularly by the press, was nearly forty years older than Jack's mother when he married her, his third wife. This was the stuff of novels.

Johnnie Lee Macfadden, the groom's mother, was present, and it was impossible to keep your eyes from her. Stunning in dress and looks, she was something of a celebrity in her own right, selling health and beauty and youth, and periodically showing up on the Jack Paar and Merv Griffin shows. If I was ignorant of the back story, I still was entranced by her, as if some shimmering grace had gotten lost and plopped down in a charmless room above a steak house on Pitkin Avenue. Miriam, who talked with Johnnie Lee, told me later that there was an innuendo of sex about her conversation, and she never forgot a phrase she used about a man having "naughty eyes," which sounds like it could have come out of the nineteen twenties, printed on a card in a silent flapper film. It is odd how an old expression often hangs on in our talk, branding us to an era that later we would prefer to forget. Finally, just about a year into their marriage, Evelyn and Jack went to Belmont Avenue to visit Bubbie, who was ill. She was lying in bed, and Evelyn went in, kissed her, while Jack stood back, and extended from a distance his warm wishes. Bubbie motioned for him to come forward, and as he leaned over the bed she took his palm and slipped him one hundred dollars, quite a generous sum. The money was certainly welcome, but I suspect the gesture of acceptance from the family matriarch was even more valued, as it is preserved in the oral history of the anecdote. Although Jack's later conversion to Judaism closes the circle of the couple's story, the delayed gift, perhaps a silent admission of error, or an expression of genuine fondness, makes the most satisfying coda to the wedding.

Try to remember, *the old song begins, but* who knows where or when, *sings an even older one. The first implores the memoirist to conjure up the past, to revivify old places and feelings as if they had never died, giving our lives an unending freshness and seeming indifference to age. But the second song denies the premise, for we are so forgetful of the past—think of Maurice Chevalier's sly refrain, "Ah, yes, I remember it well"—that the way we lived comes back to us cloaked in doubt and uncertainty. Yet we still write, intent upon retrieving the essence of that which has gone, all the while hoping that words alone will bring the dead back, and resolve the inscrutable days of our unrecoverable lives. In a sense the entire project is a leap of faith, wherein the contradiction between truth and untruth either lies suspended, or totters back and forth in the author's mind. What we write is partly what we remember, and partly how we fashion that memory. For composition is a process of constricting the memory into a shape that alters its imagined reality and creates something new, a remembrance, which becomes the stuff of memoir, becomes indeed the memoir itself. In the hands of a superior writer, fashioning the past can run away with the intention. In Henry Adams'* Education *we are aware of the discrepancy between the narrative and Adams' life, and the strange irony that a brilliant historian could barely write his own story. Adams, along with his friend Henry James, whose own memoir was another version of his ambiguous fiction, is not a model for the memoirist. Both are simply too grand for emulation, as well as too distant. But the writer who comes to the form without preparation, either from fiction or history, finds himself in a borderless open field, and all he can do, to mangle an image from one of James's great stories, is work in the dark, and trust to the chaotic nature of art.*

11. LILACS IN THE DOORYARD

THIRTEEN. My age just after the New Year in 1952. Having a birthday on the second of January has always been off-center. An hour earlier and I would have been a New Year's baby, with everybody celebrating the holiday as if it were mine. But a solid two weeks of seasonal revels, ending on the first of January, leaves no one with a desire for anything more than a slow reentry into ordinary life. Yet I came to relish a birthday that started the year, even if a day late. It was better than making resolutions, which I disliked, for my new age was itself a resolution as it marked a fresh beginning. And so I got used to keeping my birthday quiet. But all this came much later. At thirteen you do not think closely on the meaning of your birthday. What you focus on is your imminent bar mitzvah, for which you are barely prepared. My cousin Art and I were to have a joint ceremony in the Watkins Avenue *shul*. Since he had been attending a yeshiva he was fluent in reading Hebrew, which had to be done from the Torah scroll stored behind the ark. Someone came to the apartment on Belmont Avenue to prep me, my grandmother must have hired him, for I see myself in the bedroom near the window, where I later used to read on my own, and can visibly make out a bearded man hovering over me with an open book, pushing a passage, over and over, which I would later repeat on the raised platform in the center of the *shul,* the massive scroll unrolled before me just enough to reveal the beautiful script, and swaying a bit as if in imitation of men at prayer.

You would think, coming from the world of my grandfather, I would have a memorable picture of that quintessential rite. But with his death a year earlier, and my own laxity, most of the practices were gone. Bubbie no longer made Passover seders, and so what was left of Jewish observance? The kitchen was kosher, and there were the high holidays, and I made a feeble effort right after the bar mitzvah at laying *tfiln,* or phylacteries, the small boxes filled with scripture that you strap to your left arm and around your forehead at morning prayers. But that lasted less than a week, and was the last Orthodox ritual of my life. Somehow it seems so long ago that it has been eclipsed if not erased from memory, part of a life I once had but cannot now summon up. It is as if my coming of age as a Jewish male both culminated and concluded on a Saturday morning in a small synagogue on a side street in Brownsville. I am sure there was pressure during the preparation, for studying from a book was not the same as reading the scroll, and you had to chant the words, but the passage was not that long, and memorization alone could get you through. As it turned out, I performed creditably enough, and Art read with ease. Oddly enough, he has no better memory of the service than I do. At one moment we were photographed together under a large *tales.* The synagogue was rigidly segregated, the women all upstairs, looking down, and at the end they threw candies at us from above, which was a traditional custom after the conclusion of this seminal day in our lives.

The most indelible impression was not the ceremony, but the presence of my mother. She was very ill, and it was uncertain whether she would come. I do not know how she got there. I imagine my father brought her, yet I cannot even see my father as I try and picture the morning. But I see my mother clearly, for she is sitting next to my sister at the front of the balcony, her head covered with a large white bandage, as you might see on the skull of a person in a hospital scene in a war movie, and she must have been silent through the service, because I remember no disruption, but when it was over, and everybody relaxed, and the candies fell, I looked up and saw her trembling, unable to control herself, and people were trying to help her, taking her by the arms, and she was quickly if awkwardly led downstairs and out of the *shul*. I did not follow, and I remember nothing after. I did not ask about her, or what happened. Whom would I have asked? It astonishes me now how I could stay silent, although at the same time nobody talked to me, or asked anything. It is as if my mother did not exist. Yet it was she who insisted on getting to her son's bar mitzvah, and what it took for her to manage that I can only begin to imagine. I never thought about it at the time, and I believe I felt nothing when I saw her suffering in the synagogue. I wish I could remember, but all I felt was relief at finishing the Torah reading, being pleased with myself, maybe even a bit cocky. And hard as I try I can retrieve no feelings at seeing my mother in agony. I was as if frozen in place, numb to any sensation, with absolutely no idea of what to do or how to respond, as I stared blankly up at the balcony,

Sometime in the next month, possibly the middle of February, on a weekday, my grandmother told me I should go and see my mother. I had a queasy feeling about it, but there was nothing I could say, for since my move to Belmont Avenue I doubt if I returned even once to Kosciusko Street. It would be a long ride, through the commercial strip of Pitkin Avenue, onto Eastern Parkway, switching to the trolley at Nostrand Avenue, crossing the remainder of Crown Heights, and ending at Dekalb Avenue in the heart of Bedford Stuyvesant. But it was not the trip that unsettled me. It was the thought of seeing my mother, not knowing what to say or do, and unsure, maybe even frightened, of how I would feel or what I would think. For the truth is, however hard or cruel it sounds, I had put my mother out of my consciousness, and if my grandmother had not issued her injunction I would not have moved myself. But she did. And so I went. On the bus and trolley I tried to think of anything but what faced me long minutes away, and whatever disjointed thoughts scrambled through my mind they at least served to pass the time. When I got to 503 Kosciusko I walked up the flight of stairs, entered the apartment, and was surprised to discover no nurse anywhere in sight. Mama was laying in bed in the small room next to the kitchen, facing the back yard, the room my sister Ann had slept in years before, mine for the short while I lived there, and the one she would now never leave upright. The smell in the closed space was pungent, and I instinctively felt it was the smell of death. Mama was in such pain that it was all I could do to keep myself from bolting out of the room. Miriam said that when she was there Mama had asked her for morphine, could barely speak, and yet still uttered, "I have to *mutshe* for a little bit more." And suffer she did. At first I was not sure she knew who I was, and then I thought she wanted me to do something, to tell *them* to help her die, or maybe she just wanted them to kill her. And all I remember thinking was why did they not kill her, which would at least bring peace, instead of making her suffer so? But if Mama could *mutshe* a little bit more, it was more than I could do. I bolted, running away from that coffin of pain and getting myself back somehow to the apartment on Belmont Avenue. To this day I cannot remember how. I know I was afraid to take the trolley and bus back because it would be too fast, and my grandmother would want to know why I had not stayed longer. I thought that if I walked the entire way then the time would easily be accounted for, and everyone would think that I spent it with Mama. I did not have the courage to tell my grandmother, or anyone, that I could not bear it, that I was simply not strong enough to stay in the room with my dying mother.

On March fourth, very early in the morning, it could not have been an hour past dawn, I was asleep for some reason in my grandmother's bed, when I was awakened by the ringing of the heavy black telephone in the dining room less than six feet away. Bubbie answered the phone, and after a short pause I heard her say quietly, as if to herself, *Blanchie ist geshtarbn.* I have no idea who she was speaking with, but the words are still in my head after all these years, "Blanche is dead," as is the stillness I felt in the room, and even a sense of heaviness in my grandmother's being. I made believe I was sleeping because I did not want to hear the news out loud, because I knew I was not going to cry, and I was afraid if I did not cry my grandmother would wonder what was wrong with me. Through the next few days, at the funeral especially, and sitting *shive* after, I was obsessed with the matter of tears: I could not bring them on at will, and yet I believed they were the most important sign of my feelings. I remember nothing of any service, but I cannot forget the cemetery, the casket lowered by straps into the newly dug ground, my being told to recite the *Kaddish*, which meant reading it from whatever pamphlet I was handed, which was another test, would I be able to read it properly, and all the while keenly aware that I was not crying, had not cried, which could only mean that I had no feelings, or must not have cared. And many years later, in one of the rare moments when Miriam and I talked about Mama's death, she said to me, "I didn't even think you were affected, you didn't seem to be upset by it at all." So I suppose I was right to connect tears with emotion, for even my sister thought I was untouched. As for the rest of my family, my father, aunts and uncles, even my grandmother, I did not receive a single word or gesture of condolence or consolation. In a way, my dry eyes seemed to call forth what I had feared the most, that my mother's death had no effect on my life.

Decades later, after the breakup of a long relationship, I was told to write a letter to my mother. I thought the exercise foolish, but I was smarting enough to go along with almost anything that was asked of me. And so I was brought back to that room, and the telephone call, and the cemetery on Staten Island. I needed to say goodbye, I was told, a thought that would never have occurred to me. Although I was addressing thin air, in my head I was talking to my mother, and I found to my astonishment that I had no inhibitions, and could say whatever I wanted. The pitiful part was that I had so little to say. I told her about the last time I saw her, and how hard it was for me to stay there, and that I thought I had blocked the memory of it out of my mind, yet it was not the case: I could never get the room and the bed and the smell out of my senses. But then I wanted to step away from that tortured place and tell her about the warm remembrances that stayed with me: how I cherished her small acts, like getting me a puppy to cushion the blow of taking me away from my neighborhood after I got back from camp, or buying me roller skates when she had no money, and how I was never sure if it was the skates or the gesture that

I cared about more. There was so little I could draw up to tell her, except that I knew she loved me, and then she was not there anymore, and I was sent to live with Bubbie, and she got sicker and sicker, and finally died. *And I missed you so much only I made myself believe that I really didn't, that I was tough, and could go on living without you, and it didn't matter. What did you really need a mother for? And living with Bubbie the year before you died, and even after, I felt as if I were betraying you because I knew you didn't get along with Bubbie, and by living with her I was rejecting you. But it was not my doing, although I came to tell myself what I was told, that it was necessary and for the best. And all those years after you died I tamped down all thoughts of you so that over time I came to forget that I ever had a mother, and acted as if I were born from nothing, or hatched from an egg. But then suddenly I started thinking about you, and crying to myself, and I could no longer push you away. I didn't cry when you died, but I did many years after, and I think of you now without tears, as the mother who loved me when I was a child, and who was taken away from me when I was still a boy. I'm writing to say goodbye, and to tell you that you're no longer buried deep inside but are a part of who I am, of who I've always been. And more than anything I hope you've been at rest all these long years, and that you'll think a kind thought of me once in a while.*

12. FAIRY TALES, FATEFUL ACTS

THERE IS a black and white photograph of my eighth grade class taken in May 1952. Thirty five students and two teachers, standing up against the sparsely posted back wall of the classroom, and seated in five rows, myself one of two wearing glasses, and one of three, with Goldie Drucker and Eleanor Imbriale, without a smile. Goldie is indifferent, or bored, while Eleanor's large eyes look aslant from the camera, away from the direction of all the other faces, and betray in hers just the faintest hint of grimness. Mine is blank. It is strange to see all the smiles, beaming or shy, some few forced, all of us in white shirts and blouses, the boys wearing the ugliest striped ties, and most of the girls with bows accenting their collars. This cracked photograph, "presented with the compliments of the East New York Savings Bank," stares back at me as I recognize faces and names yet cannot give them any more reality than their flattened images. I once knew these people, yet I am unable to breathe life into them. Why does it matter? We were all thirteen years old. Why care about people who passed our lives like fireflies, and had no more significance to us than those same fleeting flashes of light? Yet we want to remember, for seeing the faces and names reminds us that we played together, probably fought together, and forgetting where and when means that we have lost a part of our past, and something of ourselves to know. Better to have lost the picture. There are few, like Proust, who can recover so much of their past as to invigorate it with new life, and one unlikely to die. The memoirist is in the position of Keats in the *Grecian Urn*, trying to preserve youth and beauty while warding off age and morbidity. Remembrance is all we have, and in its recovery we find its own form of imagining. I see Carol Kaplan sitting in the next row in front of me, a very pretty face with a slight, sly smile, and I am drawn to her, can barely keep from folding my arms around her, yet not a single moment was shared by the

Class 8-3, Mrs. Cecil B. Tiber, Math.Tr; Mr.I.Joseph Geduld, Off.Tr., Public School No.2; Photograph presented with the compliments of The East New York Savings Bank - May, 195.

STANDING: l. to r. Doris Alleyne, Alice Strassberg, Eileen Baron, Patricia Mathews, Jackeline Mitchell, Leona Schmerloff, Louis Aronowitz, Milton Wyche, Joel Messelson, Hubert Alston, Melvin Meyerson, Lawrence Miller, Robert Spoolick, Martin Rubin. FIRST ROW: top to bottom. Irwin Schatzman, Melvyn Moskowitz, Leonard Shapiro. SECOND ROW: Bernard Rashbaum, Raymond Messelsoln, Stanley Seigel, Bennett Cohen, Third Row: Paula Perlman, Goldie Drucker, Eleanor Imbriale, Janet Klinkowitz, Minnie Reeves. FOURTH ROW: Joan Schoen-wetter, Judith Messenger, Sandra Lesser, Beatrice Morris, Carol Kaplan. FOURTH ROW: Ralph Di Cupero, Harvey Sherman, Steven Berkman, Barry Menikoff.

two of us. And so the past rests in a brittle photograph that is nothing like a representation of who we were. Nobody came to school in a white shirt and blouse. Nor were we ever seated so neatly and formally. This was a framed moment, both artificial and real. We all knew it. But some had wider smiles.

The first love letter I received survives as an artifact from the same year, dated "Oct. 27, 1952," addressed to me at "503 Kosciusko Street B'klyn 21, N.Y." and bearing a three-cent "Indian Centennial" commemorative stamp. A dozen brief sentences, typed in red ink, with a colored bob of flowers imprinted in an upper corner of the small sheet. The back of the envelope has "S W A M K" scrawled across it in large blue letters, a couple of "X"s thrown in at both ends, while the discolored tape pasted along the twin legs of the flap, security against the loss of that single page, still holds fast to the edges. Even more, the lipstick kisses planted on the envelope have lost little of their color, and might pass today as if blotted on a tissue between two pressed lips. Having spent a career in archives reading old letters, I am hardly surprised at seeing one aged sixty years. But this is *my* letter, not a library's, and while *life is short and art long* may be a good maxim in books, to see your thirteen-year old self in the eyes of a girl all those years ago is far from a small thing. For the letter cannot help but draw you back with wonder to a boy who exists now only in that sheet.

> *Dearest Barry,*
> *How are you? I am fine. Since you did not write me, I took it upon myself to write. I like this boy in my class, Neil, but you are still tops TO ME. I am enclosing a picture of myself, which I think is one of my best, and I hope you will. I am praying I will find a letter in the mailbox from*

you within a week. This week I had my hair cut and had a permanent. I hope you'll like it when you see me next. Well that's about all for now.

LOVE AND KISSES
Carol [signed]

P.S. IN your next letter please send ME a picture of yourself.
P.S.S. I miss you terribly.
Love Carol [signed]

The picture is long gone, and the years, far from dimming the words have merely deepened their sweetness. Yet I remember nothing of Carol. Neither who she was nor what she looked like. Her last name appears nowhere on the envelope, and the only clue to her address is the postmark, "GREAT NECK, N.Y. Oct 28 5- PM 1952." It opens up a story that cannot be completed and whose parts are random puzzle pieces. The summer I spent at a day camp on Long Island, where I acted the role of Tom Sawyer, provided an experience I never forgot. One of the boys there invited me to spend the weekend at his house. He lived in King's Point, the most exclusive section of Great Neck. It was my first time in a detached house, other than Miriam and Harry's Cape Cod, which even I knew was ordinary at best. Driving through Great Neck to King's Point was a winding trip amidst a world of homes far from the tract monolith of Levittown. For starters, I was given my own room to sleep in, and I was awed by the spaciousness and fullness of the room, as well as being self-conscious about not having pajamas, and certainly not a robe to put on for breakfast. My friend's mother kindly gave me both, and I pondered thinking about the plenty of the boy's wardrobe. There were large trees around the house,

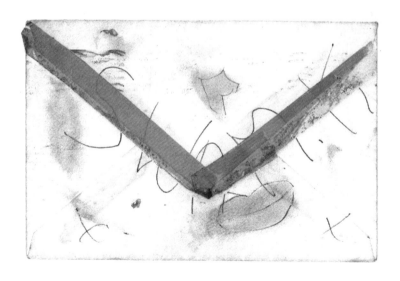

and looking out the window I felt as if I were in a private park, but the unforgettable event was the breakfast. All the family gathered in a bright room, including my friend's older sister, it was her sixteenth birthday, and sometime between the orange juice and Danish she was given the keys to a car. The scene might have come out of a film, or a novel, but none that I had ever seen or read.

Yet what stays with me now is not the present itself but my reaction, behaving with a placidity that defied the thoughts racing through my head. Of course I was an outsider, brought into this close family's life for a few passing moments, but still my manner was revealing. Over and over, as I draw upon long gone incidents, that habit recurs with regularity: no matter the situation, or the strangeness to my experience, I affected an attitude of impassivity, or imperturbability, as if what I had just witnessed was the most ordinary thing in the world. A composed face was the only response to these discoveries. Sometimes I wonder if it was a manner I deliberately adopted or if I never fully appreciated what was happening. That people lived in tree shaded houses with multiple bedrooms, and garages, and had conversations in bright breakfast rooms, was altogether normal. What was there to be surprised at? And yet as dispassionate as I appeared, as normal as I wanted to seem, in my head I had been transported as if on a magic carpet to another place where people who looked like me were not at all like any people I knew. And I could not put my finger on what the difference was, the manners obviously, the politeness and ease that went around the table, that the mother in particular seemed to impart, so I ascribed it all to the place and the setting and to everything that was outside my sphere of knowledge.

It was during my visit, to pick up one stray puzzle piece, that my friend gave a party, and it was there that I met Carol, we played spin the bottle, and I can only guess that we kissed. We exchanged addresses, although I cannot seem to get the time and sequence of events just right. But it does not matter. The more intriguing question is why I have the letter at all? What compelled me at that age to keep a mash note from a girl I had no chance of ever seeing? A thirteen-year old boy could hardly be expected to muse on the meaning of those lipstick traces, or appreciate the plain innocence of the writing, yet on some visceral level his heart must have been engaged, and the single leaf of love was a place to assuage the soul's hunger, and even if none of that was thought, could not possibly be understood, it was still known while being unknown, felt without feeling, yearned for with no yearning. The spare story of Carol and Barry is an interrupted or broken fairy tale by Scott Fitzgerald—-Bedford Stuyvesant meets Great Neck—-long before the boy ever heard the name, or could possibly know what a Fitzgerald fairy tale entailed.

I remember almost nothing about junior high school. I took the bus on the corner of Stone and Pitkin, in front of a large yeshiva high school, as it made its way west on haberdashery row to Eastern Parkway, where I got off at Rochester Avenue and walked four blocks north, past Lincoln Place, St Johns Place, Sterling Place, until I reached 210 at Park Place. The daily trip stays in my mind, but what went on in school escapes me altogether. I am certain that no book learning happened. There were a number of shop classes, all the boys were required to take at least one, on the theory that we needed to find our natural abilities, those who would wind up using reading and counting for work, and those for whom manual dexterity would prove decisive. I remember taking a woodworking class and making a square, hardwood board game, with a heavy metal arrow that functioned as a spinner drilled into the center. That was the best thing I ever made, or even did, in junior high school. I know I wanted to go on and make something else, but of course nothing came of it. I was geared for the reading and counting track, and the class satisfied the shop requirement. The strange thing is that the leather briefcase I made in elementary school and the wood board game in junior high stayed with me as subliminal experiences, and I always believed that I was good with my hands, and if I only developed the skill I would have made things over the years that might have given me pleasure both in the making and in the things themselves.

I think of my wonder and admiration when I first read that Arthur Miller was an accomplished woodworker and made his own furniture. I would momentarily delude myself into thinking that I could have done the same thing. While the idea is preposterous, it is absolutely the case that the school system had no clue as to what they were doing with us, or what their educational objectives were, if anyone that we came across in 210 could even have mouthed that cliché. Maybe Arthur Miller's woodworking was a hobby, although I doubt it, for I have it in my head that *hobby* was a very big word in my time, long after Miller's period, and having hobbies was a mark of our well-roundedness and a sign of our potential for happiness as grown ups. Successful adults had hobbies. Those without were narrow, limited people, unable to express any aspect of a personality apart from the one that lashed them to their work. I was aware of the word because it would regularly show up on tests that were designed to tell us what we were qualified to do with our lives. *What are your hobbies?* the forms would ask, and I felt painfully embarrassed, even guilty, because I had nothing to write down. I played no instrument, I could not sing, and I never learned to tap dance, which I badly wanted to do ever since I first saw Fred Astaire and Gene Kelly in the movies. Whether these activities qualified as hobbies or not, I would have listed them if I could get away with it. As I think of it now, I am struck by the ludicrousness of it all, and can only attribute it to an education culture that was empty at best and hostile at worst. Our families, at least the ones I knew, had no idea of this mania for defining and classifying their children: most were happy if we were not getting into trouble, and all hoped that with a little luck we might grow up and get away from where we came from.

John Marshall was the first school I attended with a mixed black and white population. It had a reputation for being tough, straddling the border of Crown Heights and Bedford Stuyvesant, and before entering I remember worrying about how I would handle myself. But it was not that dangerous when I was there. Five years after I graduated it became notorious. A girl was raped in the school basement; the principal jumped off the roof of his six-story apartment building; and a reporter for the *World-Telegram & Sun* posed as a teacher for two months, wrote a series of articles about the place, and won a journalism award. John Marshall became a byword for uncontrollable students. The school had gone from borderline functionality to a blackboard jungle in just a few years. In my time, the most that could be said was the potential for violence was there. One of my classmates, Lenny, cited just such a moment: "A black kid walked up to me as we were going home. He was smaller than me, and he punched me in the stomach. I didn't feel anything and he looked shocked, then ran away. But he conveyed a hostility toward whites that taught me a life lesson." Another, Harvey, told about the general safety of the place: "I remember playing pool in the afternoons after school, and ticking off one punk named 'Junior.' I told him to fuck off and I remember going to 210 the next afternoon and Jacobson telling me not to show up. Well, to the expression 'never eat at a place called Mom's and never play poker with a guy called Doc' must be added, don't play pool with a punk called Junior." He added: "Marvin and Bernie always got me out of trouble." Bernie was very tall, and Harvey, like me, very short.

An Italian boy whom I barely knew approached me with an offer of protection. Anthony was a stylish kid who wore his sleeves rolled up two or three times to show his forearms, and in the graduation snapshot he is captured with the only bow tie in the class. I have no idea what prompted his offer, but he was insistent that if I ever needed help he would be there. I learned only recently that Anthony was the best friend of Irving, who in later years became an important person in my life. Irving would go to Anthony's house and sing to his friend's piano accompaniment, a skill he put to use in Spanish class one day when he got up in front of the room, and in a resonant voice belted out *Solamente una vez / Amé en la vida / Solamente una vez / Y nada más*. I can still hear him, and even more see him, as he placed a bandana over his head as a prop for the performance. Irving had a wonderful voice, but a tumultuous relation with his father, so any kind of musical training was out of the question. I am unaware of any of my friends who went to dance or music classes. I never thought about it growing up, but unless you were in your friends' homes you had no idea of what went on there. And nobody talked about life at home. Nobody talked about what his father did for a living. Or about their mothers, who mainly were at home.

I am struck by how unknowing we were of our friends' families, or even that they had families. To learn in the course of writing this memoir that one classmate was beaten throughout his childhood, and another's father threw a bicycle at him because his wife hurt her hand when the boy raised his elbow to prevent her from smacking him, comes as a shock. In the latter incident the boy's mother went back to hitting him with a whip, but one with studs. The instrument was called a *lokshn* or noodle strap, because of its shape, and as my classmate bitterly gibed, "everything always got back to food, even child beating." How is it we were so ignorant of everybody else's home life? Through all these middle years I never set foot in a classmate's apartment. It is true I was always taking the bus home, but even in elementary school, when I lived in the neighborhood, I never went into anybody's home. It is as if there was an unwritten rule that nobody knew but everybody followed: life on the streets, and that included school, was communal, fair game, while life at home was private, off limits. Reflecting back, our street knowledge was an open and ongoing work in progress, but the lives of others were closed and sheathed in silence.

Sometime in my first year at 210 all the students were called together for an unannounced assembly. On an ordinary weekday morning this was unusual, and an aura of suspense hung over the auditorium. A teacher briefly addressed the students, telling us someone had a few words to say. As it turned out, that someone was a dean. In truth, I did not know what *dean* meant, but it carried a sense of importance about it, and in a young teenager's mental hierarchy it trumped a teacher. And so the auditorium was permeated with even more tension. The man's name was Abraham Squire. He stood before us, not on the elevated stage but on the apron a wide step below, and to the side, which supported a large piano. He varied his stance, awhile upright, at times leaning slightly with his arm resting on the piano. His suit was dark brown, with a pattern, something like a herringbone weave, I would not have known to call it that, except that it was not a solid. Most of the teachers wore solid suits, even in high school, and it was not until college that I first saw faculty in coats with weaves. This alone distinguished the man before us. I was sitting very close to the proscenium, perhaps the second or third row, and had a very clear view of him.

At this point memory dims as to what he said exactly, but the tenor of his remarks remains clear in my mind. It was all about the Constitution, and freedom, and individual rights. Most of this was far too heady for a seventh grader to comprehend, let alone process. And I doubt that my classmates had any clearer idea of what we were listening to or why. But if the meaning was gauzy certain details soon became crystalline. The speaker had either been fired or was on the verge of being fired. And the issue driving the dismissal was Communism, although the word was never mentioned, as if it were taboo. While his talk was largely abstract, even a twelve or thirteen year old was conscious of the swirl of newspaper stories about people who were investigated or fired or blacklisted. This was the high point of the McCarthy era. *Red* was the chief epithet of the day, followed by its less robust yet equally gripping cousin, *pinko*. All those stories were now concentrated in this single man standing before us on our own local patch. I have no doubt that I was especially sensitive to the matter because my aunt Irene and the Goldman side of my family were sympathetic to causes identified with the Communist Party. Even if none of them was an actual member, people suffered from *guilt by association*, another ubiquitous phrase that virtually wrapped its target in a red flag.

I remember being advised or warned by someone in the family to use a brown paper bag if I were carrying a book by anybody suspect, like Howard Fast, whose novels *Citizen Tom*

Paine and *Freedom Road* I avidly devoured. How I was supposed to know who was suspect baffled me. I read Fast's novels and tried to figure out what I was missing, why these riveting stories about American history made the writer a person to be shunned. It might be comic if it were not so serious, because I always associated the brown paper bag as the carrier and covering for the beer or rotgut that down-and-out men and winos drank in the open against storefronts and tenement walls and below the street on supers' steps. Much later, after 210 had faded from my life, I learned that the Board of Education, spurred by superintendant William Jansen, had run "departmental trials" of all public school teachers who resisted testifying about their past, chiefly their putative Party membership, but also the people they knew, and dismissed them for "insubordination and unbecoming conduct." Cockamamie charges carrying serious consequences. But of all this I knew nothing at the time, and did no more than watch and listen as Abraham Squire talked to us, it could not have been more than fifteen minutes, and then walked up the aisle straight out of the auditorium. We never saw him again. For myself, long after McCarthy became an eponym, I would sign no petition in front of any supermarket no matter what the cause.

My memories of reading during these early years are scant at best. There were no books on Lincoln Place, Miriam said the "dump" was so small there was no room for a book, not that I cared much since I was always in the street. And Belmont Avenue just had Zeyde's Hebrew texts. But there was a great library on Stone Avenue, one exclusively for children's books, and no one growing up in the neighborhood could ever forget it. I remember thinking it amazing that such a wonderful building was only for kids. It was a freestanding structure, but unlike the beautiful Eastern Parkway branch near Utica Avenue, which had a classical design, this one was far more exciting to a young child. It had brick walls outside, faced with stone decorative trim, two entrances on the corners of the street that formed the base of what could only be called a tower going up two stories, with bay windows on the tower's sides, floor to ceiling windows on the lower story, and smaller windows along the second floor. The interior had delightful decorative features. I can remember walking around the main floor of the library, and occasionally going up a small set of steps to an alcove, where books for older children were shelved. What seems odd is that I remember almost nothing of checking books out, and yet I know I did, because I can see myself walking back from the library to Belmont Avenue, and the journey went past all the blocks that had been razed to build the vast projects, and it was unnerving for me to walk by myself along Stone Avenue, beside these beanstalk buildings,, with their wide and empty spaces, and think about all kinds of potential encounters with the Blacks that lived there. My excitement at going to the library, and I am not sure whether it was the building or the books I most looked forward to, was chastened by the prospect of the walk, both going and coming, and in the end I gave up the library, although I cannot have been much more than seven or eight at the time.

I have no memories of picture books, which were never read to me, and I know that when I was in the branch I looked at books with a lot of print, either because I was a facile reader or perhaps I thought picture books were only for small children. In any case, my few checked books from the Stone Avenue library, unrecoverable in memory, are far outweighed by my nostalgia for the place itself. For I like to imagine that massive, ornate castle, built on the edge of Brownsville for kids like me, as having jump-started my long and abundant life in libraries. As I look back now, it is almost head-shaking how little the city gave us in these our green days. The libraries were close to the best that Brooklyn had to offer. But even here it was not altogether the city's generosity. The three libraries of my early years, before I became a regular at the great main branch on Grand Army Plaza, were Carnegie gifts. Each was an architectural treasure in its own way, and they all provided a lifeline to a boy who had no other resources but his own will and desire to learn something of the world beyond the boundaries of his limited bus and trolley lines.

When I try and think back on how I learned to read in school nothing comes to mind. And I have no memories of reading anything in class as I was going through the elementary grades. But in the sixth grade, my last year, I bought two books that were sold through the school. These were part of Grosset & Dunlap's "Illustrated Junior Library" series, and the first was *Tom Sawyer*. The book had a cream cover, a red spine, and lovely bright colored drawings. I read the story with so much pleasure that I eagerly signed up for the next book, which was *Gulliver's Travels*. I found this harder going, and am not sure I finished it, but I can still see the gorgeous graphic of Gulliver tied down by the Lilliputians, a great hulk of a man bound and made immovable by an army of smaller beings. These were the first hard cover books ever bought for me, and as I write this the color of the covers, and the drawings, and the feel of the bindings in my hands returns to me, but even more the pride I felt in having such beautiful books, and knowing that they were mine alone.

These artifacts, of negligible value, seem to take on a weight out of all proportion, and it is a toss up whether the detail warrants the attention or is merely an occasion for retrospection. There is no doubt the memory is real. But does it need to be filled with meaning in order to justify its recovery? For memories with no meaning are terrible to contemplate, like a plaque-filled brain discharging scattershot images, telling us in their randomness that all is for naught. Or perhaps the mere existence of memory, and the exercise of recall is a cry of the self against fate, a reminder that we were there, as Whitman put it, and our remembrance is sufficient unto itself.

13. A NUDE DESCENDING

Kosciusko Street had books, a meager few, and my earliest recollections of reading by myself at home date from that time. There was a complete set of *The Wonderland of Knowledge,* twelve volumes published in the middle thirties that Mama had bought for Miriam when she was a girl on Christopher Avenue. That they survived the moving when all the exciting books that Miriam owned disappeared is one of the knotted twists of a younger sibling's life. The *Wonderland* passed itself off as an encyclopedia, although it would never have qualified as such, even then, but pictorials were its strong suit, strewn liberally throughout the pages, and each volume, with a rich navy binding and gilt lettering, featured a colored drawing on its face. The style was of the period, Art Deco, not that I knew anything of that, but the binding and pictures were captivating. I sometimes wonder whether I remember them simply because they existed, and I could say there were books in the house. I read in bed, in the front room next to the kitchen that looked over the small backyard, the room my mother later died in, and mostly in the morning, when there was daylight, for there was no reading lamp, and I would sit back against the pillows, engrossed in the stories I found in two or three books. One was the *Arabian Nights*, a single volume of tales, and the wonderful thing about reading as a young person is you have no idea where the text comes from, and you would not even care to know. The story that stayed with me was "Ali Baba and the Forty Thieves," because of a glorious picture of treasure spilling out of chests, and filling up higgledy-piggledy all the space laid bare by the incantation of two magic words, *Open Sesame*. It is curious that a boy who never saw children's books when little should somehow retain his earliest memories of books largely because of their pictures.

But it was not just pictures that held me. There were three writers bound up with me and K Street, and that fatal room, whose pieces filled me with thoughts and feelings that I had never before gleaned from words alone. The first was Rudyard Kipling and "Baa, Baa, Black Sheep." I was riveted by the story of a small boy sent away by his parents from his home in India to live in England with a woman who turned *abuse* into a term of affection. I am sure I was galvanized by the figure of Punch, almost my age by the end of the story, and his brutal Dickensian childhood. Although I had no knowledge of that word, I was aware of Oliver Twist because he was pictured on every box of *H-O* oatmeal, a cereal bowl clutched in his hands as he looked up pleadingly into the cook's eyes. I remember being transfixed by that graphic, with its faux Victorian style, the closest I came to Dickens at that time. I was also affected in the story by the condition of the small boy's eyes, given my intense self-consciousness about my own myopia, as he nearly read himself blind as a way of escaping from his tormentor. And I remember thinking that in the end, even with his mother's return, the boy was not altogether the same, because the terrible damage inflicted by that twisted woman's malice could not ever be undone. The story may not have been a tragedy, whatever a tragedy was, but it left me alone and nowhere.

The other two pieces implanted in my mind strike me even now as odd for a boy of my age to have been reading. They must have been outliers in the house, the only print that was not a shrill pamphlet about politics or war. I remember trying to read some of those documents, and resisting them, whether I was wary of their message, afraid to ally myself with a point of view I knew was suspicious, or if I was unconsciously resistant to the prose, which was deadening. I do not know where sensitivity to style comes from, and young readers certainly do not engross themselves in books for an aesthetic high. Yet we can be moved by art without being aware of it, as I believe was the case when I read John Dos Passos' "Art and Isadora," another in this trio of tales, rounded out with Dorothy Parker's story, "Big Blonde." I keep trying to see the books that held these two writings but I am unable to conjure anything up. Although the details of "Big Blonde" are thin in my mind, I have avoided revisiting the story in order to keep from mashing memory with present knowledge. What would an eleven year old make of the blonde? I am sure there was a risqué element, the picture of a woman lounging in bed, barely dressed, except that there was no real eroticism, nothing that would spark an erection. I was rapt instead by the squalor, the alcoholic stupor, an apartment in disarray, and the sad portrait of a blowzy woman, desperate for marriage but doomed to dismissive sex. Not that I understood anything of the sex, or really what was going on, but I felt bad for the woman, and while a part of me realized that she was bringing it all upon herself, another part thought it was unfair, and that she never really had a chance. I knew nothing of Dorothy Parker, or *men never make passes*, or the Algonquin Club, but when I later learned all that, I always remembered her story, and thought first of "Big Blonde" whenever the lady of the corridor came up in conversation.

As for Dos Passos, I was enthralled by the riff on Isadora Duncan, this beautiful, rebellious woman, starting out in San Francisco, throwing off her shoes to dance in her feet, sheathed in flowing, diaphanous gowns, winding up an adulated star swirling on stages in filled spaces, talked about, famous, indifferent to criticism because she was an *artist*, and art conquered all, and then showing up in Europe, the continent falling before her, flowers abounding, riches in her chest, yet still yearning for more, for love, romance, I was too young to know it as sex, so that one day she impulsively picked up a man in a café in Paris, they went for a ride in his beautiful small car, she was thrilled, happy in her life, when her long scarf got caught by freak chance in the fast turning wheel and instantly snapped her neck. I never forgot Isadora Duncan. And a few years after, in high school, when we played Botticelli to pass the time, I would choose "I. D." when it came my turn to pick a famous mystery person, and no one could guess her name, for there were no modern dancers in our group, and no one had ever heard of John Dos Passos.

As I said earlier, I remember nothing of any junior high classes, neither teachers nor courses, except for Mr. Geduld's Spanish class, and that only because his classroom was chaos beyond measure, a free-for-all within four walls that at times required Mr. Ball, the other Spanish teacher, to enter the room and rein us in. We were not an unruly group at rest, but Mr. Geduld managed to bring out the worst in us. While it seems odd that I can call up nothing of any English class, I have a searing memory of a single hour. Our regular teacher told us that we would have a substitute one day the next week, and we should bring a book of our own to read during the period. What bliss! No instruction, not that any imprinted itself anyway, and an entire period to be left alone to read what we wanted. But what to bring? There were no books at Belmont Avenue, and at this period I was not checking anything out of the library. As it turned out, I found myself with two paperbacks by Thorne Smith, *The Bishop's Jaegers* and *The Night Life of the Gods*. I have no idea where they came from. I knew nothing of Thorne Smith, or of *Topper* the novel, or the movie, but by then I had already read *The Bishop's Jaegers*, vaguely deciphering "jaegers" from the context as underwear, and not thinking to look it up. It now strikes me as a bizarre joke that I never used a dictionary then, I doubt there was one in the house, because later I lived surrounded by lexicons.

In any case, that racy book, with its cast of eccentrics thrown together on a Staten Island ferry, lost in the harbor fog, and landing on shore at a nudist camp, kept my eyes focused on the page, even though I was keenly aware I could barely penetrate the story. The nudity was what I was interested in, what I hoped to see pictured in print, and sex to go along with it. As for Thorne Smith's teasing dialogue, the relaxed imbibing of alcohol as a finger in the eye of Prohibition, and the celebration of sex over morals, of all this I was clueless. What a fourteen-year old boy was interested in was writing that would elicit sexual excitement, wherever and however it came. I had no way of knowing that Thorne Smith was too sophisticated for me, his books more subtle than salacious. But that was neither here nor there. I had read one. I would bring *The Night Life of the Gods* to class. This novel was even more ribald than the other: the alcohol free flowing, the sex lauded, and the central conceit, a madcap inventor who can turn stone to flesh and back again, nothing short of brilliant. I sat next to a boy named Melvin, a buddy, and our desks were pushed very close together. I was there with Thorne Smith, and he had a copy of Mickey Spillane in his hands, I think it was *Kiss Me, Deadly*. I thought it gutsy of Melvin to bring that book, for the writer's name was one with *sensationalism* and *violence* and *lurid sex*, although I was blank as to what *lurid* meant, except to imagine it as something thrilling and forbidden. And while I thought Melvin brave, I also thought it reflected a lower level of reading, although I could not have put it in those terms and would never have used the word *taste*. It is strange to ponder, years later, how we absorb cultural attitudes when young, a mash-up of the moment and our own peculiar psyche, even when we are unaware that we have such a thing. I had picked up the denigrating comments about Spillane, of which there were no shortage in the papers, and internalized them in my own mind. The sex and violence did not bother me, but the charge *hack writer* did, and that was enough for me to consign his books to a lesser shelf, one I never stooped to choose from. Writing this now it smacks of intellectual arrogance, but that assumes an active will, and I had no idea why I thought as I did. Looking back it strikes me with wry amusement that Melvin, with his pulp fiction, was enjoying all that action, while I, with my elegant stylist, had no idea what I was reading.

So there we were, the two of us, side by side, each hoping for some small bit of excitement, or pleasure, to pass the hour. And what did it matter what we read, for who would know as we sat at our desks, each person screened by the one in front of him? On this last count we were too young to be aware of the implacable determination of grownups to oversee everything about our learning. You would have thought the fact that we were reading at all, that we managed to find books to keep our mouths quiet and our hands in view, would be cause enough for small mercies. Enter our teacher for the day. She was a short, rotund woman who wore her hair in a bun, sat behind a desk at the front of the room while we were all in our seats. Suddenly, to my utter surprise, she told us that each student would come up to her desk and show her our books. I am not sure if I was more worried about her disapproving of my choice, or disturbed by the intrusion on our privacy. I cannot say I was outraged, or that I thought of it *exactly* as spying, because that would suggest I had a more developed sense of what was allowable or appropriate. None of us considered that we had any rights vis-à-vis our teachers, so any protest would have been unthinkable. There was nothing to do but sit silently and wait until we were called. As it happened, Melvin went up immediately before me. He carried his copy of *Kiss Me, Deadly,* she inspected it, and sent him back to his seat. At that point I might have guessed that she was not your run of the mill teacher, for only a Martian could have been ignorant of the pulp colossus whose book she just examined.

But I did not have time to think, because I was called up right after Melvin returned. I do not know if I had a bookmark in the pages, or the paperback cracked open at just the spot, but she saw the title of the chapter, "A Nude Descends the Stairs," and went ballistic. For the next minute or two I was on the receiving end of a shrill rant about my reading such a vile book. There is no point in imagining her words. Sex was at the heart of it, and a single word, *nude*, set that dim woman off on her tirade. I could have lived with that, and returned to my seat no worse for the wear, for by then I was no longer shocked by teachers going round the bend. But she refused to give me back my book. I could not care less about her silly harangue, but I wanted my book. And as I write this now I still get angry at her highhandedness, and irritated by her stupidity—that she let Mickey Spillane pass blissfully by but stopped the traffic with the cultured Thorne Smith. Many years later, when Modern Library reprinted *The Night Life of the Gods,* I assigned the book in a course. I had never finished it all those years earlier, and I did not search too deeply into what impelled me to read it anew. I was looking for something *funny* for the class, but it is possible I wanted to recover something I had lost. And reading it again, or maybe for the first time, I could appreciate Thorne Smith's intelligence and his great gift for humor. But an unexpected discovery came when I got to Chapter IX, "A Nude Descends the Stairs," and it suddenly hit me, as all the statues in the novel were being brought to life in New York's art museum, that the title was an open allusion to the stunning Modernist painting by Marcel Duchamp from the 1913 Armory show, "Nude Descending A Staircase." And I had to smile inwardly, for the reference would have been obvious to the writer's contemporaries, and wonder to myself that I thought to read that book in the eighth grade.

When my mother died, early in March 1952, I stayed home from school, sitting *shive,* for all that meant to me, for even then I realized that what I knew of Jewish rituals was rudimentary at best. Actually, it was not even knowledge but a collection of bits and fragments picked up in passing. Nobody ever explained the meaning of sitting on low chairs or stools, or covering the mirrors, or walking only in slippers, which I did not have, any more than they explained why we put stones on the gravestone a year after the funeral. As I sat on the couch in the living room on Belmont Avenue, looking blankly at the white sheet hanging haphazardly over the mirror, I wonder that I never thought to ask anyone what these things meant, or how they might help me understand my mother's death? But whom would I have asked? Certainly not my grandmother, and my father's conversation never went beyond necessities. Sometimes I marvel that I felt so warm towards my father, that I loved him as much as I did when there was so little presence. But I remember his general kindliness, which as I think of it now reflected that of his own father, and his warm smile, which was a part of his nature. Miriam has a different feeling. She remembered the years on Christopher Avenue before I was born, when Mama wanted her own house, apart from her mother-in-law, and our father paid no attention. And Miriam bore the brunt of taking care of Mama when she was just a teenager, largely because our father ceded that to her, or simply abdicated responsibility. She resented it, and carried that grievance for long years after. And this does not account for my sister Ann, whose attitude was even more intense than Miriam's. Is one or another of us more right than wrong? Or are we all tied to our own interactions with our father, at different times, under different conditions? And if we factor in our distinct personalities, and consider that our father may have changed over the years, is it any wonder that there is never one correct view, and not just of our father but of ourselves? It is a wry recognition that the process of remembrance yields more uncertainty than resolution, and what was sure knowledge for most of a lifetime seems suddenly no more solid than sands at ebb tide.

At this point, reflecting on what I have written about these years, I should be inured to the idea that there was anything to be learned in my household, or anyone to teach me, yet strangely it continues to astonish. But at the time I never thought anything odd, for it never occurred to me that there might be other ways of connecting with each other. My two sisters were left to their own devices, and so was I, seven years younger than Ann. But to return to Belmont Avenue, I was sitting *shive* alone, my father back in the store, when the bell on the street door was pressed. Since my grandmother and I formed the only traffic up or down the stairs, the doorbell rarely rang. I buzzed back, opened the door of the apartment, looked down the stairs, and to my amazement saw a group of classmates carrying a large basket of fruit and flowers wrapped in a shiny yellow-orange paper covering. There were perhaps four or five boys and girls. I see them sitting on the armchair facing the couch, one on the seat, one on an arm, another leaning against the back of the chair further up, and the others joining me on the couch or standing near the television. The teachers obviously made some announcement, but I have no idea how it was managed, whether the whole class chipped in to buy the basket, or how the kids selected among themselves to show up. Since everybody lived near school, they would have had to take a bus to get to Belmont Avenue, far enough from their home turf to have made the trip more than a small gesture.

Whatever the circumstances, I can still remember how happy I was to see them, and how grateful I felt at their coming. At the beginning there was some unease, perhaps even discomfort, since they were there because of my mother's death, and had no idea what was appropriate, and at the start nobody knew what to do. I think my grandmother was around but she left us alone in the living room. After we loosened up, we wound up jabbering, and then started telling jokes, not without some initial trepidation, and the jokes remain in my memory, because we turned to telling dirty ones, as young adolescents will, and I was telling them along with my friends, and I can remember thinking to myself, my mother has just died and here I am mouthing smutty stories while I am supposed to be in mourning. I am not sure how I rationalized it, but I thought that it was okay, what else were thirteen year olds supposed to talk about, death and the consolations of philosophy? That was far outside our competencies. My classmates came out of an impulse to give comfort, although I doubt they even thought in those terms, or simply to say they were sorry for what happened, and then we got carried away being who we were, and put aside the terrible fact of the moment, that I was now without a mother, which was nothing I could understand, and certainly not my friends. But for a couple of hours, which was a long time, they made me forget what I was doing, which was nothing, and brought me back to myself as an eighth grader, doing what eighth graders do, which is cutting up and getting laughs, however. I have no idea what that late morning visit intended, but for me it was a balm brought freely not by adults but by people my own age, who knew nothing of condolence or resignation or the ways of God, but simply that something awful had happened to someone like them, and for those few who made the trip to Brownsville, to share those long minutes, in bawdy humor and silly chatter, it was never forgotten.

As for graduation from John Marshall, almost nothing can be salvaged. Harvey and Lenny pull a complete blank. Irving believes he was never there. But I know I attended, because I can see the Catholic school where it was held. It took up an entire block along Eastern Parkway, with stone steps leading up to three entry doors, tall columns and sculptural details. I could not get over my awe at the building, which was a girls' high school, and I remember thinking to myself what must it be like to have classes there, on one of the most beautiful streets in Brooklyn, as opposed to the soulless place that was John Marshall. Although it never crossed my mind that buildings were designed before they were erected, I know that I was moved by architecture, judging simply by my visceral responses to the Stone Avenue and Eastern Parkway libraries. And so the Catholic high school, across from Brooklyn's grandest museum, ensured that I would not forget the occasion. But while this memory was of the stone, a far lowlier object stayed with me as a memorial, even as all the rest of graduation dropped into oblivion. As we waited to funnel into the auditorium, two abreast in a narrow passageway, I wound up next to Irving, and the space was so tight, and we were so close, that I could not help but look down and notice that he was wearing sneakers, plain gray high-tops. We all wore coats and ties, as well as Irving. The thought occurred to me that maybe his shoes were scuffed, or being resoled, and like me he probably had only one pair. And I asked him how he could come to graduation in sneakers? I wonder that I made so much of a bit thing, as if I were invested in the protocol and ceremony, when in reality none of us cared about it at all.

BOOK TWO

1. FATHER AND SON

AFTER MY MOTHER'S DEATH my immediate family was living in three separate households. Miriam and Harry on Long Island, myself on Belmont Avenue with my grandmother, and my father, sister Ann, and aunt Irene on Kosciusko Street. I was in my own world. The major event in the late spring of 1953, before I entered high school in the fall, was Miriam's giving birth to identical twin boys. There was a bris at their small Levittown house, which filled to the walls with uncles and aunts sitting on anything with a base, because the rented tents were useless in the constant rain. What I remember most is the *moyel*. Even though I did not want to think too closely about what he actually was about to do, I wondered about his skill as I tried to remind myself that this was a festive occasion. I liked the idea of having twin nephews, even though the reality of it was largely lost on me. Early in her pregnancy, Miriam's doctor asked if there were twins in the family and she said no. But a week before delivery she remembered that our grandmother had two brothers in Kentucky, each of whom had twin boys. It was then said that twins ran in the family, and usually skipped a generation. How did you prepare for them? Get help! was the doctor's advice. For triplets there was the possibility of baby endorsements, but for twins, zilch. So two elementary school teachers were suddenly faced with double of everything. Harry had no resources from his family, and my sister could count on none from our father. I was dimly aware of the financial burden, but more intrigued by the physical challenges. How do you feed two babies at the same time? Or change their diapers? But in truth I was as far removed from their actual life as Brooklyn was from Long Island.

When it came to Kosciusko Street it was a similar story. Ann started going with an engineer from the Bronx, Ed Sloan, who was a part time boxer. That amazed me, the idea that my sister was dating someone who fought in the ring. When he picked her up I remember looking at him surreptitiously for any signs of a darkened eye. Ann worked for a part of this period at the Hotel Lexington in Midtown, which I thought glamorous, because Arthur Godfrey broadcast his show from the Hawaiian Room there, and I would prod her to tell me if she had ever seen or met him. It is odd, even funny in a way, for I was no particular fan of Godfrey, whose folksiness I found a bit off-putting, and the Hawaiian Room meant nothing to me, called up no pictures of palm fronds, but the name sounded an exotic note, as if a word alone could induce an image of magic that had neither form nor color. For years after, the street itself, Lexington Avenue, would call to mind the hotel, and in turn the show room, and at last my sister's nearness to Manhattan glitter.

One of the odd things about my family life was the almost palpable disconnect between my presence and my experience. I was there and I was not there. Living with my grandmother was a little like having a roommate who was never underfoot and made no demands. She was in her early seventies, tired, the ever-jockeying relations with her children finally settled, and that strong maternal instinct, now turned quiescent, was not to be revived for a fourteen or fifteen year old boy. If this makes sense to me now, what I find strange is that it never occurred to me at the time. She rarely made meals for me, as if I were invisible within my home. And yet the flip side is that I felt free to do as I wished. Back then I was glad to be on my own, but now, as I write, I am struck by how my entire family, aunts and uncles, could have been so indifferent to my situation. And mine was not unique. Almost all were equally indifferent to my three cousins whose mother died young. When their father brought home a new, cold wife, the two girls, both in their teens, learned to fend for themselves and take care of their younger brother, a boy of seven. As for my sister Miriam, at sixteen riding the trains from Brownsville to the Bronx during my mother's hospital treatments, not an aunt or an uncle made a gesture to ease her burden. Miriam's resentment never abated. She succeeded in tamping it down, burying it under a lifetime of activity as teacher, wife and mother, only to have it raised up, after its long dormancy, in her brother's story.

My father was at a loss after my mother's death. That statement has a fine note of certitude, but in fact I have no idea if it was anywhere near true. He was sleeping at K Street, and while I saw him at the store on Belmont Avenue, nothing suggested that life had in any way changed. He certainly never spoke about his feelings. And he never uttered a word about Mama. I doubt that it even occurred to me that he ever pondered such matters, so what was I to think? As it happens, I thought nothing, in my fashion, and life continued, until I learned that he was looking for a new wife. The idea of it made no impression on me, I was quieter than might have been expected, and unlike my cousins' father, snared by an uneducated immigrant who repeatedly turned up at his grocery in East New York, mine at least waited until after the unveiling on Staten Island, where my mother's grave may as well have been consigned to oblivion.

A digression: Some years later, in college, on an early April day, I had this inexplicable desire to visit her. I corralled two friends on campus, Marty and Judy, and we set off in my 1953 Ford for that borough in the bay, driving along the Belt Parkway to take the ferry at 59th Street. Of a sudden it started to pour, and I could barely make out the lanes through the wipers, not to mention that I had no clue how to get off the beltway to the terminal dock. Somehow, through the torrents of water, we managed to find the ferry, and by now my friends, having had no choice but to stay with me, asked if I knew where I was going. I did not. Neither the name of the cemetery nor where it was located. I paused, and wondered about the compelling urge that had brought us to a standstill, sitting in a car while sheets of rain pounded the roof. But all that was now moot. When the ferry docked, we had to drive off somewhere. As strange as it sounds, I went straight onto the street that caught the ferry traffic and drove for a fair distance until we reached a road that I turned right on, and from there continued until we came to a cemetery. It was Jewish, we drove in, my friends remained in the car, and I went out searching for anybody who might tell me if my mother was buried there. How I found anyone working on that torrential day is beyond me, but somehow I was given directions to the grave, and after all that nerve-wracking driving I felt I owed it to my friends to trudge through the muddy rows of gravestones and find my own. By then all I wanted to do was get it over with, and I had no idea any longer why I felt impelled to come in the first place. I stayed just minutes, perhaps imagining I might conjure up my mother as if from a clear well in a green forest. Nothing showed.

The only visible light was the glistening water running down the stone. I returned to the car, nodded to Judy and Marty, and drove back to Brooklyn. When I think about that day, what amazes me is that I found the place without directions or detours. Yes, I was unconsciously retracing in my mind the drive to the cemetery that I had made sitting in a car some seven or eight years earlier. But a part of me cannot shake the uncanny thought, the Scots have a word for it, unco, that someone was with me in the sedan, guiding me to that resting place in the far reaches of the city, where no one I knew had ever gone before.

Returning to my father's courtship, the first I learned of it was when he took me to the back of the grocery one day and asked me to help him with his classified notice in the *Morgn Zhurnal*. This was clearly a modern variation of the traditional custom of the *shadkhn*, only instead of hiring a marriage broker you listed yourself in the newspaper. My Yiddish was barely passable, but he was more interested in how he should present himself, although why he thought I had any insight into what he might inscribe in two-three sentences is beyond me. As to the time, my best guess is that he placed the classified in the first half of 1953, a year after my mother's death. I remember being intrigued by this world of the marriage-go-round, carried on in the closet language of Yiddish, which made it both exotic and parochial, and at the same time undismayed by any thought that it might be unseemly. I did wonder silently what my mother might feel, but I resolved to myself that she was dead, my father alive, and he had no choice but to go forward and find another wife. I had no thoughts about a *stepmother* as a category of person, and I am not sure that the word ever ran through my head. I knew that my cousins had one, whom I never met, but I rarely saw them and they were not at the forefront of my consciousness. The salient point for me was that I lived with my grandmother, my home was on Belmont Avenue, and I never thought of my father and any woman he married as having any tangible bearing on my life.

It is almost quaint, from the vantage point of today, how a phrase like *second marriage* had no existence, and not just the phrase, but the meaning wrapped in the words. In the families I knew, there were marriages, period. Who knew from second marriages, and what they entailed? I am struck by how blind I was to the fact that Bubbie was old, and could die at any moment. In some strange way, despite all the deaths that I had witnessed up close, I lived in this blithe world of invulnerable solitariness, where I could go my own way with no one to hinder or vex me, oblivious of anything outside that might bring me to a stop, or a fall. It never crossed my mind that if my father remarried I would live with him and his wife. I failed to see that his pursuit would have a confused effect on a son he no longer lived with, as it would to a lesser degree on Ann and Miriam. But this may have been a function of the splintered lives we led, separated from each other, the one not knowing how or what the other was doing. My father's life was just another thread in a tangled skein, Miriam in Levittown, Ann in Bedford Stuyvesant, while I, at fourteen, had no other thought than getting ready for high school in East New York.

Does it matter that all I have of my father's casting for a wife are nothing more than two-three scant details? Should I be turning over rocks to find out where and when and how? One could conceivably uncover a marriage record, although locating a sixty year old classified in a Yiddish daily might be a stretch, but to what end? Miriam knew nothing of the events. Ann did, but she has a blunt resistance to calling up any of that past, and even the word "Brooklyn" stirs up unwanted feelings. So I am left with what I know, or rather what I remember. And what I remember is that my father suddenly looked modern, even a touch fashionable. He bought a new suit, and sported a dark brown overcoat, something he never wore before. Next to my uncle Max he was the best looking of the Menikoff brothers, with a good head of hair, attractive light eyes, and a wide yet pleasing face. I remember thinking how good he looked in those spanking clothes, and wondering why he had to wait until Mama died to dress that way. I even found myself torn between admiration and resentment, for when I looked approvingly on his dress I felt disloyal to Mama, and when I was harsh in judgment I was unfair to him, who wanted nothing more than to go on with his life, which really meant to have another, different one. If clothes were the currency for that new life, then he was on his way.

I cannot say for sure that I wondered where he got the money, since that would assume I was aware that he had no money to spend, but the only cash I ever saw was in the register. Even then I knew that the store was always on the verge of going under. My father kited checks, even if I never heard the word, as I would occasionally be asked to postdate payments that he made out to creditors. I knew it was not a kosher practice, but it was a pre-electronic period, and you could safely factor in a delay for mail delivery and check processing. The serious problem was not the time lapse, but the uncertainty of whether there would be funds to deposit that would cover the checks. Still, if at the time I did not dwell on where the money for my father's clothes came from, what I clearly remember was his purchase of a new car, a dark green Pontiac coupé, with two sets of chrome strips running down the hood, separated by a gorgeous ornament depicting the Indian chief in a late Art Deco style, his head modeled in an amber colored Lucite, with two silver vertical flaps that looked like rudders standing up on each side. Any thought of my father and what this minted splendor was for went clear out of my head. All I cared about was the beautiful Pontiac. Some two or three years later, before I could get my license, my father would let me start and move the car when it was parked on the street alongside the store: I would pull the handle in behind the steering wheel, sensing the grooves on the chrome and black shift knob, move downward into first, and "drive" several feet or one car length along the curb. How could I not be thrilled?

A narrative can suddenly surprise its author, and only recently I learned about the money. My sister Ann, seven years older than me, lent our father five hundred dollars. That would not have been enough for clothes and the car, but he bought the Pontiac on installments, which I know because the initials GMAC were forever imprinted on my brain, General Motors Acceptance Corporation, having no idea what "Acceptance" meant but fully aware that GMAC was the finance arm for GM. And so a mystery was solved: Ann was the source of our father's new look. But as I processed this information I wondered to myself, where did she get five hundred dollars to lend? She was not a professional, and cannot have been earning serious money. It turns out, according to my brother-in-law Ed, my sister was an extraordinarily diligent saver, a habit he illustrated with a story. Ed was a collector, of objects high and low, and he bought a red Pulver gum machine that Ann remembered from childhood, one of those ubiquitous penny machines that could be found drilled into the pillars on subway stations. Ann told him that as a child she would take out a penny, make a gesture to put it in the slot and start the action, a policeman who twists a STOP-GO sign to release the gum, and then pull back at the last minute, sacrificing the treat and saving the penny. How would I have ever known that about her? Or that she paid half the cost of the twelve hundred dollars for her own wedding just two years later, mollifying her father-in-law, who wanted our father to cover the affair, as was customary. We never lived in the same house long enough for me to become familiar with her habits. I see now that her propensity for saving was a fierce impulse to manage her life, since who could she depend upon? Mama was gone, and in any case she had long before given up any ability to offer support. As for Irene, forever busy with lost political causes, she would in just a couple of years sell the house on Kosciusko Street and move to California, leaving her niece to scramble for a room at the 92nd Street Y. And yet Ann helped our father. I know she expected to be repaid, but never was. Any more than I, after lending him two hundred dollars when I was in college, after a moment's hesitation, wondering whether I would ever see it again. For some reason, borrowing from your children must not have felt like a debt. Blanched now of all feeling, and indifferent to the detail of the incidents, what strikes me is the absence of any common sense of obligation, an attitude not restricted to my father. We were told to help out, and we did, but there was no return. When Miriam worked in the store on Rutland Road she was never paid, any more than working on Belmont Avenue put money in my pocket. It is as if we had no needs, no individual wants. In a way I almost wish that behavior had been deliberate, as it would allow me to feel resentful, but there was no deliberation in any of it. My father's actions may have been thoughtless, but they were not ill-intentioned: it is just that children's lives and what they entailed were outside the realm of his consciousness, and beyond his understanding.

It is something of a marvel how little I know of my father's marriage. I never met any of the women he went out with, nor did Miriam. Ann was more aware of them. He dismissed one woman because he did not like her looks—she was *mies*. Not that he chose the opposite, *a sheyn ponem*, which was par for the men in my family, who got cataracts when choosing wives. But the whole process was wrapped in such secrecy that I knew nothing of my father's dating, and the first inkling I had of something odd was when he appeared in the apartment on Belmont Avenue, having summarily moved from Kosciusko Street.

Nobody told me in advance, and as there was only Bubbie's bedroom and my very small cubicle, the only place for him to sleep was in the single bed with me. He said nothing as to why he was there, or how long he expected to stay. And I did not ask. All I remember is that he stayed for a short while, married in the interval, and then left for his wife's home in Jamaica, in a borough as foreign to me as another country.

What strikes me as strange now is that none of it seemed so then. Perhaps my father was worried about how we would respond to his wife. There was after all the example of Hilda, my late aunt Nettie's successor, who moved into my cousins' home and proceeded to cleanse the place of their mother, throwing out her deft embroideries, tossing her dishes, and even dumping my cousin Laura's piano books in a frenzy of exorcism. But as Mae Kaufman moved my father into *her* home, for he had none of his own, no similar cleansing was necessary. She managed instead to divest him of his children. I like that sentence, its statement, its sound, and yet it softens and conceals the harshness of the woman, and the rigor with which she separated my father from his kin. When I was long gone from New York, and in a convivial mood, I would joke that my stepmother stepped out of the pages of the brothers Grimm. But when I drop the smart dart, it seems so senseless, as I thought even then. Miriam was married; Ann had her own life; and I was living with my grandmother. Mae had a profitable business selling carpets and linoleum on Jamaica Boulevard, run by her elder son, and she lived with another son, Paul, who was four or five years older than me. What did she have to fear?

Yet I can count on one hand the number of times I saw Mae in the twenty-five years of their marriage. Ann and Ed saw her twice. Miriam comes up with three as a number. It is not even correct to call her a stepmother, a word none of us ever used. So how explain her behavior? Miriam and Harry were invited to lunch at her house, the twins were toddlers at the time, so Mae and my father could not have been married more than a year. Well, as toddlers will, they wandered, discovered an old vanity dresser with perfume bottles resting on top, and tipped them over. Mae screamed. And that was it for lunch. The scream, or maybe the voice, must have run in the family, for I took the train out there one Friday night, after my grandmother died, thinking I would see my father for dinner. I rang the bell, was buzzed in, and just as I was standing inside the door, her son Paul, looking down from the top of a half-story staircase, asked me what I was doing there. I told him, and was instantly held in check for several minutes by a shrill harangue about daring to show up at their home unannounced without so much as a prior call. It was a dressing down from on high by the lord of the manor. I left and never went back. Years later my sister Ann and her family were invited out to Long Island, by then Mae and my father lived in Stony Brook, to see the house that Mae had bought for Paul. As Ed tells the story, my father was on the porch when they arrived, and was sitting there still after everyone returned from admiring the new home. My niece Lydia, a teenager at the time, vividly recounts the visit, mainly because she did not get to speak much with her grandfather. "Mae didn't let him speak to anyone. She was so bossy with him! I remember being surprised at that even at that time. She crowded him out, pushed him aside and just put her son front and center. We were only 'allowed' to talk to him." Lydia also recounts my father calling her mother at their home in Illinois: "He always called collect because Mae would yell at him about the phone bill. He seemed quite frightened of her. One time he was on the phone w/Mom and Mae started yelling at him, I could hear her in the background and I was across the room. Funny, because it was a collect call, anyhow. She must have been a bit of a control freak."

But the story about Mae is as much about my father, perhaps even more so, and layering two-three incidents of her tantrums and tactics does not explain their relation. After my father married he began a slow but steady retreat from my life. For three years, from the time I was fifteen until my first year in college, Dad still worked the store on Belmont Avenue. But the grocery was unprofitable, while Mae's carpet store piled up cash. He really had no need to keep it going, and possibly he stayed because as long as my grandmother was alive the store was part of her life. She may even have had an ownership in it, which only indicates the murkiness of my knowledge. Yet the immediate consequence of the marriage was indiscernible. Life for me went on pretty much the same. But after my grandmother died, during my freshman year, it changed utterly. One incident stands out. It was very late in the afternoon, my father was still in the store, and I asked him if I could come out for dinner that night. He seemed just a little uncomfortable, if I am not imagining that in retrospect, but he said that would not be possible, went to the register, took out a couple of dollars, and said I could go to a restaurant. I cannot account for what came over me, but I rushed to the store shelves, grabbed a can of tuna fish—I am puzzled as to why tuna fish always turns up as a default dining option—and ran upstairs to the apartment. I found myself in tears, uncontrollably so, and as I was opening the can of tuna my father came into the kitchen. That was the first time I ever saw him contrite, or simply aware that I was more than just a moveable object.

And it was the only time I held him responsible for treating me as a complication in his relation with Mae. I realized that he had thrown in his lot with her, and it was useless to try and counter it, not that I had any idea how to do that if I wanted to. At the time, and long after, I thought it a weakness of him, I thought that he was frightened of Mae, but that thought only confused me the more. Because I always felt my father was afraid of very little. Opening and closing the store on a street that was always on the edge of some potential act of violence, my father seemed to me fearless. And I knew the story, in bits and pieces, that when he was a young man in Russia he was abducted and thrown on a train for conscription in the army, it was during the civil war, but he picked up a lesson from another conscript on how to fall and roll, and he jumped off the train, escaping forced military service with his life. If not, he might have been fighting for the White army, and ended up a nameless victim of the Red Terror.

But he did not end up a Cheka corpse. He jumped the train and, in two or three years, made his way to New York with his sister Nettie, brought his father over six months later, and in another four years his mother and the rest of his siblings. And then in the middle of the jazz age he married a Manhattan high school graduate, and bought a car at a time when the dealer who sold it gave you a quick lesson on how to drive, sending you into the streets with little more than crossed fingers. And soon my father had several stores, and was awash in cash, while the Depression was something that other people were ensnared by. In brief, Frank Menikoff had some experience of the world. But as I said when I began this story, all that was before I was around, and even though oral tales fill the interstices of the narrative, and are even part of its fabrication, as a memoirist I cannot recover any past that was never mine. And unlike a novelist I cannot enter the mind of another person. That Mae daunted my father seems clear, but it is a mystery why she was so adamant on the displacement of his children. My sisters wanted nothing from her, and I never considered living there, but it was as if our mere presence, and not even that, just the *thought* of us, was enough to set her off. What she wanted, as a well-to-do widow, was a man to escort her in life. And my father, after he gave over the store, accommodated that wish. Perhaps they had a good sexual connection, but it was impossible for me then to conceive such a thought.

At all events, they began to travel seriously, I do not know where, I do not even know how I know, but I would on occasion think to myself how unfair it was that he was going places with this large and overbearing woman when Mama, as far as I knew, never went anywhere. And yet I was not angry with him. He was doing what he could to survive, and with no money himself he was dependent upon the largesse of a woman who had more than enough. As Ann's husband Ed bluntly put it, our father had found himself "a meal ticket." But despite the expression I doubt that Ed had any more severe a view of my father than I did. It is hard to convey the experience of people without resources trying to contend with the scarcity of daily living, which was a constant struggle. No money for Ann's wedding. No money for school for Miriam. No money to pay his son for working in the store. Mae waved her wrinkled wand and all that went away. Her new husband did not need money. He did not even need a store. Break free from your past and start your life over in Queens. But doing nothing proved problematic for my father, and he wound up tending another store Mae had, selling small household items and odds and ends such as might be found in a five-and-dime. When Dad visited Miriam on Long Island he brought with him knick-knacks from the store for the twins. But those visits were fraught, and made my sister angry, because they were made in secret, without Mae's knowledge, and Dad was never at ease, for he always worried about staying too long. So having given over the material worry of finances, he now had the mental worry that the financier exercised over his life.

But I was ignorant of most of this. I would hear of him infrequently from Miriam, so it seems reasonable to conclude that he did not want to be cut off from his children completely, but once I left Belmont Avenue, and was living on my own, I rarely saw my father. It was not by choice, but I would not go out to Jamaica, and he rebuffed any suggestion I made over the telephone to meet in a restaurant. In effect, my father left my life sometime in my late teens. But it is not as if I put him out of my mind. I would call, and it was during one of those calls that he asked me for the loan of two hundred dollars. I would send Father's Day cards, on occasion a gift, and sometimes Mae would send an acknowledgement, which I always found strange since there was never any communication between us. She seemed to hold on to these rituals of social manners, which struck me as the most bizarre contrast to her compulsive drive to control everything. And of course when I left New York the opportunities for contact with my father were nonexistent. I barely saw him during the four years I was at Brooklyn College. In fact, I am at a loss to conjure up a single meeting in all that time, certainly no lunch or dinner out, no visit to any of my apartments, not even an encounter at Miriam's on Long Island. Yet there was no specific crisis that precipitated a break or rupture. What strikes me most, as I think of it, is how our relation just ebbed away, without any great wave washing over the shore, a process of gradual dissolution, but a process that had been there from early on. Dad was never involved with my life, and once he partnered with Mae, and I was out on my own, we no longer shared any physical space, so there was no need for any pretense.

And still I could not dispatch him from my head. Many years after, when staying in Woodbury on Long Island, in my sister's beautiful home, enjoying the comfort and familiarity I always felt in that place, my children were then in their early years, I was divorced, and I wanted to see my father. Miriam refused to let me borrow her car, but Harry, ever the conciliator, said go ahead, visit with him while you have the chance. So I drove out to Stony Brook, where they were living, and when I arrived Mae, true to form, said she would leave us so we could have time together. It never occurred to me that she meant no more than fifteen minutes. But that was probably enough. I suspect that part of my desire to see him was self-protective: I always had a nagging thought that I would get a call in Hawaii telling me of his death, and I would have to debate in my mind whether I should pay for a premium ticket to go to a funeral for a man I had not seen for years on end. And what was the protocol for that decision? If I did not go, what did it say about me as a son? And if I went, was I acting out of regard for some desiccated ritual that would cost me more dollars than I could afford? Talking with him that afternoon as he sat on the couch, in what appeared cramped quarters, as I was never shown any other room, that worry of mine was finally resolved. My father never once asked about my children, I am sure he did not know their names, and I wonder if he even knew of their existence.

And then he said to me, this came within our fifteen minutes, "the best thing I ever did was marry Mae." I was not taken aback, or at least did not show it, and I responded that I was glad for him, but he should not then expect anything from his children, that we all made our way accordingly. Actually, I do not know what my words were, but they were an attempt at a truce of sorts: he had made the decision that suited him, and we all came to live with it. But he could hardly expect any sympathy in return. I always thought that he married a woman who bore a similar characteristic to his mother, that is, controlling, but in truth I never knew my grandmother that way. It was a behavior that affected her sons and daughters, long before my time. And it was so different from what I associated with my mother, who despite her sickness I always thought of as sweet and kind. In any event, Mae came back to the house in those few minutes we were in the small living room, and I took leave of my father. It was the last time I saw him. Mae called my sister when he was dying, telling her he was crying and calling out for her, but she did not go. When he finally passed, Mae never told Miriam. She had a call from our uncle Max, and immediately phoned me in California, catching me in a library. I could think of nothing to say, and made a stupid joke, telling her she was now an orphan. But I remember going through the day thinking to myself, "my father is dead," saying it over and over as if the phrase could be intoned like a mantra, and I could draw up from some unknown deep a thought or feeling that would be appropriate and make sense of it all. But nothing came. And all I could think was that I had been an orphan for a very long time.

2. BARRY AT FIFTEEN

"*MY DARLING BARRY*" — so begins a packet of letters written over a three-week period by my girl friend Jean in the summer of 1954. She was at a Jewish girls' camp in the country. Anything outside the borders of New York City counted as country. The site in Westchester was the former estate of a Jewish businessman, complete with swimming pool, tennis courts, and bungalows, who ceded it to the YWHA in the early Twenties. It sounded better to me than Surprise Lake, but the mission was the same, providing a touch of country life to street-bred girls. But as the old saying goes about taking the girl out of New York, they carried the streets with them all the way to Mt. Kisco, and "in the city" rolled off their pens as if it were an automatic expression: "There doesn't seem to be anything doing in the city" (Jean), or "How are things in the city?" (Janet). I write this because it is important to know how we understood where we lived. The *city* encompassed everything that was New York, except possibly Staten Island, and it identified Manhattan when you said, "I'm going into the city." Everything else was a *town.* I remember standing in the cold, late at night outside the old Hudson theater in Midtown with Eddie Fishman, waiting to get in to see the "Tonight" show with Steve Allen, and two slightly older guys were behind us, from Buffalo, and I blurted out in a spasm of cordiality, "That's a pretty big town, isn't it?" What did I know from Buffalo? I had never even stared at the Tappan Zee Bridge..

My memories of the three-week period when Jean was at camp are slim at best. Yet I have a batch of autograph letters that document the days and weeks running from July through early August. How does the memoirist capture an intimate story when only one person has a voice? Jean is alive in every line she scratched, while Barry is framed by those sentences alone. In a sense, the rebuilding of a summer romance too old to be remembered is part material recovery and part imaginative fabrication. That a fourteen year old girl would write to a fifteen year old boy for eighteen days straight, anywhere from two to four leaves a day, makes an indelible statement about the girl. It is one that even now, after long years, deserves its own generous tribute. For Jean's are lovely letters, open, innocent, and with a simplicity and fluency matched only by its beautiful hand. Reading them I find it stunning that they were dashed off by a teenager hunched on a bunk bed, her best friend below her, and a roomful of girls all noisily engaged in the same activity ("If I make mistakes don't worry because I'm sitting here in the dark and slowly going blind").

Writing letters was what we did, Jean's just happened to be better than most. They chronicled the daily life of the camp, the food, alternately good and awful ("breakfast shitty, pardon the expression"—we were not prudish, but used profanity sparingly), the sports, swimming, which Jean loved, tennis and volley ball, arts and crafts, hikes, in the evening games and singing and social dancing, and Friday services, when the girls had to wear white ("Very religious camp this is"). Yet those details were the smallest part of the story, for almost every sheet is a register of deeply felt emotion, and taken together they form an unending song to the beloved. "I miss you and wish you had your arms around me again," or, "I miss you terribly and wish you were here," the last phrase echoing Eddie Fisher's popular song—*They're not making the skies as blue this year / Wish you were here / As blue as they did when you were near / Wish you were here.* They bring back our shared time with friends ("I was thinking of Eddie's backyard and 'us' rotten teenagers") and our own private moments ("I was just thinking of our 27 second kiss"). And always the letters themselves, sheets of script that were the transit for intense feelings ("Please write me mushy love letters. I know I'm being blunt but <u>please</u>"). The word has lost its currency, but it was ubiquitous that summer, as the girls all sat around and "read mushy parts in each others letters." In any case, I must have obliged, because she read my writing to her bunkmates: "After I told them what a doll you were I had to read them your letter. I just kept reading it over and over because it was so wonderful."

Jean returned to *my* letters again and again, saying that they were "gorgeous," that each one sounded so much like me it made her "homesick." Her favorite was "the letter with 'Yours'," an allusion that stymied me until I read further along in the correspondence: "I've got the girls in my bunk singing 'Yours.' It's a beautiful song and I wish I was there to hear it with you." *(Yours till the stars lose their glory / Yours till the birds fail to sing / Yours to the end of life's story / This pledge to you, dear, I bring.)* I thought, how could they possibly know that song? I knew Helen O'Connell's early forties recording with Jimmy Dorsey, just as I knew the words to her other Dorsey hits, because I loved her lilting voice, even tried to imitate that sultry, drawn out *cool and limpid green eyes*, but those songs were well before the music we listened to on the radio. I must have written out the lyrics in a letter, Jean read them to the girls, and they were teasing her a bit by suddenly singing it aloud in the bungalow. But if "Yours" was before our time, Jean's letters were filled with the music of our own day, the songs we danced to feverishly in Eddie Fishman's backyard. A radio was our lifeline to music, and from her "counselor's room" Jean heard through the walls Patti Page singing "Steam Heat," as she wrote, "and I really need 'your kisses to keep me from freezing each night'." In fact, *The Pajama Game* had two more songs that were charting, so it is small wonder that we were all anxious to see the show as soon as we could: "Are you taking Jean to see The Pajama Game? Is Henry taking me?" (Janet)

There were other tunes that carried over the airwaves in the Peter Pan Bunk and filled the lines of Jean's hurried missives: *Blow me a kiss from across the room / Say I look nice when I'm not / Touch my hair as you pass my chair / Little things mean a lot.* Once she ended a letter with lyrics from an old standard that was covered by a new group: "Nothing else for me to say And so I'll close But by the way I am thinking of you P.S. I love you." As I think of these songs, the words still imprinted after all these years, I wonder about the role they played in our lives. I knew that many of them were idiotic, like "Doggie in the Window," I could not abide "Tennessee Waltz," and I thought "Que Sera, Sera" was a song for little children. Yet all the singers had talent, however ludicrous the material, and not a few were accomplished musicians. Some I had a particular affinity for, like Peggy Lee, whose rasp gave her renditions of "Golden Earrings" and "Lover" an eroticism that I subliminally recognized but could not have articulated. Also Kay Starr, whose voice had an edginess that cut its power, almost an aching, as she held and drew out those vowels, that we would now associate with country music, which we then were clueless about. Jean wrote: "Right now the radio is playing 'If You Love Me' (Really Love Me). 'I would make a mountain fall, Do anything at all if you only say you care.' Those are the words I just heard and they're very true." The song was Kay Starr's version of Edith Piaf's "Hymne à l'Amour," and although I knew nothing of the French original, I was aware of Piaf peripherally, as the girl friend of Marcel Cerdan, for I remembered the front page splash when the champion fighter went down in a plane on his way to visit the Little Sparrow in New York. I think Piaf lodged in my mind ever since that disaster, and much later, living in Madison, I would haunt an undecorated artsy storefront dive on State Street, plump quarters in a tabletop jukebox, playing "Milord" over and over, and all the while imagining myself in some exotic place elsewhere.

The summer of 1954 was spent at Brighton Beach. It seems strange, after years lived near the soft sands of slender Hawaiian beaches, its warm waters tinted blue-green inside the coral reef, that I should be drawn back to the beach in Brooklyn, its vast expanse of hard sand that spread from the boardwalk to the sea, the chill of the Atlantic that faced you as a test of courage, and its pungency, inhaled the moment you stepped off the elevated train. It was a place afar, in the city but not of the city. Yes, there was Coney Island, and in college Irving would pester me in the evening, and make me drive to *Nathan's* for a hot dog. But we never went swimming there. Brighton was our sanctuary and our playground, we loved the water and the waves, body surfing before we ever knew the term, and tanning away the hours with Coppertone, years before we learned about the danger of the sun. I have a picture of three teenagers standing on the beach: myself in the middle with shades, a crew cut, waist high swimmer's suit, tilting slightly to the right while my left hand rests easily on my upper leg; Eddie Fishman in trunks, with his infectious smile, head leaning in the opposite direction to mine; and a third person whose face I recognize but whose name eludes me. Although the picture is static, there are apartment buildings in the distance, people in canopied chairs directly behind us, the ease and comfort in the scene is visible on all our faces. Brighton was our limited escape from the streets, our small yet unalloyed pleasure. And Jean, like the other girls in Mt. Kisco, was herself thinking of the sand and the sea, both as remembrance and anticipation: "I am waiting until I see you and until we can go to the beach again." But that

was not to be. I do not know how long after she returned before we stopped seeing each other. I have no idea why. What remains after so many years are just these letters, words detached from the writer, who knows nothing of them, but graved on the page in pencil and ink, with lipstick splotches on the envelopes, no longer eliciting the thrill that they then carried, although that cannot be altogether stilled, but now, drained of their blood-life, they are hieroglyphic testimony to a moment in time when two very young people, who knew nothing of life, were once bathed in love, alive with the language of popular songs, and the vocabulary of teen longing.

Barry at fifteen and sixteen presents the memoirist with an unanticipated perplexity. For while we remember more of these years than of our early boyhood, there is a perceptible difference in our experience of these memories. Those farther back often have a sharpness that seems missing from later reminiscences. Why should my sensory images of Ray Bolger and Isabel Bigley be more piquant than my remembrance of "Damn Yankees," which was a thrilling musical? Is it an example of Stevenson's assertion that the first experience can never be repeated, the first love, the first sunrise, because it touched what he called "a virginity of sense"? Maybe the first Broadway show is in that category, strange as it seems to compare a show to first love, but they both have a wonder about them that you cannot explain, yet they stay somewhere within you never to be lost or forgotten, even though the show, like the love, has long since gone dark. How do we convey later memories with the same vivacity as those farther back? Can we even do so? For the memoir progresses by steadily shedding a virginal self, and supplying a carapace for that lost skin, harder, shrewder, even judgmental where no judgment existed before. And so the narrative undergoes a transformation just as the boy transitions into high school. In a way the memoirist wants to hold onto the early tone, the bright wonder of discovery, for recollection is discovering the past as if for the first time, and making it new. There may even be a touch of poetry in this, granted the talent of the writer. But the nearer the past, as the subject adds years, the farther we find ourselves from Wordsworth's child, and wonder gives way to reflection, which is more prose than poetry. Thus begin the years of middle adolescence.

3. BROADWAY HEIGHTS

"Do THEY STILL really have prizes in Cracker Jack boxes"? That question from *Breakfast at Tiffany's* runs through my head as I stare at a number of ticket stubs on my desk. *Do they still have ticket stubs?* I think to myself, as if *Oh yes* will give me the same satisfaction it did the Tiffany's salesman, *a feeling of solidarity, almost of continuity with the past.* Yes, people still really do get those tickets that always felt to me as vital items, not like the flimsy pasteboard punched out by the automatic machines in the movie houses. For me, a theater ticket was the tangible evidence of an occasion, marking a moment set apart from the ordinary. In a way it seems odd, for what could be a more quintessential New York experience than going to the theater? Why shelter these torn stubs, artifacts of a distant time, their colors and typography so distinct from today's computer generated tickets? I look at them with blank wonderment to think how much the theater meant to me. They survive in a small 2¼ x 4" ticket envelope from the *Majestic Theatre, 245 West 44th Street Telephone: CIrcle 6-0730.* The phone number brings back

memories of those intoned telephone exchanges, whose New York names—*MUrray Hill, PLaza, GRamercy*—were so much classier than the *PResident* and *DEwey* of my neighborhood. John O'Hara must have privately crowed to himself when he hit upon *BUtterfield 8* as the title for his novel, exulting that no one had thought of that before.

I sometimes think it all had to do with Manhattan, which was a special, even magical world. I have an image of a quiet Sunday morning near the Battery. Harry and Miriam were taking me to the Statue of Liberty, I was nine, the song going round was *I'm Looking Over a Four Leaf Clover / That I overlooked before,* and I have always associated the jingle with the day. That morning stayed with me, for I imagined I could reach out and touch the air, as if it were gauze that covered the strangely silent streets. The stillness and clearness, the scent of the bay, pierced me in a way I intuitively knew was all about place, and the place was the city. I believe that feeling returned, perhaps subliminally, when my eyes were fixed on Audrey Hepburn, sitting on a stone ledge before a small fountain, surrounded by canyons of skyscrapers, a cigarette nestled between her fingers, as she says, "Oh, I love New York." No song to the city could match

Hepburn's voice. But I knew no one who lived in Manhattan, and in those years in early high school, I could not have imagined myself living there. That changed when I was in college, and my great dream was to move to the city. *Saturday Night Fever* shone dizzying lights on John Travolta's dancing, but its core was a Brooklyn story about crossing the East River. In high school Eddie Fishman and I would travel to the city during Christmas, just to walk around and absorb the atmosphere, the lights and gaiety, the throngs of people jostling each other on the sidewalks outside the great stores, all the while smiling and wondering what took so long for the season to come around. There was nothing like that in the Brooklyn we knew. I cannot think of a section that ever looked decked out for a party. Admittedly I was not familiar with downtown, and the odd occasion that I wandered there was to buy chocolates at the *Barton's* store on DeKalb Avenue, marvel at the Brooklyn Paramount Theater, even if I never went inside, and maybe walk over to *A&S*, our borough's answer to the city's department stores. By this age, fifteen and sixteen, we were all aware of Brooklyn as a distant second sister to the island across the river. It was not a point anybody argued, or felt badly about, and I remember no long riffs by anyone raising the standard for the hometown. Nor did anyone take any particular pride in growing up in Brooklyn. That would have to wait, for long years and longer lives, when the borough could be spied from a glass, and at a distance, that took in far more than a narrow body of water separating two worlds.

And so we come back to the ticket stubs, each one the result of a long subway ride to Times Square. It was not the same if you lived in Manhattan, and could take the train three or four stops to get to midtown, or a bus, or maybe even a taxi, and as I write this I realize I never took a taxi, one of those basics of New York life that had nothing to do with me. But traveling to the city was part of the fun of it all. Rising out of the dark into the raucous center of town, looking up at the massive Bond sign with its two enormous mannequins that towered over the Square, arrested by the waterfall and oblivious as to how it worked, then passing your eye to the right on the chance you might see giant smoke rings coming out of the other spectacular billboard with its immortal line, *I'd Walk a Mile for a Camel*, meandering along Broadway with a show of purpose, and wondering all the while where everybody was going and what they all did, for I was excited by the clothes and carriage of the throngs jostling their way forward and back, the only people not moving being those who would save your soul or skim your wallet. And finally sidling onto 44th or 45th Street, finding the Belasco or the Lyceum, picking a seat at the box office, which was a bit of a sham since I was never out of the second balcony, and for $1.75 I was granted entrée to a legitimate Broadway theater.

I know it gave me a grown up feeling. I am sure it had to do with going into the city by myself, entering play houses where I imagined the people all around lived in wonderful apartments in Manhattan, overlooking the Park or the river, or on an uptown side street, the mark of city chic, and bought seats that were not in the last rows before the upper exit. I was always attuned to class differences. I could not say to myself *I want to sit downstairs, in the orchestra*, for those seats were for others. In a strange way, I held two ideas in my head that chafed against each other—that I could experience the play solely as if I were alone in the theater, while at the same time nursing a keen sensitivity to the social divide in the place itself. It comes to me now, years later, how self-conscious I was of the family and streets that bred me, how I carried that beyond the borders of the borough, and how even the excitement of a Broadway show was suffused with the sense that there were separate seats, and lives, among the people that shared that closed space.

Although I could have listed from memory five of the eight plays I saw from October 1954 through May 1956, the torn tickets let me piece together the names of all the shows. I saw *The Pajama Game*, right after the girls returned from camp. What stays with me, sitting four rows from the back of the large St. James Theater, was the dominating presence of John Raitt, standing on the left-hand corner of the stage and directing his soaring tenor to Janis Paige at the opposite end, as he belted out *There once was a man who loved a woman* and dragged out the pronouns in the refrain: *They say that nobody ever loved as much as he—ee / But me—ee, I love you more.* And who that was there could forget the breath-stopping "Steam Heat," the dancers with their bowler hats, skinny black suits and white socks, twisting and bowing low as they mouthed those marvelous words whose barely concealed eroticism was perceptible even to a teenager—*The radiator's hissin' still I need your kissin' / To keep me from freezing each night. / I've got a hot water bottle, but nothin' I've got'll take the place of you holdin' me tight.*

Of course I knew nothing of Bob Fosse, or that this number ushered in his signature style. I am not sure I ever used the word "choreographer," for I paid no attention to anyone other than the stars, and I could not tell you who wrote the songs they sang or orchestrated the moves they made. And it was not only Fosse I was ignorant of, but George Abbott and Jerome Robbins and Richard Adler and Jerry Ross. It would be years before I attended to the composers and lyricists, the people who wrote the books and directed the scenes, but then I was no longer in my middle teens, in love only with the performers and lights, and oblivious to the artists who made it all happen. As for the show, I can see Eddie Foy leading the group in the "Seven and a Half Cents" number, and thinking to myself the "union" in the plot was nothing more than a skeleton on which to hang some singing and dancing. But the music was so memorable—Rosemary Clooney already had a huge hit with "Hey There"—that only a grown up would have cared about anything else. Years later I saw a revival of *The Pajama Game* by the New York City Opera. It had become a storied part of theater history, and as I was sitting in the grand orchestra of the New York State Theater, I found that despite my best efforts and ardent wishes, I was unable to recover the view from the balcony of the St. James.

The letters from camp make clear why I went to *The Pajama Game*, but I have no material evidence for any of the other shows. I can only speculate as to what motivated a sixteen year old as he bought tickets to a varied group of plays. I saw *Tea and Sympathy* at the Ethel Barrymore because of Deborah Kerr, who was a major film actress and brought a new kind of sexiness to the screen two years before in *From Here to Eternity*. I was naturally drawn to glamour queens like Rita Hayworth and Ava Gardner, but no scene in any of their movies compared with the beach shot of Kerr and Lancaster in Hawaii, their lips locked together, bodies in a vise-like, horizontal embrace, while the waves sounded and rushed over them. It had to be the most visually erotic coupling in my movie experience, though I would never then have used the word *erotic*. And so the prospect of seeing a movie star in New York compensated for the sleep-inducing title of the show.

The play was controversial, but I knew nothing about it and was disappointed, for if I expected sex in the person of Deborah Kerr, all I got was a mundane set with a lot of dialogue that left me blank. I did not read a review, but I doubt any would have talked openly about homosexuality, or in a way I would have understood. As I think of it, if the word had been used I would have had no idea what it signified. All I knew is what I picked up from the street, slur terms like *queer* and *fairy* and *fag*, and the Yiddish *feygele*, literally "small bird." What being a homosexual entailed, apart from some kind of unknown perversity, was beyond me. I am sure my ignorance explains why I never recognized my best friend in high school as gay, and I balk at using this descriptor because it would be an anachronism here, for *gay* had no other meaning to me than *carefree* or *light-hearted*. The word stuck in my head from Louis Jourdan's number in *Gigi (She's so* gay *tonight / She's like spring tonight / She's a rollicking, frolicking thing tonight)*. Clearly I was dense to all that pertained to the play, if I read the *Playbill* I might at least have learned about the actors, but I had a stubborn habit of not reading any preparatory material, as if I wanted to test myself to see if I could make sense of what I would be watching without the help of a crib sheet. The result: I was bored or bewildered throughout, and in the final scene, when I suddenly had a glimmer that Deborah Kerr had slept with the boy, I could not for the life of me figure out why.

That was not the case with *Lunatics and Lovers,* a farce I climbed to see at the Broadhurst Theater, and all I can remember is looking down and trying to catch every wise-ass word that came out of the mouth of Buddy Hackett. He was a short, rotund man, with a mobile face that he screwed up when he spoke while the words and sentences peeled out from the side of his mouth. Hackett was a Brooklyn native whose voice carried the street yet had an inimitable sound, like a cross between a screeching truck and a high-pitched chorister. A Catskills apprentice, an all-purpose comedian-actor, he was a guest on Jack Paar and a fixture on Johnny Carson. He came armed with one-liners and ad libs that were usually off-color, and routines that were offensive even in those deaf-and-dumb times, but he was hilarious, part Don Rickles, part Jonathan Winters. I remember him vividly from television, and whenever I watched him on Carson I would at some point think to myself *I saw him onstage in that absurd show that exists nowhere now except in my head,* as if I took a quiet pride in having seen him live before he became a major celebrity. And that was the sole reason I went to the show, for even a sixteen year old knew that the piece was nothing more than cotton candy, and the only thing I retained from it was its star and the title, a variant on some poetic lines about *lunatics* and *lovers* and *poets* all being touched by overactive imaginations. I did not know it then, but years after I read the original verses in *A Midsummer Night's Dream,* and instantly connected them with the farce I had seen as a teenager, it gave me an odd satisfaction, as if I were the keeper of a bit of useless information, that the title of a show nobody ever heard of was a Shakespeare allusion. But what perplexes me about *Lunatics and Lovers* is that the show opened a full two years before Jack Paar went on the air, so how on earth did I even know from Buddy Hackett?

There was no such perplexity for *Will Success Spoil Rock Hunter?* or so I initially thought. My ticket stub for the Belasco Theatre is dated a week after the first performance, while my others have dates anywhere from two to eight months after the openings. Why did I buy such an early ticket? The thrill of ogling Jayne Mansfield might explain it, but as this was her first stage role, I had no idea who she was. Ditto for Walter Matthau. Curiously, Orson Bean stayed with me, partly because his name was odd, his voice had a peculiar timbre, and I would see him often after on Johnny Carson, and always think he was the man who stood in the middle of the stage in that play with Jayne Mansfield, who by then had become round-the-clock news for her breasts and her turntable publicity. In effect, the ubiquity of her presence supplanted Bean in my mind, and though I never forgot him, Jayne Mansfield superimposed herself on my memory of the play, which in actuality was pale. But as I piece together why I was so quick to see a show whose principals were unknown, I was fascinated by the title, and could not help thinking Rock *Hunter* was far too close to Rock *Hudson* to be coincidental. I was puzzled as to how they could get away with faking such a known name, as if they were winking at the audience and telling us the *real* subject of the play. Long after, I learned that Rock Hudson was indeed the intended original, but the actor's agent put the kibosh on using his name.

What most held me about the title was its question mark: could success truly damage character? For in my mind, as far back as I could count, I equated success with fame, and fame with authors and books. It was the author of the play that drove me to buy an early ticket. I knew George Axelrod because I saw *The Seven Year Itch* earlier in the year. Now personified in people's minds by Marilyn Monroe's white halter dress, it was an exciting film for a sixteen year old, for the risqué dialogue and the scent of illicit sex that steamed over the scenes. But I also saw it as a *New York* movie, with its sticky heat, Tommy Ewell in a seersucker suit, the emblem of summer in the city, the subway rumbling under the sidewalk, and the claustrophobic apartment that any native would instantly recognize, and that the director, Billy Wilder, memorialized just five years later. So when a new play by George Axelrod was announced, what could I do but rush out for a ticket, hoping to find stimulation in the theater, where the language was freer, and forbidden words spoken aloud carried a shiver of a thrill.

There are three more ticket stubs from my Broadway year, 1954-1955, and a fourth just before my graduation from high school. *Anastasia* at the Lyceum and *The Diary of Anne Frank* at the Cort both draw blanks: I had no memory of them before tracing the stubs to their titles. The name "Anastasia" brought it back, a lost daughter of the last Russian czar who had only to prove her identity and a small fortune awaited her. This minimal recital placed me back in the theater, and I remembered the end of the play and my bafflement—*was* Anna a true Romanoff or merely an imposter? I did not see the movie with Ingrid Bergman a year later because, as with *Rock Hunter,* I felt smug about seeing the original on stage, and turned my nose up at an adulterated film version. It strikes me now as ironic and self-defeating, for I would certainly have followed the movies more easily than I did the live performances, but that thought never occurred to me at the time. As for *The Diary of Anne Frank*, it is odd I remember nothing of that show, yet when I say the words "Susan Strasberg" I imagine myself at the theater, and hear again all the buzz about the young actress, scion of theater royalty, in her first starring role on Broadway.

And now, as I am pushing to call up Susan Strasberg-Anne Frank, what slips into my mind is *The Member of the Wedding,* I was eleven years old, and I see that weathered kitchen, planked down on the left hand side of the stage, Ethel Waters, stolid, comforting, sitting on a plain chair in a corner, and Julie Harris, off to the center, fidgeting and moving, full of questions, all inflection in her voice. I felt an immediate attachment to her, as I did to most actors I first saw on the stage, and I later went to see her as Joan of Arc in *The Lark*. She was mesmerizing, looking up to the top of the theater, as if she were trying to break through the roof with her eyes and soar up to the sky, the darkness on the stage, the light illuminating just the single actor, and her voice, so memorable that I wondered if it had stayed in my head for six years, and I am sure I told myself I was watching an extraordinary actor, in no common play, and I had to commit it to memory.

What remains are stubs for two dynamite shows, *Cat on a Hot Tin Roof* and *Damn Yankees.* Since the old Morosco Theatre was torn down I cannot calculate how many rows from the back I was when I saw *Cat,* but I was likely near the roof. The nosebleed tiers did not bother me because I considered a theater ticket a great buy. I remember going on a date in high school to the *Paris* movie house on 58th Street, which I thought the pinnacle of sophistication, that glorious sign with the "P" sloping to the left and the name written out in cursive as if by hand, and if I have no memory of the film I have a clear picture of the demitasse that was served in white cups and saucers, not that I knew how to drink demitasse, but I took my cup to a cushioned chair in an uncrowded lounge and waited for the film to begin. The movie theater was on a quiet side street, not far from Fifth Avenue and the Park, and as I remember it the ticket was $1.85, because I had it in mind that a Broadway show and a *Paris* movie were virtually the same price. For some reason I thought going to the *Paris* was the most elegant thing imaginable, whether it was the coffee in the lounge, or the suave street—Broadway was many things but classy it was not—and the memory of that evening never faded. What I think held me was the ambience, quiet block, movie house nestled in the middle, arresting sign, lounge, coffee, cushioned seats, even the evening felt as if it were alive and could be touched. And there was clever me, taking a girl away from Brooklyn to a foreign movie in a foreign theater. Yet all I could think was how strange it all seemed, as if in a dream I had punched through a giant screen and found Gene Kelly and Leslie Caron on the other side. I wanted to be there, and understand that language, but for all my desire, my strutting and singing *I'll build a stairway to paradise* in mock imitation of Georges Guétary, it was beyond my reach.

So I return to *Cat on a Hot Tin Roof* and *Damn Yankees*, two shows that were the antithesis of each other and at the same time the best of Broadway. I had no idea that the people who put together *The Pajama Game* also made this wonder, but my memory of the production is of the dimmest, and hard as I try I cannot re-visualize Gwen Verdon's star turn *(Whatever Lola wants / Lola gets / And little man, little Lola wants you).* That is not the case with *Cat.* I can see Burl Ives at the front of the stage as if it were yesterday, slightly off to the right, his voice carrying up to where I was sitting as he boomed out *mendacity,* a word I could not define but viscerally felt as more than *terrible.* I knew of Burl Ives as a folk singer, and I half knew something about his politics, but I remember trying to get my head around the idea that this man who lilted *On top of Old Smoky* was the thundering voice of Big Daddy. For the rest of the play, I was largely at sea, since I could no more have penetrated the sexual maze onstage than I could figure out the plot. And as I think of it, I am not sure I even knew who the playwright was. If you asked me then who was the author of any particular play I would not have been able to answer. I knew the name Arthur Miller only because my mother saw *Death of a Salesman* with Lee J. Cobb, who made a profound impression, and it was the only play I can recall her mentioning. It is the oddest thing, but any snippet of my mother's seems to have lodged itself like a filament in my brain, forever undisturbed, until suddenly, like now, it lights up in some inconsequent manner, and reminds me that I was not always alone.

But what does a year and a half on 44th and 45th and 46th Streets add up to? I went to musicals that I obviously enjoyed, and plays that were exercises in ideas. The strange thing is how little of those plays I could genuinely understand, and yet I continued to buy tickets to others. That I remember almost nothing of the actual shows, of what I was seeing while in the theater, jars me somewhat, and makes me wonder about my memory. I can see myself straining in my seat to hear the words and understand their meaning. And yet clarity eluded me. It was as if I were in a place where everybody was running around on stage and jabbering in another language, and I was watching them and thinking I could understand what was going on by their movements, but in fact nobody was saying anything that made sense, and I could not even figure out the plot. Yet somehow that did not bother me, it did not seem to matter that I sat through triple acts with incomprehension, for the theater experience was its own reward. But the thing that strikes me most when I look back on those Broadway nights is that I see no one in the seat next to mine in any of the houses, or riding with me on the subway under the river and to the Square. It is as if I had gone to all the shows by myself, and the experience had been reduced to several torn tickets that I kept for some long forgotten reason, and that now remain odd mementos in having survived at all. And yet these green and blue and yellow stubs have unveiled the past and shored up unstable memory, prodding the recollection of emotion for a transitory moment or two.

4. MY BEST FRIEND

EDDIE FISHMAN lived at 658 Wyona Street, just below
New Lots Avenue and a few blocks from our high school. It was
the heart of East New York. For someone who was my closest
friend for three years I find it strange that I have no idea how
we met. All these tiny tales need beginnings, else how would we
make sense of their endings? It is as if we imagined ourselves
living in a world of perpetual cause and effect, racing to link
our scattered actions, when the slightest reflection tells us that
causation may be undiscoverable. Eddie was well liked, and a
group of regulars congregated at his house for dancing. On the
face of it, he was the last person you would have picked for a
dancer, heavy-set, I do not say fat because he never really looked
fat, a large head, full face, and an utterly disarming smile. Lenny
remembered: "He was a sweet and kind guy and was always
smiling when I was around him."

But he had a passion for dancing, as our mutual friend Harvey recounts in a story no one could make up. Meeting him for
the first time at the Utica Avenue train station, Harvey joined

Eddie on the way to a dance party in the Bronx. When they got there the girls, who all knew each other, would not go on the floor with boys whose tripping skills they were doubtful of. So Eddie, with the aplomb of a born sophisticate, asked Harvey if he could "follow," and Harvey, having learned to dance from girls who were older, said that he could. "Eddie got up, bowed, and in a loud voice asked me to dance. I curtsied and said yes. He threw me over his back, under his legs and under his arms. The girls stopped dancing with each other and stared at us. When we finished we bowed to each other and went back to our chairs. For the subsequent dances, the boys and girls danced together." If I could not be dragged to the Bronx for a party, Eddie was always game for a good time, and he could turn the pall of a room into instant glee by an audacious display of skill and a joie de vivre that was nothing like East New York. Well, that was also Danny Kaye's stomping ground, so maybe there *was* something in the water.

Eddie was maestro of his basement and backyard, our own private *Roseland*. It was just before long-playing vinyl came into vogue, and a small record player holding a stack of 45s was all the equipment needed for our slow embrace of pop ballads or the frenzied rhythm of Lindy songs. We lived for dancing, yet the songs that moved us from our chairs to the floor are murky in my memory. Pull up a list of charted tunes and I can hear them as if I were listening now, yet for the most part I cannot say what was on the record player when we were dancing. One exception was "Sh-Boom" *(Oh, life could be a dream /Sh-boom, Sh-boom / If I could take you up in paradise up above / Sh-boom, Sh-boom)* which still resonates in my head. The strange thing about that song was that it made no sense, I thought it one of those novelty tunes that popped up on the airwaves and made you wonder who ever thought them up, yet all the while you sang them over and over *(Put another nickel in / In the nickel-odeon / All I want is having you / And music, music, music)*. But "Sh-Boom" was more than just another novelty tune, it had a propulsive beat that picked you up and drove you to your partner, where you quickly locked your right hand around her waist, your left holding her bent right arm, and then leaning in you hit down hard with your left foot, swaying back and down on your right heel, until the two of you were turning and turning and turning, just like Kay Starr's "Wheel of Fortune," never letting go, holding fast and hoping there was not another couple to break the whirling twisting bodies *(If you do what I want you to / Baby, we'd be so fine / Sh-boom, sh-boom / Yada da da da da da da dada)*. It was the best dance record we had until Bill Haley came along soon after.

But when I look back at that time I am struck by our simplicity: nobody in that basement knew anything about where the music came from. For myself, even the mildest sexual innuendo in the songs escaped me, like a line from "Mr. Sandman" *(Then tell him that his lonesome nights are over)*, or "Tweedle Dee" *(Mercy mercy pudding pie / You've got something that money can't buy)*. As for the world of R&B, whose records were copied by white singers, I knew not a whit. As we swirled to the Crew Cuts' "Sh-Boom," who knew that four Black musicians from the Bronx wrote and recorded it first, or that the repeated title, with its jackknife nonsense syllables, referred to an explosion like the one that took place thousands of miles away on a Pacific atoll. Joe Williams, who I listened to on the radio, was to my mind an authentic Black singer *(I'm going to Kansas City / Kansas City here I come / They got some crazy little women there and I'm gonna get me one)*, and I had no clue that the composers of that song were white. Of course within a year all that would change, and pop music would never again be the same. In the meantime, we danced in our ignorance.

Eddie was never content with just two dance numbers. We did the rhumba with Dean Martin ("Sway"), the samba to an old Jimmy Dorsey-Helen O'Connell recording of "Brazil," and the tango to an arrangement of "Hernando's Hideaway" from *The Pajama Game.* The mambo was all the rage, and Rosemary Clooney hit the chart with "Mambo Italiano," a schlock dialect song that had on its flip side, as I discovered later, a lovely ballad that became a jazz standard ("We'll Be Together Again"). Nobody was at fault. We knew what we knew, no more, no less. Years after, when it became fashionable to call us a silent generation, which I always took as shorthand for all sorts of moral failures, the failure to address racism, a word that had no currency at the time, or sexism, which nobody would have understood, or possibly just failures when placed beside the huge numbers following us. Historians write the past, never the past *they* lived in, and few were as prescient as Scott Fitzgerald, who had the genius to make of his personal history a chronicle of his own fabled generation. For those of us dancing in the basement on Wyona Street, aware of where we came from but oblivious to where we were going, our ignorance was our knowledge, and our knowledge lasted only as long as the dance.

As I think back on my friendship with Eddie, I remember that he was the only companion who enjoyed unfettered freedom. This was no small factor in our relationship, for I spent stretches of time in his home, partly because his mother was sympathetic to a semi-orphan, and partly because he had a kind of free rein there. His family life had its own special dysfunction, unique yet of a kind with all the other twisted and thwarted lives behind closed doors that keep erupting haphazardly in this narrative. For me, not having a mother set me apart, and it never occurred to me that my friends might have their own tortuous if not broken relations within their families, making my own situation seem relatively benign, and on occasion even upbeat. My memories of Eddie's mother are dim, and I knew nothing of his intense closeness with her and a childless aunt who indulged him, a trucker father who was baffled by his son's style, and a gorgeous sister who disappeared from view for several months. But Eddie was always up for going into the city and soaking up the excitement of Manhattan. It was this open attitude that spawned our scheme to take a trip beyond the reach of the subway. Our plan was to get four or five friends and travel to Washington, D.C. The details of who we asked, how we intended to travel, what we planned on doing there, all escape me. But what soon became clear was that everybody else dropped out, the trip nixed by all the parents, and Eddie and I were left standing.

We could have joined the others and thrown in the towel, but he was as anxious as I to see if we could pull off an out of town excursion on our own. We made one concession to the changed circumstances: we altered the site from DC to Philadelphia. Neither of us had been to either place, and the prospect of going to another city, one familiar by name, was incentive enough to move us forward with the project. I am sure I told my grandmother that I would be gone, since it would have been odd if I simply disappeared for two days. I cannot remember what I used for a suitcase, since I have no memory of even owning one. Although the dates are blank, we were both sixteen. We went to New York, bought bus tickets to Philly (we took some curious pleasure in saying "Philly" rather than Philadelphia, as if we were smooth city kids who knew the score), and within a couple of hours found ourselves in an altogether strange place. In fact, it was so quick that it took some time before we could adjust ourselves to being in a city where the streets even *felt* as different as they looked, so used were we to New York sidewalks. But the first order of business was to find a place to stay. We headed for the local YMCA, which served as our base for the weekend. I remember the weather was overcast, and we were restricted to going everywhere on foot. I know we did not take city buses since we had no idea where they went, and we were not in a position to take taxis, which you could not hail in any case, so we wound up walking for two days from the site of the Y.

But we were excited. We had broken out of our tight circle, we were in a place where nobody knew us, and many things seemed strange. I remember trying to get my head around the "cheese steaks" that were advertised everywhere we turned. The idea of melted cheese on a steak was so alien to me, although I was not kosher, that I wondered what kind of place, or people, could come up with such a comestible. Eddie and I had a trace of arrogance that we carried with us, as if we were from the big city taking a sauntering look at this smaller town, with an indulgent and slightly jaundiced eye, but in truth we took in with eyes wide open whatever we passed along the streets. The thing that quickly became a source of amusement to us was Benjamin Franklin—his image was all over the place and everything was named for him. Whenever we passed a building, or a long street or parkway, we would smile and say, "Benjamin Franklin," and more likely than not it was so. I cannot say for certain if we went to the art museum, but my one unforgettable memory is of the Rodin Museum. That was a wonder, and for me the highlight of the trip. I was astonished that the city had an entire museum, small as it was, devoted to one sculptor, and I thought to myself even New York had nothing like this. Although I knew zip of

Rodin, except for The Thinker, which everybody knew, whether as art or joke, that museum was magic to me.

Since then I held a special feeling for the sculptor that was separate from the appreciation of his art. He was part of my weekend in Philadelphia with Eddie, much like a song you identify with a person or place, that becomes merged with you forever, and you can never forget them. It was the same several years later, in college, when I would go to the Museum of Modern Art on 53rd Street, long before the invention of MOMA, and the building on that quiet block was a refuge, with a lovely sculpture garden, pieces by Henry Moore plunked down on the grass, and shortly after entering I was confronted with two enormous paintings, *Guernica* and *Demoiselles*, works that became identified in my mind with a place that I loved, a kind of meditative shrine, more accessible and intimate than the Metropolitan. Those Picassos stayed with me, and whenever I saw an exhibition of his my mind returned to them, and to the building on 53rd Street, just as years later, in another town, after climbing the wide steps of a grand museum on a broad parkway, and peering at Duchamp's famous artifacts, I was carried back again to Rodin, and especially to Eddie, with his brown hair, broad shoulders, and ever endearing smile.

What happened to the boy with the twin gifts for laughter and dance? It is not always the case that you can recover anything of an early friendship after long years and the absence of communication. When we graduated from high school Eddie declared for science and went to CCNY while I opted for Brooklyn College. I never saw him during those college years, and soon after I learned that he had gone to Arkansas for graduate study, the picture in my mind of this city sophisticate living in a small town in the Ozarks was beyond comprehension. But the story I have to tell is of long after, when I reunited with Eddie for another memorable weekend. It was during a summer when I was living for a short time in Princeton, and getting progressively bored. I wanted to spend a weekend in the city, but I no longer knew anybody there. Oddly, and I have no way to explain it, I thought of Eddie, whom I had not seen for more than twenty years, and I found his telephone number in the directory. I called, and his infectious enthusiasm smoothed any minor qualms I may have had. He told me that he would meet me at the bus terminal and we would drive to Brooklyn, where he lived, and I would stay for the weekend.

After he picked me up, and we crossed the East River, he asked would I like to see a great restaurant with a spectacular view? He took me to the *River Café*, and the view of Manhattan, as we looked out from under the Brooklyn Bridge, and the smart feel and sound from the restaurant itself, made me gladder than I could express for having made that call. Having a drink at the bar was what I imagined being in *Sardi's* was like if we had ever gone there in our time, although I am certain it was far hipper and much more fun than that theatrical outlet could ever have been. It struck me sharply that here was a place, in my home borough, that I could haunt, and feel smart doing so, when all those years ago nobody thought it anything but dreary to stay in Brooklyn. Leave it to Eddie. Although we did not talk about it, I had an uneasy feeling that although he knew the *River Café* he never actually frequented it. I thought it might have to do with money, for Eddie's car was old and low end, and his apartment was barely modest. But it was hard to engage him in serious conversation, I could get no concrete idea about what he actually did for work, and he seemed to prefer playing the role of cicerone to this quasi-exile from the big city.

But I had something of my own to contribute to the weekend. Before the summer, in California, I had my eye on a gorgeous and brainy art historian, Susan, whom I had gone to dinner with once but who was evasive for all that. Still I had hope. She was going to be in New York for the summer, living with a friend in SoHo, a fabricated place with lofts for art and galleries for show that was just being put together. My plan was to meet Susan for lunch, with Eddie and her friend as partners. We called on the two women at their walkup flat, and they took us to a restaurant nearby. The place was filled with greenery, plants in pots and vines hovering over the tables, it was a lovely afternoon, the conversation was easy, and I could see nothing beyond Susan's eyes and her full chest, and hear nothing other than her smartness. The meal moved fast for the chatter never flagged, and before I knew it the waiter was taking dessert orders. He served coffee, and as I brought the brew to my lips I suddenly noticed, with something of a shock, that I had a green glass cup in my hands, and there was a green glass saucer on the table. I quickly put the cup down and said, louder than I realized: *What is this? What kind of restaurant are we in? Why are we being served coffee in glass cups?* And the knowing women smiled and said, *That's Depression glass.* My reaction was quicker than my thought: *Depression glass?* I blurted out. *This is the kind of junk that was in my grandmother's kitchen!*

Eddie and I returned to his flat, and for the remainder of the time I tried to think a little about his life. He was in New York but he seemed to be living on the edge of the city. He had endured a number of family tragedies, any one of which might have broken a less resilient man. I knew none of this at the time, any more than I was aware of his conflicted sexuality. A friend who knew him well told me that Eddie had dated a woman for years, but considered himself too careless with money to ever propose marriage. Maybe. But I am grateful for that found weekend. Eddie took me into the city on Sunday, where I could pick up the Princeton bus, and I saw him for the last time as he drove away in that old car, back to Brooklyn, to those old habits that brought him small pleasures for a while longer, and kept his face forever one to smile at.

5. BARRY ON HIGH

HIGH SCHOOL. Are there another two words in popular lore that can conjure up such alternating if not divergent pictures of the way we were before we were? For every person who harbors an unending series of petty humiliations, there is another who finds a spiral staircase of social success. But if those are the tropes evoked in movies and song, they had little reality in the overlapping circles that made up the cast of young people from East New York and Brownsville, some slipping in from the edges of Crown Heights, who attended Thomas Jefferson High School. Unless you took a test for Stuyvesant or Brooklyn Tech, which were both off limits to girls, you went to school where you lived. That might have been a mistake. One classmate, prodigiously gifted in mathematics, thought that he was destined for Latin and never bothered to take the test. It was not until scoring at the top of math meets in his senior year that it occurred to him that possibly he made the wrong choice. Another future mathematician was warned away from Brooklyn Tech by his older brother, who told him his social skills would be arrested, a bent way of saying he would go bonkers without girls. For myself, I knew nothing of Stuyvesant, Brooklyn Tech was far too technical for me, and I was aware of the Performing Arts high school only because my sister thought I should go there after my star turn as Tom Sawyer. No teacher in junior high talked about these schools in any of my classes, and I give a plus to whomever in John Marshall pushed Irving, later my college roommate, to apply to Stuyvesant.

In all fairness, there were teachers who recognized children with talent and urged them to seize chances far beyond their narrow blocks. Miriam had been encouraged to go to the High School of Music and Art in Manhattan, a prospect that caused her anxiety, but which our parents, to my amazement, apparently did not dismiss out of hand. Perhaps that was because Mama herself liked to sing and had an attractive voice. When young she used to enter competitions in the city, and *her* mother told her to always aim for second prize, because first only brought a trophy while second came with cash. It sounds like Little Bubbie, at one with a generation unmoved by useless sentiment. I am struck by stories like these, of a classmate from deep in East New York who had been selected for Hunter, the most élite public girls' school in the city, but whose parents would not allow her to travel the distance from Brooklyn by herself. Or another, as brainy as she was beautiful, and conscious as I was not of the tonier schools, like Midwood and Erasmus and Madison, but who faced the hostility of a mother who resisted or resented her daughter's natural gifts. Two tales of how many, yet I am reminded of them when I hear the endless paeans to the Jewish love of education, as if it were a genetic trait. In the interior of Brooklyn, where Jefferson was located, there were enough leftover families in the early Fifties who were struggling, and for all those who wanted their children to rise in the world, however clueless as to how that might happen, there were others too tired or indifferent to care, or simply unable to see past the blinds that shuttered their windows.

The great hulk of a building at 400 Pennsylvania Avenue was already thirty years old when I went there, and its best days were clearly past. But it had an instantly identifiable name, unlike Samuel J. Tilden or Franklin K. Lane, people nobody had ever heard of, or one with no name at all, like Boys High, which I always thought a little odd, as if it was a school for little boys. In the corridor when you entered there was a life size bronze of the president, seated, yet for some reason I cannot visualize it at all, which seems all the more strange because it was the only object of distinction in a building that was altogether without feature. Maybe all the city schools were featureless, but as I said earlier, it was only the Carnegie libraries in my boyhood and early adolescence that figured in my imagination. Jefferson, as a building, was just a larger version of John Marshall, and no teacher ever remarked about the space we inhabited, let alone said the word *architecture* out loud. And none of us thought to question the "look" of the school, I guess because the streets and apartments that most of us knew were cheerless enough themselves. That would change when I went to Brooklyn College, promoted by word of mouth for having a "campus," which was as far as my thinking on urban design could reach. Everybody who went to Jefferson had been going to city schools for nine years, and got the routine. Uninspired. But why, since I never thought of the building when I was there, am I writing about it now? Because it strikes me that the sense of a drab and colorless space existed subliminally, and the vast storehouse of boxed classrooms made an impression on my mind even though I appeared impervious to its stamp.

One room alone, in all respects unremarkable, imprinted itself on my visual memory simply because it had posters tacked up on the walls, the only place that drew the eye away from the dull blackboard up front and the dreary walls on the side. They were tall, with a beautiful ink script that transcribed lines from poetry and could be read at a distance. There was only one I still see vividly, it was high on the wall facing my seat, so I never missed it, and I would look up at it often, and read the lines over to myself because I could never understand them, even though I knew the words, and I thought if I only kept reading and thinking I would be able to make sense of them. *O chestnut-tree, great-rooted blossomer, / Are you the leaf, the blossom or the bole? / O body swayed to music, O brightening glance, / How can we know the dancer from the dance?* I am certain I never heard the word *blossomer,* had no idea what *bole* was, or how the tree turned into the body, but the line that stuck in my mind was the last, perhaps because it was the easiest to remember, *How can we know the dancer from the dance?* I remember sitting at my desk and puzzling over it, the dancer dancing, yet at the same time separated from the dance, and while I could not unravel its meaning the line stayed in my head, and it all came back to me many years later when I read "Among School Children," the beautifully scripted poster, the adolescent transfixed by the baffling lines, and Mrs. Olga Kahn sitting atop her desk, elderly and small, carefully dressed, hair pinned up in a bun, her entire being imbued with literature.

Everybody remembered Mrs. Kahn. One classmate, an expatriate in Paris, could not forget an hour spent on Plato's *Apology,* "when she drove us crazy asking us questions for almost the entire class, and finished by saying, 'Now you know how people felt about Socrates.'" Another, a poet and professor, tells of the time we were asked to write a poem and one student "swiped the lyrics to 'Unchained Melody' and presented them as his. We all stifled our laughter, particularly when Kahn said that it sounded like a song lyric," but somebody "ratted him out, and he was made to confess and apologize to the class." At the time, few of us knew anything of Roger Kahn, but years later many read *The Boys of Summer* and learned to our surprise that the chronicler of the Brooklyn Dodgers was the son of our 10th grade English teacher. Her influence was profound. The senior editor of the school newspaper, by admission a voracious reader, considered her "literate life" to have been inspired by her. For myself, the incidents related so vividly in my friends' memories are utter blanks, and I had no special relationship with Mrs. Kahn. Yet the class was crucial to my life, although I could not have known it then, for it was there that I began to read again. Through all of junior high I can barely name a fistful of books, and that would be a stretch. Dickens, whether *A Tale of Two Cities* or *David Copperfield* I am not sure, and Twain's *The Prince and the Pauper*, but if I am a bit tenuous on the titles, I nonetheless have a graphic picture in my mind of those abridged paper novels with their hideous bottle-green covers that the school passed out for our instruction or moral uplift, it is hard to know which carried more weight. And the funny thing is that we knew it. Even as twelve or thirteen year olds we could see through the pretense of "education" in the guise of fiction.

There were no books I was burrowing into on my own. For better or worse, I had simply stopped reading. In Jefferson that changed, and it was in Mrs. Kahn's class that I read *Crime and Punishment,* which I finally confirmed with the help of my classmates, because for years I tried to piece together in my mind how I came to that book, the first serious one I can remember poring over on my own, and I dated my new-found literacy from it. I could never get the picture of Raskolnikov out of my head, as he finagled the ethics of murdering a mean old woman, worth nothing herself, but whose money would provide for his benefit, while the murder would exemplify his superiority. Whatever I understood of the debate, and the religious dimension was certainly beyond me, I avidly followed the plot, as the detective slowly and methodically fused himself into Raskolnikov's conscience. But mainly what stayed with me was an odd joining of the idea of the novel and the fact that I had read it, and over time the latter thought dominated. I was more conscious of having read the book than of the book itself. There was a sense that I had done something I never thought to do, had in fact never done before. *Crime and Punishment* proved the lodestar for my new life, even though within just a few years I could not even say where or when I read it.

61 Glenmore Avenue, corner of Watkins Street. The Brownsville branch library, a bare two-story brick and stone building, was nearly half a century old when I started using it. I was aware that the structure was smaller and plainer than the Eastern Parkway library, the model of sedate style, my visceral response to the elegance of the building. Even the Stone Avenue library, which I had not entered in years, carried a trace of its faux castle in my memory. If 61 Glenmore was nothing like these, it was closer than Crown Heights, and ranged beyond the world of children. It exactly suited, and years later, when I read how Jack London and Richard Wright found in local libraries the furniture they needed to find themselves, I traveled back in time to Brownsville, and that simple edifice whose shelves I scoured, but whose interior yielded no more than a single memory. All I can think is that it was a repository rather than a hangout, since I never saw any friends there. I carried the books home to Belmont Avenue, where I read them, occasionally in

my grandmother's bedroom, because it faced the street, pulling up a hard chair next to the window, to catch the light, and disappear into pages of print until it got too dark to see.

I can watch myself now sitting there, gripped by Knut Hamsun's *Hunger* as the character wandered the streets trying to find a way to satisfy his gnawing appetite, and spellbound by Charles Jackson's *The Lost Weekend,* my knowledge of the terms *DTs* and *delirium tremens* coming straight from the novel, as I remember it. I have no idea how I chose these books. The film of *The Lost Weekend* was too early for me to have seen, I thought the title intriguing, even if I cannot say for sure that I knew it was about alcoholism, or whether I was just curious as to how a weekend could have suddenly up and disappeared. I would never have spoken that thought out loud, but in truth I had a kind of literal mindedness that I never quite lost, and I sometimes think it a reason for not connecting with science fiction and fantasy writing. As to where the Hamsun would have come from, that escapes me. Maybe I learned he was a Nobel author, but I am not sure I even knew then of the Nobel. One writer I was devoted to was Albert Camus, who was all the rage in the Fifties. Just the word *Existentialism* carried an aura of excitement about it, and saying it made me feel part of a world of serious thinking, even if I was mostly blank as to what it meant. I never thought that reading novels, which gave me immense pleasure, was an image making activity, but reading Camus created the illusion of being smart, even though nobody would even know.

Another foreign author I will never forget taking home with me was Antonio Moravia. Somehow I heard that he wrote about sex, and it is hard to recapture the language in my head or how I thought about it, "dirty" would not have been the word although we had no other term for talking about books that brought on an erection. Strangely enough, I never read *The Amboy Dukes*, but I devoured Harold Robbins' *A Stone for Danny Fisher* when I was much younger. In any case, I was determined to check out a Moravia novel, but when I found a title in the catalogue, I think it was *Two Adolescents,* which sounded just right to me, it was not on the shelf and had to be specifically requested from the librarian. I was a little uneasy, but the idea of the book being hidden away because it was too sensational for the open shelves gave me the courage to approach the librarian. The circulation desk, as I remember it, was in the center of the library, I asked the woman behind the counter for the Moravia novel, I can still see her face, a cross between disdain and distaste, and she told me that it was adult fiction, as a way of dismissing me. I do not know what I said, perhaps the imagined excitement of those pages dug my feet into the ground, but she relented, as if with a shrug, and gave me the book. It was a victorious moment when I walked out of the Brownsville library with a dirty Italian novel under my arm.

My other place for reading was the living room, where I could sit in a small armchair, but there was never a good lamp, and I was dependent on the daylight that could be caught in the room. The chair was opposite the sofa, pushed up against the wall, and at a right angle to the cabinet television. It was here that I followed my own bent, losing myself in books I carried home from Glenmore Avenue but unable to say how or why I picked them. Some seem to have been obvious, like my binge reading of Steinbeck, although by today's habits it hardly approached a binge. I remember *Of Mice and Men*—who at sixteen or seventeen could forget that?—and *Tortilla Flat* and *Cannery Row*, and I think *The Red Pony.* By chance I read today of Richard Llewellyn's birthday, and I thought of *How Green Was My Valley,* and wondered if the movie title made me aware of the novel, but for long after that book was Wales to me, and when I knew of Richard Burton, and found my way to the White Horse Tavern, not a shrine so much as a place where Dylan Thomas went, I would always come back in my head to *How Green Was My Valley.* I think that the titles of books often stay with you longer than the stories, which fade in memory, an unchanging talisman to a world long lost. *You Can't Go Home Again* was the longest book I took home with me, determined to finish it through, and did, with avidity, but in this case the title entered the culture. It is clear that I was not pulling books off the shelves pell-mell. Authors' names were driving the selections, but those names, and their titles, are now stray puzzle pieces, fragments of a life connected by threads to a time long gone, when once they suffused the consciousness of the boy, impacting his life in ways no longer understood, and irrecoverable. Except for the one rare book whose story never died: *A Farewell to Arms.* Much of the dialogue eluded me as I sat in that armchair, as did the careful playing with sex, but I could not escape the pull of those last pages, two of the most beautiful people I had ever encountered brought down by their love, I followed the print as line by line there was pain, and death, and in the end nothing but aloneness. Tears were streaming down my cheeks as I finished the book, and no other novel evoked that response. I have read the book since, more than once, without tears, but never without a silent memory of that armchair on Belmont Avenue.

But love, even high school style, was not easy to find in days when *sex* was not a word that was spoken out loud, and I can recall no conversation about it with anyone. I felt drawn to girls as if by a magnet, yet I was like a filing that never stuck. I am inclined to say this was the case with most of the boys I knew, although oddly enough several remember me as someone far more at ease with girls than they were. As I thumb through *Aurora*, our yearbook for 1956, I am struck by how good looking so many of the girls were, even in those dour stamp size head shots, and how many faces I vividly remember, staring at them as if I could almost reach out and touch them, the remembrance tinged with a strange wistfulness, a regretful puzzlement that I knew nothing of their bodies. It would be easy to riff on the dance without music that we all performed, often awkwardly, mostly unaware, but as the writer warned, if you start to write about a *type,* or in this case a cultural-sexual moment, you wind up with nothing. This is my story, and the silent dance was one

THE FRONT OFFICE

I fumbled on my own. I remember a moment in the dining room on Belmont Avenue, where the cast iron telephone that brought the news of my mother's death sat on its own small table, I was talking with a girl, my grandmother had answered the phone, and after I hung up and moved away I heard Bubbie say, in Yiddish, to no one at all, that I would bring grief to girls. I stood still in that room, taken aback by the sorrow in the words as she slowly shook her face side to side, and the sudden recognition that this old woman, who spoke an old language and came from an old country, had thoughts about the dance between boys and girls, and the sharpness to see through it. The remark never left me, and even though I felt it as a slight, I would return to it time and again over the course of years, either marveling at its prescience or inverting its meaning, for despite my grandmother's prophecy, grief turned out to be a road that ran in two directions, and at any one time it was a toss-up as to who had the right of way.

At sixteen and seventeen I looked for girls where I could find them. An afternoon ball game at Ebbets Field remains vivid in my mind. I have no memory of who was playing, I feel sure that Eddie was with me, but just behind us sat two or three girls, one of whom took my eye. After some chatter that I initiated, it turned out her name was Linda, and so I started to fake-croon, à la Buddy Clark, *When I go to sleep / I never count sheep / I count all the charms about Linda.* Whether that impressed her, or just made her laugh, it kept the chatter going, and my back to the diamond for most of the game. She had gorgeous blonde hair that came down not quite over one side of her face, but close, and it reminded me of Veronica Lake, so I blurted out "Did you ever see *I Married a Witch*," the only movie I could at once identify with the actress, before realizing almost immediately that the compliment might have sounded like a barb, and I quickly contorted some explanation. I remember thinking to myself that I wanted to see her again, it seemed so easy to just start a conversation, but I was unsure how to do that. It may have been one of the first times when I tried to pick up a girl, found us both engaged, and concluded in my mind that she was just as eager for us to continue.

It is strange how that idea stayed with me over the years, against all odds. At times I am amazed how the same action can be repeated again and again, without success, and always as if for the first time, like the living version of a comic strip, Charlie Brown, Lucy, and the football, all destined to show up every fall in a familiar scene, and ending each time exactly as the year before. In a way, my belief that the girl would be equally engaged reflected a desire that ran so deep as to be unrecognizable, a bit like Charlie Brown's love for the red-haired girl, and barely saved from being desperate by its complete unconsciousness. While it seems absurd to make sentences out of some floating and fleeting minutes, decades ago, in a ballpark that has shrunk in form to a couple of small words, the perplexing question is why I remember it at all? Maybe it was the song, for years later, in Madison, I was invited to a sorority dinner by a beautiful Wisconsin undergraduate, her straight blonde hair came down to her shoulders, flipped into a wave, eyes wide and bright in a fair face, and she was Linda, only this time I did not try to sing, and there was no need to ask for her number. Yet when she first called, and told me her name, my mind flashed back instantly to Brooklyn, a lost stadium, and a girl I never knew.

Still we tried. I have two small pictures of Brenda, a tall, full figured girl who lived in Brighton Beach. In one, shot at an angle so that she is seen sideways, but very upright, on a concrete walk, an apartment building rising in the distance, and a clear sky filling the background. Brown hair brushed straight back, a loose shirt draped over jeans rolled up to her calves, and flat slip-on shoes. This open-air picture was taken near the beach. The other is an indoor shot of the two of us, Brenda sitting on a chair, a short sleeve sweater filling her form, myself standing slightly akimbo next to her, right hand on hips, a pose that I seem invariably to have adopted before a camera. My dark hair was brushed back just like hers. There is a television set to the left, and a large bureau framing us from behind. The photo, snapped in her apartment, is unimaginably common, as if it were recorded by some itinerant in the early period of photography, except that we are both smiling, and appear happy. There is nothing more ordinary, and nothing stranger, than staring at a photograph of someone you no longer know. I can piece together a bit of story from a classmate whose girl friend lived near the water, and what I *do* remember is walking long past midnight in the empty streets close by the Brighton Beach elevated station, waiting in the cold on a deserted platform, hoping a train would come before anybody showed up to keep me company, and the endless ride home to an even more desolate station on Livonia Avenue in Brownsville. While the memory of the night and the cold and the station is vivid, I can remember nothing of the evening with the girl whose pictures are in front of me now, nor of saying to my classmate, who reminded me of it recently, "Boy, there is nothing like a house date with Brenda." And I am sure that was true, for why else would I have clacked along above and underground on the IRT to see somebody who lived at the end of the BMT line? But in fact I knew nothing of this beforehand, and it was only the prospect of making out with a big-breasted girl that impelled me. I did not repeat it. Wonderful as the house date must have been, it was trumped by distance. Yet the pictures make for a strangeness that emerges from them as if out of nowhere, and Brenda takes on a presence that she never possessed in my memory. I see a lovely young woman, easy and casual, self-assured in the solo shot that takes in her long lines, and I wonder why I cannot bring back our time then when I see her so sharply now. Is the photograph a trigger that releases the past? Or is it an object that creates its own memory, supplanting the oblivion of a seaside house date with the impalpable presence of a conjured girl?

At some point my grandmother rented the flat above us on Belmont Avenue to a young couple. The wife was English and the husband American. It would be hard to overstate how exotic this was to a sixteen-year old boy who knew few people beyond the inner streets of Brooklyn. Foreigners were common enough in his experience, distant relatives, or customers in the grocery store with ink on their forearms, but all were washed in from the old world, with distinct accents and a generally dispirited air that was reflected in their somber dress. As for the Puerto Ricans who were slowly making their way in Brownsville, I cannot say I knew *exactly* where they came from, and I certainly had no idea about the status of the island, but they became part of the streetscape so quickly that I viewed them as no different from everybody else who made up the sidewalk life of my world. On two occasions there were visitors to Belmont Avenue who struck me as coming from places that seemed stranger than that of the refugees. Once it was a young man from Winnipeg whose family settled in Manitoba after the war. He was only there for a day or two, but I remember listening wide-eyed to his talk of living in a wild country, where wolves loped within sight of the door, and the snow and cold were so extreme that it sounded like an ice world. The second visitor, my grandmother's nephew, was from Kentucky. A Navy man, on duty briefly in New York, he came to dinner in uniform, and there was nothing more exciting than seeing a live sailor, very tall, white pants, white shirt, and a white Navy cap that he held in his hand. From that time forward I wanted to go to sea. But what was more startling was his speech: he sounded like somebody from another planet. It was a Southern accent, of course, slow, deliberate, a honeyed softness to it like nothing I had ever heard in real life. But the strangest thought ran through my head, that the person opposite was related to me, and Jewish, but looked and sounded like no one I knew. I never forgot him. Several years ago I saw him again, he talked fondly about that distant visit with his aunt in Brooklyn, I think he had the vaguest memory of me, but I heard that quiet Southern note once more, mellower with age, and I could not help but go back to a long vanished dining room table, and a boy who had been awe-struck by a man in white.

If the visitors from Winnipeg and Louisville succeeded in breaking for an hour or two the monotony of Belmont Avenue, it was as nothing next to the fair and slender blonde with the lilting English voice. I have no idea how the apartment was rented, but one day I discovered a couple living above me. It is odd how little detail I had about the pair, where they came from, how they wound up on a street one block from the pushcarts, what the husband did for work, even their names escape me. The young woman was certainly a war bride, not that I knew *exactly* what a "war bride" was, but the phrase had such wide currency, especially in the movies, that it was easy enough to make out its meaning. I would find my way into her apartment whenever I had the chance, as she seemed always eager for company. My cousin Eileen, who was eleven or twelve at the time, remembers being befriended by the woman, who was at most in her early twenties: "I used to watch her put on make up all the time and she liked to show me her lacy underwear. My Mom would always tell me not to go up to her apartment.

She obviously had her eyes on you and Artie for more intimate types of sharing." Eileen's awkward delicacy does not indicate whether she knew as a young girl what pleasures the woman had in mind, but in fact the soft fresh face did indeed enjoy Artie's company, and my own, though never at the same time.

The whole adventure was wrapped in a furtive excitement. I would slink up the stairs when my grandmother was down in the store, and a titillating game of cat and mouse would begin, a laughing frisky knowing woman, and a clumsy raw boy, she in a short skirt, teasing, unbuttoning her blouse just slightly, edging me on to hold her, touch her, but pulling back, switching and taking off her blouse, showing a satiny slip, which I could feel, and all the while my body too stirred to even think about what was happening, grasping like a puppy to get hold of some sweet nectar, but no clue as to how, nor how to keep from trying. She was always laughing, not tauntingly, but in a toying playful way, and there was never any chance that I would get what I wanted, although in truth I had no idea at all what I wanted. Certainly the word sex was never in my mind. I would not have known what that actually meant. But physical touch, feeling her breasts, seemed to me the object of the game. When I was in her apartment all thoughts of outside vanished, except that on the thin edge of my mind tottered the idea of "getting caught," which meant her husband might suddenly appear. But he always went to work, and she never seemed overly concerned, although I seem to there were one or two moments when she worried about his finding out. What strikes me now as curious is that it never occurred to me that my grandmother might know what was going on, and also that I have no memory of whether I knew that Art was climbing those stairs as well. I was so intent upon seeing and feeling her that I blotted out all sense of life down below, grandmother, father, aunt, all in close proximity, while I panted about as if in a world away, alone with this ripe yet restless transplant, waif-like, lost in another country, making do however she knew how, her sweet and comely skin the scent of desire, reaching out to be touched, recognized, maybe even loved.

Surely there were girls my own age I could have gone out with. Yet for some reason that was rarely the case. For one thing, I never stayed after school as I was always working in the grocery, usually in the evening, and on occasion by myself, and looking back I am a little surprised I was not more on edge than I might have been. The street was a hard one. Once a young woman was being served at the back of the store, I was in front near the register, when a man walked briskly through the door and up to the counter, took a razor out of his pocket, slashed the woman across the cheek, wheeled around and marched straight out. That was the only time, but I could not forget it. At night beer was one of the bigger sellers, and it was fine if the buyer was not drunk, but if anyone came in with a bit of a stagger it set my back up and made me want to finish the sale as quickly as possible. One of the singular things about working in the store, confirmed by my cousin Art, who traded places with me regularly, was that neither of us ever got paid. Art thinks it was a *duty* that was expected of us, but I certainly did not see it that way. Simply, it never occurred to my father that he should come up with cash out of his pocket for anything. When I was smaller, I saw an ad in a magazine for a Western by Zane Grey, *Riders of the Purple Sage,* I believe the price was just over two dollars, so I clipped the coupon and ordered the book. It arrived, I read it voraciously, and immediately subscribed to the entire series, agreeing to buy four volumes at a time. I plainly did not think it through, how many books there were in total, how much it would cost, I just wanted more *Riders.* When the first set came, and I remember it clearly because I was in the store *helping out,* the phrase that always stood in place of *working,* and when my father saw them, and the price, without so much as a word he made me send them back.

And so, as a teenager, I decided to stop *helping out* and look for a paying job. I found a grocery not much different from ours, walked in, asked for work, and the owner hired me. He was a fat man with rimless glasses and a receding hairline, who was always leaning back against the small wall that enclosed the cash register and checkout counter. I was hired at the minimum wage, 75 cents an hour, and he quickly saw that I could do just about everything in a small grocery. I could slice lox from a long slab of salmon, no small skill, candle eggs, cut butter from a tub, use the electric blade to cut Swiss, American and Muenster cheese, and of course do all the shelving of canned goods and sorting of bottles, since there were deposits on the glass, and everybody brought back their milk and soda empties for several pennies apiece. Well, I worked in that store for two weeks before getting paid. It was late in the afternoon. The owner was in his regular place, behind the counter, his back against the wall, the register facing him on his right. When I asked for my pay, he handed me a check, I looked at it in some puzzlement, calculated quickly, and said that it did not account for all the hours I worked. He then said, with a greasy smugness I will never forget, that the hours were correct, but the pay was based on 50 cents an hour. I could not believe it and stood stupefied. I looked at his fat face, a toothpick hanging from his mouth, and walked out of the store as if I were grossly insulted and intent on upholding my dignity. If I had not been so well behaved I would have come up with some act of retaliation, but what exactly I cannot even say. I think at that moment I regretted not being a *juvenile delinquent,* the all inclusive phrase for anyone who exhibited rebellious tendencies, for at least I might have concocted plans on how to get back at the creep. Alas, I had no imagination along those lines. All I had was my silent anger. But I never forgot, and the episode taught me a lesson, albeit one that at times proved more costly than smart.

My first date came about not through high school but via the Brownsville Boys Club, a neighborhood institution that had erected a new building the year before. In truth, I have no idea how I heard of the place, especially since it was far from where I lived, but I was so anxious to meet a girl that at first I paid no attention to the distance. I crossed those nighttime streets not to play ping-pong but to find someone who was other than me, but I was grounded enough not to expect or even imagine a dream walking. If the main purpose of the Club was to keep teenagers off the streets, it also functioned as a quasi-crucible for integration, drawing Blacks, Italians, Puerto Ricans and Jews together under one roof, a fact of which I was dimly aware. I doubt it was intended as a social mixer. Still, my head was turned by one girl, Julie, long dark hair that she wore in a ponytail, not slender but strongly built, and a face that fixed and held you. At this point in my narrative I succumb to conjecture: since the BBC was distant, and it was dicey to walk those streets, I doubt I went there more than the one time, but if so I would have asked Julie for a date shortly after meeting her. That strikes me as way too cheeky to be plausible, yet I see myself talking to her unbidden in the noisy lounge, spurring conversation, and somehow asking for a date. She agreed, and specified a particular Saturday night. What seemed strange was that she lived on the edge of Bedford Stuyvesant, and I could not figure out why she was at a rec center miles away. In any event, I took the bus from home, retracing my old route to junior high school, and walked half a dozen blocks to her street.

The building was one of those old, stately apartment houses never found on blocks deeper in the neighborhood. I reached the apartment and rang the bell. Within moments the door opened and a tall Black man stood facing me, his hand on the knob. Instantly I thought I had made a mistake, but rather than excuse myself I said simply *Is Julie here?* and he answered, *Yes, please come in.* So I was not in the wrong place. He ushered me graciously into the living area, invited me to sit down, Julie introduced me to her mother at the farther end of the large room, who was tending to her new baby. It was just such a moment when I was grateful for not appearing surprised. If I thought about it beforehand my eyes would have widened. But I acted as if it was the most normal thing in the world to ask a white girl for a date and find a Black man open the door. This was 1955 after all. Yet that was not my most remarkable discovery. It took just several minutes for me to realize that the place I was in was more sophisticated than any I had known. A high fidelity sound system, classical music on the turntable, bookcases that ran along the walls, all made for a suffusion of culture that felt as if it could be touched. Julie's father was my first personal experience of a Black man different from the men I saw on the street and in the store. I did not say any of this to her when we left, but I never lost the picture of a serene mother with her baby, and a father still and strong, with a smile creasing his face as he sized me up as a date for his daughter.

Julie had two tickets to Carnegie Hall. The show was a Hootenanny. I had some vague idea of the word, that it was connected with folk singing, although how an entire program of folk singing could be put on at Carnegie Hall puzzled me. Not that I thought about it that much, it was clearly Julie's game, and I was going along for the ride. I had never been to Carnegie Hall, so this was a grand occasion, but it was nothing like I had imagined. I thought the place would be filled with people sitting quietly, attentive to the concert artists, all understanding of that serious music that was foreign to my ear. But of course this was no longhair concert, and nobody was sitting still. The audience was raucous and energetic, responding exuberantly to the action onstage. I remember very little of the show, we were sitting way in the back, but the finale is vivid in my mind, for the Weavers and all the performers came on stage, and Pete Seeger led everyone in a rousing chorus of *This Land Is Your Land,* joined in by the audience. Julie was thrilled by it all. I am sure I reverted to an awkward silence, for I have always had an aversion to singing out loud with a concert sized crowd, a habit I never completely broke.

But the show at Carnegie Hall was more than just a concert. I knew who Pete Seeger was, I had vivid memories of the riots at Peekskill, and if I could not have defined hootenanny precisely it did not take much to know that it was infused with politics, indeed that folk singing itself was a form of politics. Even now I can sense the feeling I had at the time that I was taking part in a suspect political activity because of the performers and the occasion, a celebration of racial unity and political solidarity. I could not shake off the shadow that haunted me from the Goldman side of my family, where I knew more than I wanted to about subversive politics, and the specter of the government as a menacing antagonist was more real than fanciful. When I went with Julie to Carnegie Hall I did not know that the Weavers were coming out after five years of being blacklisted, that the show was a defiant act against the zealots who kept them from working because of their real or falsified Communist Party ties. The paroxysm that took hold in the early Fifties had abated, but there was no bold public headline that declared it dead. And so a part of me felt uneasy at associating with people and causes that had been vilified during those years of contagion. I did not like feeling that way, but I had no control over it. My displaced anger or confusion erupted two years later in a college class, when the instructor, remarking upon the death of Joseph McCarthy, asked what we thought, and I blurted out something to the effect that he got off easy. I was checked by him, and learned a new proverb, whose wisdom rested in its utility—*never speak ill of the dead.*

6. REEL MAGIC

I HAVE A COMPULSION to write about the movies. It is not all that strange, given how much a part of our lives they were, but I wonder about their place in a memoir. I suppose it is no different from writing about the books I read. In revisiting the pictures from those years, I can see again the imprint they made on a boy who loved movies, and found in them competing and overlapping worlds of harsh pleasure and inspired fantasy. Not that I knew any of that as I sat in the dark, transfixed by the shows, the solid houses they played in all gone, while the insubstantial and illusive flickers of light and shadow are vivid in my mind's eye. There is no knowing why one movie stays with you, it just does, or one star never lets you go, and even if you did know, while in thrall to it all, that the movie and the star were nothing but the stuff of dreams, you were powerless to dispel them, until years later, searching for the dreams that you yourself were made on, you brought them into the open world of print.

As a child I grew up on Westerns, an oater being obligatory in every triple bill I went to with my father, and Randolph Scott was my favorite cowboy. I could never take Roy Rogers or Gene Autry seriously as rivals. I thought *Happy trails to you, until we meet again / Happy trails to you, keep smilin' until then* a mawkish tune, and for the most part the man on the palomino pony struck me as little more than a mild-mannered showman. Autry I thought of differently. His signature song, whose opening line I liked to sing *(I'm back in the saddle again)* had images that were memorable, even if I had no idea what plant in the landscape he was crooning about—*Where the longhorn cattle feed / On the lowly jimson weed*—and Autry's voice had a twang that caught you, one I associated with a cowboy singer. I also liked that his horse had a strong name, *Champion,* instead of that ridiculous *Trigger,* and his clothes, unlike Rogers', never looked quite like they had been bought for a birthday party at a costume shop. Still, neither seemed to me the real thing the way Randolph Scott did. And even though I cannot name a single movie that Scott was in, the picture of that stoic and implacable hero, his long frame and sculpted face set against the wide landscape, became my enduring image of the true cowboy.

The first hard Western I remember was *The Gunfighter* with Gregory Peck, galvanizing with guns slung low over his hips, black mustache, and tired face. As an eleven year old I was gripped by the story of an aging fighter who wants to put down his pistols but is pursued by every young gun eager to make his reputation. I wanted Peck to escape the past and get back with his wife, who hated his life as a fighter. Even I knew that was not possible, but I could never have guessed that the gunfighter would be shot in the back. Years later, when I saw John Wayne's *The Shootist,* his adieu to a dying genre, I returned instantly to that earlier fable and the cheap cruelty of its ending, which had never left me. Next was *High Noon,* a mesmerizing black and white morality tale. I was too young to understand it as an allegory of the blacklisting days of its own making, but as a story of courage versus cowardice it was unmatched by any other film I had seen. Gary Cooper, *torn twixt love and duty,* looked nothing like a hero, drawn, thin, afraid, yet with no shame in showing it. The music was compelling, this may have been the first time I was aware of a film score, and the clocks ticking up to noon kept me in absolute suspense, even if I did not know what "real time" shooting meant. Gary Cooper, turned down for help by everybody in town, had to fight alone or run *(I do not know what fate awaits me / I only know I must be brave).* But he had no real choice. If I knew nothing of the allegory, I viscerally connected with the feelings of helplessness and isolation that showed in Cooper's weathered mask. It was a riveting performance. And after all the avengers were killed, as timid faces peeped from behind the shutters, and doors edged open, the cowboy hero stood alone in the center of that dusty town space, threw down his tin badge, and walked away. What more could a boy dream on? but to push against the world, if the world turned its back, not to bow or buckle, and in the end to walk away upright.

And finally came *Shane.* By this time I was more conscious of the actors, and I knew Van Heflin, but I cannot say if I was a fan of Alan Ladd or not, except that I liked him, and I wonder if part of the reason was that he was short. Clearly he was no Gregory Peck or Gary Cooper, but he seemed easier to identify with, and *Shane* was in color, so the whole film was brighter and livelier, although the story had elements similar to *The Gunfighter* and *High Noon*, a fast draw who wants to break away from his life, and a fighter who has to coerce the settlers to stand together against the greed and bullying of the cattlemen. I also liked it that Alan Ladd was nicely dressed, his clothes looking neat and clean, as if they were fresh pressed, rather than the stark, warrior-like outfit of Peck, or the rumpled shirt and trousers of Cooper. Shane was a shining hero, in bold contrast with Jack Palance, the most lethal looking killer I had ever seen on the screen, except for the indelible memory of Richard Widmark as a crazy man pushing a woman in a wheelchair down a flight of stairs. In a way he was as cool as Ladd. When he gunned down the settler who dared talk back to him, without blinking, it left me wondering for just a moment whether Ladd could actually best him. And years after, when I saw Jack Palance playing a tortured movie actor in *The Big Knife,* I had a hard time shaking free from my head the cowboy killer I still remembered as a boy. But Alan Ladd changed into his great buckskin outfit, buckled on his holster, prevailed in the gunfight, and in the end rode away from his "settled" life, leaving behind him the trailing cry of a saddened child, *Shane! Shane! Come back!*

When I started writing about the silver screen and thinking of the small screen I worried that the sentences might drop like an anchor into a bay of nostalgia, 'Oh yes, I remember that well, how I loved Judy Holliday, her sassiness and her inimitable New York voice in Born Yesterday, *or John Wayne and Maureen O'Hara in* The Quiet Man, *my first exposure to real Ireland, rather than its kitschy movie brogue, or Sid Caesar with his wonderful imperson-ations, and his unforgettable parody of Alastair Cooke as Aristotle Cookie, or The Great One himself, whose sketch characters before Ralph Cramden, like suave Reggie Van Gleason, were every bit as hilarious and touching as the bus driver, and whose orchestral al-bums a few years later would be every late teen's charm for making out, and on and on. Yet oddly I have little sentiment for these things of old, as improbable as that sounds, for a memoir by one definition is a memento, a memorial even, with a tinge of nostalgia carried in those words. But recalling the past does not imply* recovering *it, which is clearly impossible and spoken simply as a metaphor. Still it is the case that culling memory from consciousness breathes new life into it, as if past scenes suddenly appeared before me, and passed through my fingers as they moved along the keyboard.*

What of the movie musicals that meant so much to me when I was a boy and a teenager? I badly wanted to be a tap dancer because I idolized Fred Astaire and Gene Kelly, although I have no real idea why their movies resonated, I am sure the music was a big factor, as I knew the lyrics to so many songs from the films. Astaire in The Bandwagon, *getting a shine on his shoes, along with Cyd Charisse, who saw a new sun up in a new sky, and everyone else in that glorious confection of song and dance. And there was Kelly in* An American in Paris *and* Singin' in the Rain, *two gorgeous color palettes that fitted themselves gauze-like on the mind of anyone who was alive and young in the early Fifties. Kelly's signature number has become so iconic that it is impossible to recapture its originality, or appreciate that the line was lifted from* A Child's Garden of Verses. *And it was in the musicals that I fell for my first movie star, Leslie Caron. I was taken with her in* An American in Paris, *but I was a goner when I saw* Lili. *I cannot say whether it was the gamin face or the waif-like role, but she and the song, with its touch of blue, became so fused in my head that when I heard the one I saw the other (A song of love is a sad song / Hi-Lili, Hi-Lili, Hi-Lo /* A song of love is a song of woe / Don't ask me how I know*).*

After that, I watched her in Daddy Long Legs, *a classic fairy tale, and again she was a stray, in this case an orphan, but living well in college at the expense of an unknown benefactor, and if Fred Astaire was far too old for her, well, who paid attention to that when the movie delivered a great song like "Something's Gotta Give." Finally, I saw her in* Gigi, *and it was as if the sum of all those earlier musicals had been compressed and wrapped into one incomparable film, where the story and the music and the acting and the costumes and the color were beyond anything that had gone before. Every song and number was spectacular, and then came the finale, where Leslie Caron was transformed from a young girl, playfully popping her cheek in imitation of the sound of champagne uncorking, into a stunning white-gowned beauty attending Louis Jourdan on her first night out as a woman. Gigi made Cinderella seem little more than a small character in a child's story. But as I watched the movie with my friend Anna, in a small theater in Sullivan County, I had no thought that I was seeing a falling star, that the currents that came to define the next decade would replace the romantic lyricists and composers with rougher singer-songwriters. The film musical that formed my own taste, like the songbook, had exhausted itself, or its audience, and I was slow to recognize, if indeed I ever did, the newer sounds, and their deeper meaning, that soon dominated the air.*

And always there was Audrey. It seems odd to talk about a movie star as if you knew her, but as I write this, and think of the Italian poster for *Vacanze Romane* hanging in my bathroom, or the original shot of her waving to a crowd at an awards ceremony sitting on my bookcase, I have to wonder if I have always had a fetish for the girl who carried the trauma and hunger of the war years within her, but of which I knew nothing at the time. And I wonder too if suffering can lie so deep as to call forth its alter ego, a bright and luminous face that turned winter into summer, black and white into color. I had no thoughts like these, but starting with *Roman Holiday* I found myself attached to her in a way I could not explain, except that I was keenly aware of being in the minority by siding with the thin girl in designer dresses when everyone was gaga over Marilyn Monroe. I remember being transfixed by Sabrina, perched in a tree, herself transfixed by the lights and laughter in the grand party, and despairing in her unrequited love for the idle and rudderless William Holden. A Cinderella soufflé, *Sabrina* was carried along by the charm of an actress whose voice, defying imitation, made the most trivial moments shine. As when she demonstrated her single-handed egg cracking skill for Bogart, "It's all in the wrist," or, huddled in a broom closet with Peter O'Toole, who had just performed a feat of legerdemain in opening the closet with a key from outside, she whispered one word, "Marvelous," or at a press conference in Italy, when asked which European city she preferred, she paused midsentence in the boilerplate and delivered that memorable answer, both beautiful and bittersweet in its simplicity, "Rome! By all means, Rome."

If I could not understand the spell she cast, I would not miss any of her pictures, and thinking back just to the Fifties, I was amused by the silly satire of *Funny Face* and kept off-balance by the thin mordancy of *Love in the Afternoon,* each with leading men beyond the age of plausible lovers, but with Audrey Hepburn in them I never cared much. Except that I deliberately stayed away from *War and Peace* because I could not imagine watching her in a costume drama, the picture in my mind was always that of a lost or motherless child, success or happiness coming about through accident or chance encounters. It would be absurd to say that I identified with her situations, but the transformation of Sabrina from a gawky girl into a sophisticated woman, or Princess Ann cutting her hair like a flapper to start a new life, hinted to me that I was not bound forever to my life on stone streets. That these were fairy tales was not lost upon me, but that never mattered. I fell in love with Hepburn, and was a clay pigeon for the early stories.

If, as I got older, *Two for the Road* and *Wait Until Dark* supplanted fantasy with a darker reality, the enchantment of early romance never really disappeared. I was in Italy with a group of American students, screening *Roman Holiday* in a large room in an old building on a street in Florence. At first I thought I'd start the film and leave. Yet as soon as it began I was enthralled, Audrey Hepburn so stunning, and young, Rome so beautiful, and empty, as if it were a city where all the famous sites were for two people alone, and the story, sparely told with wit and humor. The end, foretold from the start, was even more poignant than when I first saw it, two people resigned to their parting, who can say nothing but keep with them their beautiful day together forever. Yet watching the movie so many years later something struck me as dated, and it was more than the empty spaces in Rome. I found it impossible to imagine a journalist

today sacrificing the biggest scoop of his life for love and de-
cency. And as I thought of that change, a kind of degradation
really, like the loss of honor, I found myself thinking of another
loss, for everyone in that movie was gone. Audrey Hepburn was
dead. And Gregory Peck and Eddie Albert and William Wyler.
As the film was nearing its conclusion I felt tears on my face,
unbidden and unwanted, I grew up with those people, even if
they were nothing more than shadows on a screen, they made
up my boyhood, and now, seeing them move and speak as if
they were alive, yet knowing them all dead, I saw instantly that
my tears were not for the movie alone, but for someone who
had been transported by it long ago, and very far away.

7. BACK AT JEFF

FROM REEL MAGIC back to chalk dust. A good opening, the writer thinks, sounding the sentence over in his head, with just a hint of self-indulgence, as he returns the story from the movies to high school. But why break the flow with an extraneous thought, like those intruders in old novels who are constantly interrupting the action and reminding the reader that someone "out there" is telling the story? Partly to capture a touch of the writing process, but I suspect even more as a silent admission by the memoirist that he cannot adequately re-present the experience he recounts. To do so would require the integration or mash-up of movies and school and family, stitching them together in a formal or helter-skelter fashion within paragraphs and even inside sentences. For experience, as Henry James once said, does not begin or end anywhere, it is one long continuous process, and its re-creation requires the skill of a novelist gifted at composing a continuous stream of writing that mirrors the concurrence of distinct actions, and fluently mixes the past with the present. But as I am not writing fiction, beginnings and endings are the only way to reconstitute those vivid vestiges from the totality of experience that was my life during those years. I am not sure I can even recapture simultaneous actions, since memories are isolated, free floating as if in a collection of transparent containers, whose covers can be removed and their contents explored as if they were specimens under glass. And so the memoirist separates and organizes those containers, schematizes them if you like, in order to recover a past of memories, and create a narrative of experience.

It is something of a shock to come back to high school, as if I had disappeared in these last pages into libraries and boys' clubs and movie theaters, when all the while I was taking the bus along Sutter Avenue and going every day to that fortress in East New York, just three stops from the end of the IRT line at New Lots Avenue. And the strange thing about this extended hiatus is that I feel a little older, as if I grew up in the course of the writing after leaving Olga Kahn's class, and I am wondering if I can recover the perspective of the boy in the ninth grade who knew no more than two or three others who had gone on to Jefferson from junior high. What became clear to him very quickly was that the chaos that was John Marshall was absent from this place. All the classes were large, but everybody was behaved, or seemed so. A friend sent me two photographs from our biology class taken by the teacher, Mr. Bernard Annenberg, whom she remembers with fondness. They are candid shots, most are smiling, some few looking down at their books or to the side, unaware of the camera, one boy sitting on the window ledge at the back of the room, all the girls in blouses and jumpers, the boys in shirts. While I recognize many of the faces I have no memory of the class, or the teacher, and yet I was there, for on the reverse of the pictures, along with all the signatures, is my own John Hancock.

As I sift through letters from classmates, talking about teachers and courses, and scroll through the pages of the yearbook, I have a momentary doubt as to whether I actually attended the school. I see myself in a photograph of the *Aurora* staff, some thirty students, and I wonder what I was doing there, since I contributed nothing to the yearbook. There are five young men in coats and ties, amid a sea of women in white blouses and long skirts, some flanking us, others sitting behind a desk directly in front, and more seated across the length of the floor with their legs propped under them and only their skirts and hands showing. I recognize several of the girls, one of whom enticed me into a furious make out session after graduation, and in the calm after the fury passed along her copy of *A Catcher in the Rye,* which I had never heard of. I knew by sight all the boys, among them Carl, part of the art staff, who just before leaving Jefferson had a small sculpture accepted and exhibited at the Brooklyn Museum. I knew nobody, aside from my sister, who made anything that approached art. And yet here was one of our own on display at Brooklyn's showcase on Eastern Parkway. Still the picture, like all the others in the yearbook, seems so dated, I was about to write *demure,* that you have to wonder where all the original thought that danced through those staged heads ever came from. In a way, the sedate pose and drab dress belied the tough smarts of the girls, who every boy knew were at least their equal, and then some.

What am I searching for as I peer through a magnifier at these ensemble black and white photographs in my copy of *Aurora?* I see so many of the same people, in picture after picture, some few I knew well, that one question keeps repeating itself in my ear, *what was I doing there for three years?* I was not in *Arista* or the *Service Council,* numbering about one hundred in each, and these were the school's honor societies. I was oblivious to the Honor School within Jefferson. Obviously the same faces showed up in the same classes, but I attributed that to the students themselves, who decided whether they wanted to take courses that prepared them for college, or opt for a commercial program designed primarily for work in the city's scrapers. That was the extent of my thinking about why we were bunched together, and if I was vaguely aware of another explanation, the word *tracking* was not part of our vocabulary. But I believe there was a deeper reason for my blankness, I simply felt out of my depth next to the other students, especially in math. In elementary school I did fine, and junior high was easy enough, but in high school I became conscious of a gap between my tested talent and practical ability, a disconnect that made me suspicious of all aptitude testing, reinforced when I was told by a counselor that I should be a farmer.

I still remember the Plane Geometry classroom, an old teacher, short, bald, moving haltingly back and forth in front of the blackboard, and me on the edge of my seat, straining to understand his mumbling lest I miss some vital theorem. It was only *plane* geometry but it may as well have been the higher hieroglyphics. And as I sat and struggled, a very smart looking student one desk over was forever turned away from the teacher, talking to the boy behind him. Why this irritated me I am not sure, possibly because *I* was at sea I could not stand the idea of anyone else being blithely indifferent. So I confronted him in class, as if I were the Warning Monitor, and asked how he expected to pass the Regents exam if he paid no attention. He never answered but looked at me oddly, as if to ask *who turned you loose?* He was the most gifted math student in the school. That shows what I knew of my classmates. I managed to do better in Algebra, which proved a false dawn, because I then registered for *Solid* Geometry, which was like signing up for Nascar after just getting your driver's license. And yet it made a kind of sense. It was the highest math class offered, I knew others taking it, although I might have paused at the thought that they were all on the math team, and it just seemed like the thing to do. It is amazing how we move along with the current, even when we have no desire to be in the water. Still, I was doomed from the start, as I sat in class, watching the teacher wildly move her hands in space as she built her "solid" models, and despite my hardest peering all I could see was air and nothingness. In memory I withdrew from the course, only to discover the inscription in my yearbook by the math whiz, *so you passed solid!*

English was another story. Although I did not shine or stand out in my junior and senior year classes, I felt comfortable there, and can see myself sitting in the rooms, indifferent or oblivious to what went on, but happily free of any feelings of competition with the others. At times I was more interested in clothes than any chatter coming from the front of the room. I remember when Bermuda shorts was the season's rage, I was determined to get myself a pair. As I think of it now, it strikes me as ludicrous: who in Brownsville would parade the streets in a Caribbean fashion statement? Nobody wore any kind of shorts in the summer, let alone trousers that looked as if the tailor had a severe eye disorder. But I was undaunted. I knew that no window on Pitkin Avenue would display a garment so outré, so I took a train to the Village, where I expected to find what I was looking for, although I did not exactly know what I was looking for. I never read style magazines, and I am certain that my knowledge of "Bermuda shorts" derived more from newspaper publicity than any pictures in the glossies. Still I liked going to the Village, it gave me a feeling of being a bit avant-garde, of walking and shopping on a turf that might have been another country.

Later on, my penchant for buying clothes in those streets below Union Square cost me dearly, because I can remember a short black coat I picked up for fashion's sake that turned out to have no lining and no warmth. The more I recover these incidents, the more I wonder at my judgment, for I always paid a price in those small, "boutique" shops, a term I never heard, and puzzle that I was driven to do so against all reason and all need. Somewhere in those jagged, off-kilter blocks that I would return to in my college years, to Italian restaurants below street level, coffee houses dark and animated, I found the shorts, dark green, the color of pine leaves, and a pair of long gray socks to go with them. As I mulled over this odd purchase on the long ride back to Brooklyn, I wondered if I was brazen enough to wear them to school? I have no recollection of how I decided, but I can clearly see myself sitting at a desk, in my green shorts and gray socks, talking with someone who was either amused or confounded by my outfit. Yet nobody ridiculed or derided me for what I would now call a minor street performance. In a way my classmates' reaction was a testament to their openness and tolerance. But I never wore Bermuda shorts to school again.

This "story" came to me out of nowhere, almost in midsentence while writing about a high school class, and I immediately reconstructed the episode. A common belief has it that the process of writing a memoir quickens forgotten or buried incidents, as if all were part of a fixed cluster of stars, the sighting of one opening a pathway to another, as the mind leap-frogs its way through the past. But instead of trying to figure out how memories beget memories, the focus should stay on those extracted, for they are most visible, and doubtlessly form, to change the metaphor, the figure in the carpet. Clearly the Bermuda shorts were never forgotten. And looking at it from afar it has a curiously strange tenor. That a boy would have been driven to buy and wear something so eccentric in his world surely needs explanation. Standing out from the crowd does not cut it, because it was more like making yourself a spectacle. Being in vogue would be plausible, but that phrase only worked in Manhattan. A deeper possibility, as I think of it, might be an even simpler one, that worldly desire is nearly as mysterious as the demon Eros, and if a pair of short, brushed cotton pants hardly qualifies as "worldly desire," it makes a perfectly good emblem. Reason not the need, said the poet, and it holds for things we most want against all understanding. What strikes me now, in retrospect, is not the desire for the shorts, which was really just a whim, but the will *to wear them, for if the boy had buckled after the purchase, and kept them to himself, the intention would have been satisfied, but the act would have been incomplete.*

My eleventh grade English teacher seemed forever bored with his students. One of them, writing recently, could not forget his signature remark, uttered at every opportunity with great disdain, "Every schoolboy knows THAT!" None of us knew the line was pilfered, which would have taken him down a peg, but in his favor he gave us the freedom to choose books on our own, and he did have us write. One assignment had an unintended result, and a lasting benefit for me. We were to do a report on *Hamlet,* I think my topic was the hero's madness, i.e., real or feigned, and for some unaccountable reason I made my way to the Grand Army Plaza branch of the Brooklyn library. I am unable to reconstruct the first time I set eyes upon that glorious building with its spectacular entrance, two massive iron doors ornamented with gold figures from American books. I know I paid no attention to the figures, or the portrait of Walt Whitman, whom I could not have identified, but walking into the library was like entering an exalted place, the imposing card catalogue in the wide open foyer, a moment's hesitation before knowing which way to turn, towards the glass enclosed magazine room on the left, or straight back to the serious, quiet reading room. The library was not nearly as monumental as the Brooklyn Museum, whose endless climb from the street led directly into a huge and dismal gallery of mummies, but it was awesome enough for a teenager, and far more accessible. I see myself sitting there at the end of a large table in the long reading room, more grown up in seeming than I actually felt, and making use of whatever "big" books were there to help me with my *research,* a word that none of us used. What we did instead was *look things up,* or *get information,* drawing mainly upon encyclopedias and whatever reference books the librarians directed us to, and then we wrote our *reports,* not *papers,* a term I never encountered before college.

So I wrote my report on *Hamlet,* and next chose to read *Annapurna* and Alan Paton's *Cry, The Beloved Country,* two stories as starkly different from each other and my own world as imaginable. I do not know why I selected them, but they engrossed me, and much later, when South Africa became front page news, I returned in my mind to Paton's novel, as if I had done something daring, even though I did nothing more than turn the pages of a book that was cutting edge for its time. I was not clueless about the social world I lived in, but my understanding was limited and shallow. For the most part, I navigated the streets and my main concern was to keep from getting attacked. There was one time when five or six of us were wandering the blocks, somewhere between East New York and Brownsville, and were set upon by a group intent upon a fight. Our side scattered, most getting away intact, but one or two were caught and beaten. Surprisingly, the encounter did not lead to a stiffening of stereotypes, an easy "moral" deduction for anyone so inclined. It simply reinforced what we already knew, that the potential for violence was always there, but only if you were careless, and forgot where you lived, and lost that sixth sense for danger that anyone bred on those stone walks acquired as a birthright.

Senior English was memorable even if I cannot cite a single book I read there. Our teacher was Mrs. Gallagher, a tall woman with ramrod straight posture and a stentorian voice that went even higher during periodic outbursts of anger. In the yearbook she is caught sitting among the Senior Teachers in a drab dress, buttoned tight up to the neck, and offset by a tiny white Peter Pan collar. All she needed was the wimple. One of my classmates thought she was anti-Semitic because of the way she corrected our vernacular, admonishing us to say *prepare supper*, which "no Jewish kid of our background would ever have heard," instead of our inflected *make supper*. His remark is a telling reminder of the range of sensitivities we brought to our encounters. For my part, the notion of anti-Semitism never occurred to me. Instead, I thought of her as a woman hostile to the mix of teenagers that faced her. Maybe she went to Catholic schools and was used to an authoritarian style. She certainly had the position and the physical stature to practice it. But she was in the wrong place with the wrong people.

Our class was very large, I would guess at least thirty-five, and there were not enough desks. Some few had to double up and share. These desks were fixed to the floor, with a top that lifted up, and an attached seat. Needless to say, the seat was barely sized for one, let alone two. I proposed to a lovely, buxom Polish girl named Pola that we share a seat, and she obliged. We were two or three rows from the back of the room, and our singular arrangement went largely unnoticed. But we were clearly skirting disaster, and while I relished sitting with Pola cheek to cheek, I could never get out of my head the idea that we were both under a cracked tree limb, and at some point it was going to break and fall right on my head. Then it happened. Mrs. Gallagher was particularly enraged at something or other, she shouted at all of us to get in our seats, I cannot imagine what we would have been doing milling around, but Pola and I returned to our home place. Suddenly she saw us, her eyes focusing as if for the first time on our single desk in the vast array of wooden relics, threw her voice at me with all her might, and demanded I return to my seat. "I am in my seat." Momentarily stymied, she turned to Pola and repeated the command, only to receive the same answer. "How long has this been going on?" she bellowed. "Since the start of the term." Barely able to contain her apoplexy, all she could do was separate us. But if I lost the memory of where I wound up, I never forgot Pola, and our blissful venture at cohabitation.

Mrs. Gallagher was determined to mold us, street kids who had gone to public schools in East New York and Brownsville, and who were one or two generations away from Poland or Italy or Russia. It was as if she was teaching in the early twentieth century, and her role was to civilize the barbarians. One of her obsessions was our manners and deportment, scolding us for our crass behavior and telling us we would benefit from a book on etiquette. Well, she got her wish. One of our assignments was a group project, to prepare an oral book report that would be acted out in class. We were a group of four, and I argued for choosing any etiquette book we could get our hands on. So the die was cast, two girls, two boys, and a primer whose title is long lost. Our "method" involved acting out "scenes" that switched between proper and improper manners. As the caboose in the train, I first demonstrated the right way to greet a girl, I have no idea what I did, and then the wrong way, which stays with me still, as I walked up to Eleanor, a serious student, thrust my arm around her waist, pulled her tight in close to me, and in a perfect street voice said, "Hi ya, Baby, how's ya doin'?" Our teacher never smiled. And singled me out among the four of us for the lowest grade.

I cannot say whether she knew how deliberately subversive we were. There is a strange disconnect that students often have with their teachers, making them unable to imagine that older people can read their motives, even when those impulses are transparent. In a way, our exercise in etiquette was part of a silent dance, for we knew exactly what she thought of us, and this was a chance for us to take a turn on the stage. After such a long stretch of time it all seems a bit foolish, but we were very young, and there were years to go before giving over foolish things. There is a coda to this story of Mrs. Gallagher, who had not quite finished with me. It was very near graduation, I was at a table in the cafeteria with some friends, she must have been on duty, saw me and asked what I was reading. I showed her my hardcover copy of Howard Fast's *Spartacus*, and she instantly went into a tirade about the author, his politics, and my choice in reading material. I do not know where I got the book, but I clearly remember its jacket, with a powerful Spartacus drawn in red outline, looking every bit like a museum sculpture. I had been feeling good about myself for carrying the book in the open, as I had not forgotten the toxic McCarthy years, and the injunction to wrap every Fast novel in brown paper. Those days were past, I thought, but a whiff of their aroma lingered on in a student cafeteria on Pennsylvania Avenue. It would be four more years before *Spartacus* made it to the screen. Of the resurrection of Dalton Trumbo, when it came, I knew nothing. But Howard Fast had been a boyhood hero of mine, and I was very glad to see his name freed at last.

Now, having waited to foreground an unusual and exceptional man, Mr. M. Gabriel Cohen, I find myself at a loss, with

the uncanny feeling I have been here before, that someone inhabited my body in high school. For I come up mostly blank
on the details of the seminars that Mr. Cohen ran in the late
afternoon after regular classes were over. Slender, nearly sight-
less, led into the room by a girl with the highest grades, this
history teacher took it upon himself to offer a prep course for
the state Regents scholarship exam. The schools in the city that
walked away with the lion's share of awards were the usual sus-
pects, Stuyvesant, Bronx Science, and Brooklyn Tech. I imagine
schools in the middle class sections of Brooklyn also did well.
But Jefferson was an outlier, in geography and population, and
these exams, we would say today, were *culturally* biased since so
many of the questions were about art and music that were outside the borders of our experience. I never set foot in the Met, or
the Museum of Modern Art before college, and as for the opera
or the symphony, you might as well have asked me about the
dark side of the moon. It seems strange to pass my fingers over
the keys and make these words come up on the monitor, as if
I were describing someone from a hidden world, tucked away
in the middle of a vibrant city but unknowing of its pulsating
quickness.

Enter Mr. Cohen. He foresaw Kaplan before Kaplan ever
existed. Armed with sheaves of pages that named names—artists and composers and writers, historians and philosophers and
scientists—he jammed into our heads a full-fledged humanities
course in one shortened spring term. If the primary aim was the
Regents scholarship exam, he provided each one of us with the
"knowledge" we needed to be a contender. I have no idea how I
got into the seminar. My major concern in the last year of high
school was whether I would get into Brooklyn College on my
average alone. I worried that I would have to take an entrance
exam. Mr. Cohen's rough ride through the glory and grandeur

of the Western world was the least of my cares, not to mention that I never for a moment thought I could win an award. So I went to class in the afternoon, surrounded by the smartest students in school, took the closely printed sheets home with me, and returned the following week to repeat the process. But while I can visualize Mr. Cohen sitting there, in a plaid jacket, at the center of a large table, facing the room with his unseeing eyes behind glasses, I cannot name the classmates seated around me, and I was clueless to any undisclosed back story.

Harvey, a very good friend, knew more. Years later, when I met him for dinner in Vancouver, and we were reminiscing, he told me that Mr. Cohen had targeted one boy in a group of five for a full tuition scholarship to Harvard, and I was among them. It was news to me. Harvey also reconstructed the format of the seminar. Mr. Cohen, as he was blind, turned to one side, asked the person's name, and then had her answer twenty-five multiple-choice questions. At the final class before the Regents exam he handed out a sheet on the "governmental structure" of the Confederacy (who could make up such cryptic queries?) asked for a volunteer, and faced with silence called on Harvey, who proceeded to guess twenty-four right answers. Mr. Cohen (Harvey continued) "then asked someone to follow me. When no one spoke up he called on you. You got 23/25 correct. I remember these numbers because they were ridiculously high. In summary, we learned how to take this kind of test." My faith in my friend's recollection is as absolute as my own forgetting. It is a mystery to me why I remember a trivial spoken line in an early class in geometry and come up blank at this shining moment in my senior seminar. Perhaps, as it was all just guesswork, I did not put much stock in it. After all, you get no credit for mere luck. Still, it did its work, as Harvey said, and along with twenty-two other acolytes of Tiresias, I won the scholarship.

What remained of Jefferson, defunct now in all but name and memory? For Barry, one or two incidents were all that was left to bring the curtain down on high school. Near the end of the month, five days before Decoration Day, as the holiday was still called, about a dozen of us "starred" in the senior play. A quartet of witty and intrepid girls put together from scratch a riff on *The Mikado,* titled *Mikaphan,* a brash pun on our principal's name, Ludwig Kaphan. I have no idea how I became involved in the production, which, judging from two small black-and-white pictures, was sparse indeed, no set, no lighting, no costumes, just teenagers standing alone on a large empty stage. Despite the bareness, one photo captures a jauntiness in the "three little maids" number, the girls clasping their right arms behind their heads, hips thrust sideways in a provocative pose, the sexiness chastened only by their very long skirts, as these were long days before Mary Quant. One of the "maids" delightfully remembered an improvised moment as they exited the stage, slipping their scarves down from around their necks, and twirling them with girlish glee in mock imitation of a burlesque number. Even so mild a touch as that gave a faculty member cause for outrage. And these were Honor School girls, no less!

In any case, the makers of this lively frolic wanted me to play the Lord High Executioner. I hesitated, self-conscious of my flat voice and inability to carry a tune. But those girls were far too clever to be put off by my irresolution or inaptitude. The smash hit on Broadway then was *My Fair Lady,* and they argued forcefully that Rex Harrison did not "sing" but "talked" his lines, and all I had to do was copy him. While I never for a moment thought I could duplicate Rex Harrison's feat, it took little persuasion to turn me around. I may have been the only one in the cast with a "costume," my own formal suit, while my hair was covered in talcum powder to give it the same white as our principal's. I can see myself even now, standing alone on that broad apron, looking out at the huge auditorium, reciting my lines, *I've got a little list / I've got a little list / And they'll none of them be missed / No, they'll none of them be missed*, and at just that moment, in a gesture inspired by those ingenious writers, I unfurled on the stage floor a full roll of toilet paper. Although I had no sense of my performance at the time, no "cast" party or any near equivalent, years later the principal creator of the spree, Iris, remembered that carefree escapade: "Barry, you were so dapper as the man, and pretty darn comfortable as the big boss of the school."

Maybe. But I skipped graduation. Over time I never thought twice about why I bailed, but writing now makes me ponder it, and as I try and return myself to that time in June when I would have been sitting with my friends in the *Premiere* theater on Sutter Avenue, a movie house I never entered, all that comes up is that I had no one to ask. My grandmother, out of the question, my father, in Jamaica with his fairy book wife, and Miriam and Harry, miles away with dual jobs and twin toddlers. Also, finishing high school did not feel like any special feat. If you had your name inscribed on a plaque that went up on the wall for all time, or as long as the building lasted, then you might have felt like a hero of sorts. But surviving three years of classes was not climbing Annapurna, and I suspect most of us felt the same. What gives me pause now, and touches me with an odd sadness, mitigated only by its being more reflective than felt, is a telegram lying on my desk, sent to me by my sister Ann, whom I rarely saw in the four years since our mother's death. CONGRATULATIONS DEAR BROTHER AND BEST WISH-ES FOR YOUR CONTINUED ACHIEVEMENTS SORRY WE CANNOT BE WITH YOU BUT WE ARE SHARING YOUR

HAPPINESS WITH MUCH LOVE ANNE AND EDDIE. If I had not held onto this half-page sheet, with its 18 point, purple printed words, I could easily have believed that nobody I knew had any idea what had become of me.

But if graduation held no allure, the same could not be said for the prom. I very much wanted to go, and I even had someone to take. I had gone on a date with a girl from East New York, Nadine, dark brown hair, cut short, a bit stylish, I remember nothing about where we went in the city, but I vividly remember our return to Brooklyn on the subway, for she was concerned about the time, our walk to her nondescript row house, which had a tiny front yard with a latched gate, and as we got there we found her father standing inside it, wrinkled white shirt with long sleeves rolled up above the forearms, and looking for all the world as if he was about to explode. It was well before midnight, but for that man any hour was too late. I cannot recall the jeremiad he delivered, but I remember feeling empty inside for Nadine, who was clearly unused to saying anything to her father, and had to stand by silent and mortified while he went at me. For any normal boy it would have scotched all desire, but I liked the girl, she liked me, and it was very near the night of the prom. If I was shrewder, I might have seen that any man waiting in the street for his daughter to come home was unlikely to say, "sure, honey, have yourself a blast at the ball." And true to form, the old man dampened the small dreams of two young people.

But Nadine was not a senior, and as I later learned from classmates, getting a prom date in our group often turned out to be a matter of chance, or even chicanery. The most beautiful girl in the class was not asked because boys were afraid she would turn them down. One couple asked each other, that is, since neither had a date they agreed to go together. And one of the brainiest guys, who had never dated in high school, was approached by a group of girls with a list of several candidates' names, and they directed him to one in particular, who awaited his invitation. And myself? For the life of me I have no memory of asking the tall and lovely singer that I went with, Henrietta aka Henny, yet somehow we got stitched together, and spent an evening that remains largely a blur in my mind. I envisage the grand room at the hotel off Central Park, as well as the requisite round trip on the Staten Island Ferry, although I was clueless as to why this was a tradition, unless it marked the cheapest thing we could do on prom night, and you could not get any lower than a nickel a ride.

But the pièce de résistance, a table at the *Latin Quarter,* which ought to have etched itself in my mind, exists instead as a blotchy black and white souvenir picture snapped by a short-skirted nightclub photographer. Two couples are seated on each side of the table, Henny and I standing at the far end, all the boys in white tuxedo jackets with black bow ties, the girls in elegant dresses, round black cigarette trays are on the white tablecloth, along with highball glasses, and standing and seated figures are visible in the background. It is almost a genre scene straight out of a 1940s Warner Brothers movie. The photographer, who was selling a memento rather than a measured composition, took a quick, candid flash. Yet its very carelessness has in an odd way become a kind of artistry, made lasting by being the only surviving object from a moment in time that has vanished into time. I remember nothing of the club, what I drank, where we were sitting, how long we stayed, who else from our school was there, and on and on. Considering that this was our one chance to be where the action was, for we all knew by name *Toots Shor's* and *Twenty-One* and *Sardi's,* you would imagine I filed the entire evening away in my head. But nothing held.

What lives instead is the photograph and its covering sleeve, a period piece itself, with a faint sketch of an 1890s cabaret nude, along with the tag lines in green ink, printed cursive style—"*So this is Gay Paree"… / Come along with me /we're stepping out to / see the / Latin Quarter.*

I recognize everybody except two girls. Eddie Fishman is there, with his infectious smile, and Arlene Mondschein, a smart and beautiful girl, looking rapturously happy. Henny, half a head taller than me, wearing glasses, looks ravishing. And I am smiling as well. But without being able to provide any adjoining story to the photograph, why do I have it framed and hanging on my bedroom wall? It is all I own of that night, along with the Gothic inscribed invitation to The Essex House, and so it stands in for the thoughts that dispersed themselves over the black harbor on the ferry, for the romantic gestures that were irretrievable if they ever existed, for the bobbing moods of a seventeen year old crossing over from adolescence, whatever that was, into another age that had a name but no meaning. Drinking in a nightclub was being an adult, but if you remember nothing was it all just a game? And so the photograph acquires a meaning it never had when it was simply an offhand relic of some couples thrown together by chance. Because over time the historic circumstances dissolved and the years imparted a resonance to the object that was absent that June night. My good friend Eddie died young, and his erasure from life is the first thing that comes to mind when I look at the picture, as it does for Arlene, who also died early. And when I see Henny's smile, I think with not a little sadness of what I missed in not knowing her. In a strange way the stories that could have been told when the photograph was taken are beyond knowing, while those that never existed are what now give it meaning. These thoughts of past and present, evoked by still images on paper, quicken the life of a boy's long stilled memory, and remind him of who he was then, and all that has gone.

SUMMER DRIFT

WHAT TO DO with all those lazy-hazy-crazy days before college? They had to be filled with work, for money, but what kind? I was long past the grocery store groove, but I had no idea of what to look for in its place. What I desperately wanted was to go to sea on an ocean liner, a notion planted in mind by my sister Ann, who had been a secretary for a short time in the office of the National Maritime Union. So without any thought or planning—what kind of planning did you do for a job?—I found the Cunard line address in the phone directory, took the subway to Lower Manhattan, and walked into that awesome building at the base of Broadway. Struck by the color and splendor of its domed interior, I realized instantly how unprepared I was, for I had no clue where to go or who to talk with. I approached a polished mahogany desk, the woman asked me what I wanted, I said I was looking for a summer job on one of Cunard's liners, and whom should I speak to? She asked me if I had seaman's papers, she might as easily have asked for a map of the moon, and when I said no she told me that Cunard only hired people with papers. *Where and how do I get the papers?* I asked. *From the Maritime Union*, she answered. I cannot remember where the hiring hall was, clearly it was not the Cunard Building, but I found it, and encountered a hard-edged man holding down a distressed desk that faced the door. I told him that I wanted to apply for seaman's papers and he asked me if I had a job. I said that I needed the papers to get a job, and he responded that I needed a job to get the papers. Joseph Heller's ready-made description for this ploy came five years later. If my sister had still been working for the NMU she would have helped me. As it was, my dream of sailing the Atlantic dissolved before it even took shape, and I was left with only photographs of the ships' interiors that I carried away in my head from that gem of a building on Broadway.

But in a quirk of fate, I wound up spending the summer in a bland building on Maiden Lane, exiting the subway every weekday at Bowling Green, the same stop for the Cunard headquarters. I had applied for an office job and was hired by Aviquipo, a company that supplied spare-parts to the aviation industry. They sent out letters describing their products to airlines and aircraft companies around the world, and they wanted the letters to read as if each one was addressed to the recipient alone. My typing skill must have gotten me the job, but I cannot remember if I was told before being hired exactly what I would be doing, for it did not take long to realize that punching out one and two page letters to the entire aviation industry was a near impossibility (the Aviquipo Rolodex was smaller only than a raffle drum). But what I learned after I started work was that the place had an automatic typewriter, called a Robotyper, something I had never seen before, and akin to a player piano, as I remembered it from old movies. A master letter was typed on a roll of perforated paper, a job entrusted to one of the regular secretaries, the roll was inserted in a machine that was connected to a typewriter, and with the press of a button the typewriter began banging out the letter at more than 100 words a minute.

And here is where Aviquipo required my technical facility: I would insert the letterhead, type the date, address, and salutation, touch the Start button, and watch breathlessly as the machine took over. As hard as I try, I do not know what else I did in that office, except to serve as a teasing object for the sly amusement of the secretaries. And for all this I was paid, if memory serves, forty-seven or forty-eight dollars a week. Yet despite the barren retrospection there was an intangible residue from those two months as a faux typist, for I was no longer a kid who stocked shelves and served customers in a Brooklyn grocery, but a person who got off a train every day with hundreds of others in the thronging world of New York, trudged several blocks to my own tall building, and settled into the smaller space within. And if my tasks at Aviquipo were mostly mindless, still I took a perverse pride in having worked for a summer in an office in the city, and years later, when I had occasion to be near the Charging Bull, cast long after my time, I invariably walked towards Maiden Lane, whose name had never left me.

What made up this interlude of two months before my new life in college began? Although I remember nothing of the time, other than the fact of a job, I have several letters from July and August, autographs from a Jefferson classmate that insist upon their place in a memoir, much as Pirandello's characters insisted upon their moment onstage. There is so little "documentation" from these years that I treat every material object I find as if it were a talisman or code that opened a cave of treasures. And these letters are visually striking, printed in green ink that has held its color, and in a style as if copied by a calligrapher. Yet when I came upon them I was struck by my complete obliviousness to the writer. Who was Shelley? What was she to me? The high school yearbook, and friends, brought back a girl who was short and sturdily built, combed her hair simply, never put on makeup, and wore button-up shirts with collars. She was part of a clique of girls who were inseparable in Jeff, even after, and she sat in Mr. Cohen's seminar, pulling in one of the Regents scholarships. Still I am unable to place the two of us together. The letters revealed one tie, if only by inference, and in the casual and desultory discourse disclosed to me a bit of my life, while failing completely to recover any joint connection. It is the strangest of things, to be aware of your presence in another's composition, and yet remain powerless to recover the author in yours. But the magical thing about writing is that it has its own being, and so Shelley lives that distant summer in these fragile pages, suspended in her words, indifferent to my memory, and in a way that was better from what came long after.

Hunkered down in a bungalow colony in Liberty, New York, she passed the time in her letters by sporting with the vernacular and apologizing for the paltry stationery, as she threw one last bolt at our old English teacher ("And to hell with Emily Post, Amy Vanderbilt AND Long Tall Gallagher!") These high jinks covered the insistent demands she made on me to write and visit, while her mock regrets for keeping one of the "Jefferson mob" out of the city and away from me brought back to mind the picture of a girl I was mad to touch those days, who had given me a brief taste of her body, but seemed blithe to spend the weekend in Liberty. I can still see her, and remember, and wonder now as I might have then why she preferred the country. Yet that clouded memory, evoked by two-three scratches on a page, pales before the lines upon lines about books that drained Shelley's green ink. It is as if we were engaged in a potlatch, and the gifts were books. I marvel at the novels and memoirs and histories that she recorded, one or two even now striking a

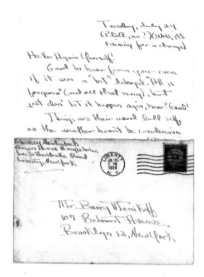

nostalgic chord, like Francoise Sagan's A Certain Smile, *which had recently been published, and Shelley declared "inferior" to* Bonjour Tristesse. *Just seeing the French title on the cheap stationery makes me wistful, for I remember devouring the novel, thinking it part of a teenager's rite of passage, although a passage to where I had no idea, but that a young woman not much older than I wrote a novel about romance and sex, got it published and became famous, seemed like a movie tale to me. But if Sagan was on everybody's tongue, I wondered how Shelley knew of Boswell's* London Journal *or Henry Miller's* A Devil in Paradise. *At the time it must have seemed normal. Yet what is most bizarre is that I cannot dredge up a single title of my own from that summer. Shelley's one reference to a book of mine, "Thomas Mann's 375 pages," brings to mind* Dr. Faustus, *though why I would have attempted such a dry and complex novel is utterly beyond me. But all this is by the by. For Shelley is gone, and the brittle leaves she wrote long ago, to a boy she thought "delightful company," are what remain of a few lazy days before the fall of our new lives.*

BOOK THREE

1. A FIELD IN FLATBUSH *1*

IN THE BEGINNING it did not feel like a new life. I was still living with my grandmother, but instead of taking the bus east from Brownsville I was catching the el going west to Flatbush. It is odd that the exact route eludes me, and I cannot trace in my head the stations and change of trains on this trip to Brooklyn College. What I do know is I began this fresh school with a declared major in chemistry. In retrospect it sounds bizarre, and it even sounded so to me at the time, but I had no idea what to write on the required form, and as I had gotten an A in high school, and imagined that chemistry would somehow lead to a job, that was what I put down. I thought of my periodic table teacher at Jefferson, a short, odd looking man with large round glasses, who would toss out helpful hints to save us money, like adding hot water to the shampoo bottle in order to extend its product life. As I think of it, others also offered strategies for protecting our wallet, like the teacher in economics who riffed one day on the good sense of a job with security, as if that constituted the greatest success in life. At the time, it never occurred to me that these off the cuff lessons, trivial and serious, might be personal, and that the obsessive concern for saving pennies and grasping security was branded on them as children in the Depression. But faced with a question that asked *me* what I wanted to do with my future, I instinctively fell back on the same necessity, *make money*, and realized that I had to choose a major that would enable me to earn a living and support myself. Yet it is not as if I was clueless about the idea of doing something that reflected my interests or abilities, although in truth I had no sense of having any special ability. A long conversation with the Jefferson classmate who exhibited his sculpture at the Brooklyn Museum sticks in my mind. I ran into him shortly after graduation on a train into the city, and the memory is so sharp because we talked all the way from one borough to the next about what we could or should do with our lives, and our conclusion was that the only work that would ensure a life of freedom was that of an artist. We were acting out, or *I* was acting out, since to my mind he had already arrived there, Joyce's *A Portrait of the Artist* long before I ever heard of James Joyce, let alone read about his coming of age in a hardscrabble city. But I told the sculptor, as the train was rumbling underground, and I was holding on to the vertical bar, that he was lucky because he had the talent to live by an art, while I had to rummage about, clueless as ever, for any other free life that might be scrounged from the ether. There was no upshot to our conversation, but I never forgot that train ride, and my wonder that someone I knew could do whatever he wanted with his days and nights.

Chemistry was a bust. I cannot recall if I received a C or D for the course, but it was enough to scratch that major from the list. Since I have no college transcript, I can only retrieve my teachers and classes from memory, many of them graphically alive, even to their gestures and inflections, while others lay buried in pitch darkness. It is probably not surprising that my Freshman English teacher, Dr. Sidney Lind, made the strongest impression on me that year. I had no idea what the *Dr.* stood for, other than it sounded important, and all teachers were addressed by their degree rather than their rank, not that the distinction meant anything to me, since *Professor* was rarely used, and in any case I would not have known exactly what it meant. It is curious how so much of the custom and culture of college life was alien when I first got there, a patchwork of esoteric practices known only to initiates as if by hand signals, like why we called our teachers *Dr.* or *Mr.* With each successive year the signals gradually revealed themselves, but never overtly, as it was not the habit of the faculty, let alone the administration, who inhabited another planet altogether, to disclose anything to students beyond the content of the course.

College was a maze of unexplained rules—*don't walk on the grass, women in pants will be escorted off campus*—which stood in contrast to the frequently unconstrained intellectual life in the classroom. At the time I never noticed the contradiction, I considered the rules but the tedious work of meager minds, and acted as if they had nothing to do with me. In my senior year I would learn otherwise. As for Dr. Lind, he was very tall, with dark hair, a rich voice, and a character actor's face. He had us for the entire year, and saw himself as something of a drill sergeant, whose role was to toughen us up for college life. And the first thing we had to learn was that none of us knew how to write. If this was a universal trope for college English classes across the land, the students at Brooklyn were not easily cowed, and within a year or two many reverted to their natural instincts and stood poised to challenge their instructors' authority. But this was the incoming semester, we were all fresh, and nobody dared say anything to Dr. Lind. And when he returned our first papers, we discovered that the sheen of high school had been transformed into the dross of Bedford Avenue. But we carried on, and I had one moment of success. The assignment, as I recollect it, was to choose a familiar object and describe it in 500 words. For some reason I tried to be imaginative, which was strange because I was convinced I had no imagination, and why I thought I could never be a writer, but in any case I put that aside. In the composition I assumed the voice of a Martian recently come to earth, who chanced upon an apartment, ambled through the bedroom, then the bathroom, and fixated on an odd object found in both places and in different sizes, a mirror. The alien was puzzled by it, kept staring at the image that returned his gaze, and could do nothing but speculate as to its use and purpose. I have no clue where the idea came from, but I remember being inwardly pleased with myself, as if I had come up with an original conceit for a piece of writing. Fortunately I never saved the essay, for the juvenility of the satire would be cringe making, while in its absence the *idea* of the piece lives on, unblemished in my memory, immune to earthly reality, a bit like the mechanical butterfly in Nathaniel Hawthorne's story. But the essay did its own work, and in the end I made the only A in class.

As far as courses that first year, there was little more worth noting, except for a series of college lectures and one art class. The school had opened a performing arts center less than twelve months earlier, a large Walt Whitman Theatre (spelled *re*), and a more intimate one named after George Gershwin. Nobody could forget the "Walt Whitman," and it had nothing to do with the size of the building. The poet's name overarched all others, indeed was second only to that of the borough itself, and this was the case even if you had not read a line of verse. As for Gershwin, he was a blank to me, for although I knew classic American songs from the radio, this was the heyday of the pop singer, and well before disc jockeys passed along in their patter the names of the composers and lyricists who made up the material. But the smaller theater, new and bright and clean, was where we were sent to hear several invited speakers in our freshman year. I can still see three of them on that elevated stage—Robert Frost, Margaret Mead, and Ayn Rand. I knew of the first two, was ignorant of the third, but it was clear even to a newbie that these were *really big* people, and as I write this I hear Ed Sullivan's profundo voice intoning his signature phrase. All three are vivid in my mind's eye: Frost, a small man on a large platform, ancient looking, disheveled white hair, in a navy suit that seemed odd on a poet, and who I flashed back to instantly four years later when I saw him at the young president's inaugural, amazed that he was still around; Mead, who seemed the most accessible, and made the greatest effort to speak to us as if we might even understand, and possibly learn something; and Rand, erect and haughty seeming even from my distant seat, wearing a black dress set off by a gold clip in the shape of a dollar sign. I cannot attest to the clip myself, but a good friend was in an Ethics class, Rand was the visitor, and he saw the shiny ornament up close. There may have been other speakers, but these are the ones I remember, as I look back in wonder that a public school should have had such unheralded riches.

Now for Art 101, or whatever the title. Why did I select an art survey to satisfy a requirement? The question is not without point, for I was missing a thumb when it came to using a pencil, I cannot remember making drawings as a child, or having a coloring book for that matter. When I was older, and tried doodling houses or trees or stick figures if only as play, they were so pathetic that I threw them away quickly rather than look at them and face my ineptitude. As a boy I was in awe of my sister's ability, and thought the caricatures she drew of her college girl friends were wonderful. I was far too young to judge their draftsmanship, but they were amusing copies of people, which to me was the height of skillfulness. Although I could never replicate Miriam's talent, I listened to her when the subject was *art*, and so I enrolled in the class upon her advice. I remember nothing of the course, except that the lights went out and color slides flashed on the screen from the Greeks onward. The instructor, Mr. Morris Dorsky, was the same one Miriam had years earlier, and one of the first things I noticed about him was his dress. Art professors looked like no other faculty. They wore sport coats more regularly than suits, worsteds and tweeds, but what most distinguished them were their shirts, dark and colored, as opposed to bland white, and accented with woven or cloth ties. They stood out so distinctly—you could spot an art teacher from the distant end of Boylan Hall—that I often wondered if they were legitimate, since to my mind their dress alone undermined the college's staid sobriety. A paper was required for the class, and I believe my sister suggested the topic, *Fauvism*, an avant-garde French movement at the dawn of the twentieth century. I am sure I drew all my "research" from art books, and although I have no memory of my grade on the paper or in the course, the *fauve* artists were always in my mind when I happened upon a Modernism show. It is strange how a slim and derivative report stays with you, as if the first discovery of art on your own can never be repeated, those dazzlingly bright colors of the *wild beasts* vivid still, so that years later, when Matisse had an explosive retrospective, I took pride in knowing he was one of the original *fauves,* and relished coming upon the legends near the early paintings, convinced that I knew what they said before I read them.

Mr. Dorsky clearly impressed me, and while the dress was part of it, there were other factors of which I was unaware. It was only in retrospect that I realized how many of my teachers in Brooklyn College were themselves from the city. Not everyone had an identifiable accent, but I can hear in my head Mr. Dorsky saying, in his inflected voice, as he sauntered down the hallway, *I come from these same streets, and here I am, a college professor.* At the time it never occurred to me that I could do that, stand up in front of young people in a classroom and talk to them. In truth, I never thought of my college professors as having jobs, let alone how they got them. It was as if they occupied another realm, separate from the world of public school teachers, who most definitely worked. Yet there were a couple of male teachers that I strongly identified with, including Dr. Lind, so why was I unable to imagine myself in their position? A superficial answer might be that there was no vocabulary for patterning yourself on someone you admired. The word *hero* obviously existed, but that was associated with sports stars and had no application to people whose jobs you might actually aspire to. And the phrase *role model,* ubiquitous in later years, was virtually non-existent then. In high school I was a devotee of Murray Kempton's columns in the *Post,* and Max Lerner's commentary in *The Reporter,* and often thought at the time that being a newspaperman might be a job for me. But in college, when I had live men in front of me to look up to, it never occurred to me to say to myself, *that could be me.* As for the female professors, Brooklyn College had extraordinary teachers, like Dr. Ethyl Wolfe, who taught Greek Tragedy from a two volume hardbound edition I can still see because of its heft and the name of its co-editor, Eugene O'Neill, Jr. At the time, I kept turning over in my head the odd picture of the playwright and the classical scholar, and thinking how hard it must be for any child growing up in the shadow of renown. But brilliant as the women were, I did not identify with them in the same way, at least not until my senior term.

In any case, I opted to register for another class with Dorsky, "Mannerism and Anti-Mannerism in Italian Painting." I had no idea what the terms meant, nor any special interest in Italian painting, but even now names like Fiorentino and Parmigianino and Caravaggio rise up from the deep, such is the flotsam of our minds, and I am carried back to that class, wondering what I was doing there with art majors who knew so much more. I went to the Met for the first time to do my research, a small pleasure for those growing up in a city where all in the world was taken for granted. I chose a Caravaggio, I can still see it hanging all alone on a corner wall, stared long and hard at the painting, and made notes. The Met had an art library, and Mr. Dorsky gave us a clear warning: do not go there during the Christmas vacation to write your paper. It filled with students on winter break from colleges in New England, and we would never find seats. We should go instead to the Brooklyn Museum library, which was usually empty, except for an antiquated German art historian who would be found asleep at a desk. Ever dutiful, I took his advice, and when I entered the library I saw to my surprise an elderly man, his head lying on his arms, sleeping soundly at the reading room table. If I did not know better I would have thought it a plant. I did not spend much time there, but I finished the essay on Caravaggio. It was returned to me by Dorsky with a qualified oral comment, that it was impressive for someone who was not an art student, but he still could not decide if the A was for the paper, or the writing.

The Mannerism class left me with an abiding interest in Caravaggio, so that even today I find satisfaction in an Italian police show like *Palermo Connection* if only because its lead detective, fixated on the painter, carries his name, *Angelo,* while the artist himself is splashed all over the screen in images and art books. But in truth much of Italian painting was a gigantic puzzle, for the saints' names might as well have been printed in Latin and the biblical stories in Greek for all they meant to me. And I had no patience for reading about them in order to understand what the artists were depicting. There were far too many saints and an endless stream of stories. Yet even then I sensed in my attitude shallowness, if not flippancy. For on a deeper level, unarticulated yet intuited, I felt alien to the huge Christian canopy that covered the art. And it was not a religious aversion since nobody cared about the painting as religious expression, this was after all Brooklyn College and not St. Johns, but there may have been in me an unrecognized or unadmitted resistance to the power and pervasiveness of an adversarial religion. Jews of infinite sophistication, like Bernard Berenson, could grandly study the art qua art, but I barely cut it as a novitiate, am sure I knew nothing then of Berenson, and as for E. H. Gombrich, whose name was imprinted on anyone who walked into an art class, no one thought fit to mention that the magisterial historian of Mannerism was a Jewish refugee from Nazism. So I turned to something that *I* wanted to learn, paid no attention to the instructor, and registered for a course in "Modern Art." No more intense portraits, no more twisted elongated figures with enveloping limbs and arms, drapery and furniture and *stuff* filling the canvas so that the whole looked like an elegant chaotic rummage room. There was something claustrophobic about those images, and I was glad to get away from them. I opted for bright skies and clear colors and familiar scenes. The Museum of Modern Art was a favorite place, and it made sense to me to learn about artists in my own century. At least it would not require penetrating the shield of the New

Testament. And the word *modern* itself fueled my desire. It had no theoretical meaning for me, I had not studied *Modernism* in any course, but wrapped within its sound and form was the world of the present, not the past, style as it was seen and felt in clothes and cars and buildings and movies. To be *modern* was to be open and filled with the desire for life. And if there was a course that went by that title, then it was meant for me.

As I look back after years of standing at the front of a room, and try to recapture myself facing that front, it is a wonder that I can see me there, eager, excited, and blissfully ignorant. At first the instructor puzzled me. He looked nothing like the other art teachers. Of medium height and build, hair thinning at the crown and cut very short, as in a crew, his dress struck me noticeably, for he wore a dark navy or black suit, along with a dress shirt, and I kept thinking he looked like a banker or a businessman. But not really, for his manner was easy and assured, never rattled, and the classroom might even be described as Zen-like, if I had ever known that word then. In any case, I was sitting in an art class, with nobody I knew, and a man at the front of the room who was clearly the antithesis of *art*. And so it began. Dark room. Color slides. I assumed that *modern* art would be 1900 forward, but I discovered we were to start in the nineteenth century. The images were gorgeous, plain air paintings of ponds and flowers and parks, shimmering colors, recognizable forms, all lovely to look at. Except that very quickly I realized every slide shown was an orphan, it came with no name or title. I thought at some point the teacher would backtrack and tell us the names of the artists, and possibly the titles of the paintings. Not so. As we moved forward, slide after slide, we got no closer to any identification. The process might have been called *Paintings Anonymous*.

Finally, I could take it no longer and raised my hand. *You never tell us who painted these pictures,* I said, thinking this would lead to some profound explanation. *What does it matter?* he replied. I was at a loss, for the simplicity of his response was beyond my understanding, and all I could do was come up with some smart remark to mask my blankness. *Well, it's important to know who the artists are, because if I want to impress some girl I've just met I have to know their names to talk about them.* But he did not rise to the bait and stayed silent. Slowly it dawned on me that the names and titles of the paintings might have little to do with the paintings themselves. When we got to work that tossed out representation altogether, it might have been Mondrian but names were still *verboten,* I again put up my hand. *Can these people draw?* And again he responded, *What does it matter?* This time I had no smart retort, but I said that if they could draw then I would be more inclined to accept these squares and rectangles as art. It was then that he showed us slides of Mondrian's exquisite early drawings, I *think* I remember a detailed pen and ink sketch of a large tree, and learned that he was a brilliant draftsman. Our Zen master was carefully and methodically teaching us how to look at modern painting. And then, sometime before term's end, he told us he would be gone for a week, visiting a private museum in Pennsylvania to study their Modern paintings, and for the first time it entered my head that this man might be important. It was not until some years after that I fully realized who my teacher was—Ad Reinhardt. And today, if I am in a museum that has Reinhardt in its collection, I rush to it at the start, stare hard at the monochromatic canvas, and take great pleasure in thinking back on the serious and witty man in the black suit.

2. GOODBYE BROWNSVILLE

AT AGE FIFTEEN my sister lent me her copy of *A Walker in the City*. I had no idea who Alfred Kazin was, I remember being balked by the story because I never knew exactly what streets he was wandering, and I was deaf to the poetic reverie that made up so much of his remembrances. But two details stuck with me, Kazin's description of the kitchen floor being washed for *shabbos,* and newspapers put down to keep it from getting dirty again before the meal. I remembered my mother doing exactly the same thing *(I just washed the kitchen, don't walk on the floor),* and how after when you walked on the papers they would slide around, and tear apart in the middle, and I wondered what the point of it was, since it only made extra work, and then you would have to collect and scrunch all those newspapers together and try and shove them into the garbage. Yet seeing it in a book was strangely riveting, as if my mother had been followed in her weekly ritual, and then lifted from life and plopped down in print on a page. And then there was the mesmerizing effect of reading *Belmont Avenue* in an opening sentence. I see myself staring at the two words, trying to wrap my head around the idea that *my* street, just one block over, old and broken, made its way into a book because of its famous pushcarts. Who knew *fame* came in such derelict forms. That Kazin was from Brownsville meant less to me than *seeing* the street name in a book, which was a visceral experience that made my life seem more real, or maybe more important. Because anyone who was able to print *Belmont Avenue* between hard covers had gone past the street itself, and into a world far beyond my knowing.

I was still living there with my grandmother, above the grocery, my father driving in from Jamaica, where he was living with Mae, who still cared for no children other than her own. Nothing had changed for me that first year out of high school. But just before spring, in the first days of March, my grandmother, who had been feeling ill, was suddenly taken to a hospital. Nobody told me anything. I went to see her the next day and found her awake in bed. All the while I could not help thinking to myself that *I* alone in the family lived with her for six years, since I was twelve, and yet I might have been a stranger for all that it mattered. What we said to each other in that brief moment could not have been much, but I left expecting her to come home within the week. But it was the last time I saw her. She died a day or two after. And in a coincidence I could not have invented, it was exactly five years to the day after she lifted the heavy black telephone early in the morning to receive the news about my mother, and said softly to no one at all, *Blanchie ist gestorben.*

Where have all the vanished ladies gone? Rose (Rasha) Menikoff née Salutsky was the matriarch of my paternal family, the central pillar for her four sons and surviving daughter. It was in her small and cramped apartment on Belmont Avenue that everybody gathered for Pesach, to endure the service and relish the food. As a boy, I knew that her sons were attentive, and the daughters-in-law were all problematic. But in my life with her none of that had any urgency, things as they were before me had long since dissipated or ceased to matter much. After my grandfather's death there were no more Passover dinners. The dominance of the woman had declined, a natural function of age, and with it the combativeness that made her such a polarizing person in her immediate and extended families. Also, the ties of her own children were loosened a little. Still she was a presence. So how to explain the puzzling fact that her grandchildren, who grew up in her shadow, aware of her centrality, have no memory of her death? No one remembers going to the cemetery, or if there was a shiva. *It is as if there was a collective loss of memory, as opposed to the varied lapses of individuals. Given all the things that I have forgotten, as this memoir has reminded me, why should this one absence seem so unsettling? Perhaps it was not just a death* in *the family, but more like the death* of *a family. Our grandmother was the last person who pulled all the uncles and aunts and cousins together, or maybe she was the only one that everybody felt tied to. When she let go, the winds carried all else away, that long gathering that had its start in a distant country, with other languages, and continued on in a new world, but could no longer be contained within the cabined streets of a shrunken and narrow enclave. Brownsville was the home of less than a handful of us, for the rest it had become a place of the past. A death in the family might signal its decline, but on a more mundane level it may be nothing more than a harbinger of change. And with the erasure of death from memory, along with the passage of time, change can seem far more easeful. For not knowing, despite all our thinking to the contrary, might well be a salve for the living.*

What to do? A simple question, but in truth I had no clue. Eighteen years old, with no money, and in the middle of a second term in college. Belmont Avenue was the only home I knew. Moving in with my father was out of the question, as his wife would not have tolerated it, nor had I any stomach for her. My idea, more a visceral feeling than a rational thought, was to stay where I was and continue on at school. I had been doing that when my grandmother was alive, and I saw no reason to stop now that she was dead. I knew nothing of her finances and never thought of her as the owner of a building with two apartments and a grocery store. The only finances I knew anything about were the simple ones of my father, who had no money and lived on the largesse of his wife. My grandmother said to me once in passing that I should not worry when she died because she would take care of me. The remark, casual and unprompted, shook me, and was never forgotten, but its vagueness only led me to imagine that she would leave me something, and it was not until later, when I looked back, that I conjured out of air a figure of two or three thousand dollars. Maybe she had it in her mind, but I have no idea if she had a will, or if she mentioned it to my uncle Charlie, who handled all her affairs. In any case, I received no money. But that was farthest from my thought. I was focused only on how to remain in place, for I could see no picture of where I would be sleeping if I were thrown out of Belmont Avenue. Bubbie's daughter and her family lived above me. I was never invited upstairs for dinner, and I came to feel as if they wanted me to vacate the apartment, perhaps at the urging of Charlie, so it could be rented out. I felt besieged. The main door was an old-fashioned one, the kind seen in black and white movies where the top half above the doorknob is all textured glass, but there was also a wood one that had been fitted later, for added protection, which we never used. Now, for the first time, I found myself closing and locking it whenever I was in, as if I were barricading myself from my own relatives. But if in this distant silence I can summon that picture of an earlier self, sitting on a sofa, listening to the sounds from above, even then I knew the heavy door was no palisade, and I would soon have to leave.

Then I found myself with my sister in Massapequa on Long Island. Neither of us has an exact remembrance of the details, but I have a dim recollection of an intense phone conversation, with Miriam telling me in the end to chuck it all and come out. My entire stay there amounted to less than six months. During my high school years I had little contact with Miriam and Harry. They never came to Brooklyn, and I possibly visited them half a dozen times on the Island. My joining their household did not make for a tight body of five, but rather chain-linked together a young suburban family of four with a single person whose adolescent years were spent alone. Friction was inevitable, but somehow we got through the time until school ended, and since I knew as if by instinct what the better part of valor was, before ever knowing the proverb, I thought the best thing I could do for the summer was to go away. And so I landed a job at an overnight camp near Poughkeepsie. The summer of 1957 was set to be my escape from New York, and, with any luck, from that long held virginity that increasingly swallowed up my thoughts.

What was the name of the camp? To channel Ad Reinhardt, *what does it matter?* For the sake of a story the writer would like a hard noun for a place that at the time had such personal importance. But maybe the obliteration of the name is an apt metaphor for my uncertainty as to whether it was a summer to remember, or a blur to forget. I did bid farewell to my chaste self that summer, though just barely, and probably more in the jumble of my imagining than in physical reality, yet the weeks away also left me with two-three vivid images. I had been assigned to the youngest campers, ages 5 and 6, a group usually reserved for experienced counselors and any new hire that lacked the temerity to refuse. The camp directors could not have known that I liked small children, and had often played with or watched over my younger cousins. In any case, I was sitting on the wooden steps outside our cabin, early afternoon, boys were being dropped off and deposited for the summer, and as they were left you could read on the faces of their parents, *free, free at last,* when who should be standing in front of me but my English teacher for the year just ended. *Of all the camps in all the states* etc, but it was a pleasant if unexpected encounter, and I assured Dr. Sidney Lind and his wife that I would take special care to look after their son, not having the faintest idea what I meant by that.

Since I had no special skills, and these children required the most attention, I wondered what I would be doing with them, until I inadvertently discovered a talent I never knew I had. It probably started by chance one evening before bedtime when I started making up stories to keep the kids quiet until they fell asleep. It quickly became routine, the children wanted the stories, and the other counselors insisted I continue because it relieved them of the last bit of work before we were done for the night. And the storytelling continued outside the cabin, in a campout, in the dark, the boys arranged in a circle, kept close to make sure no one got lost, and I was suddenly called upon to entertain them. But the strangest thing of all was that I had no stock to draw upon, it was not as if I could call up Andersen's tales at a moment's notice, I think the Pied Piper was the only one I knew, or Greek myths, of which I was ignorant. As best I remember, I made up everything from scratch, I was constantly badgered to tell of ghosts and things that go bump in the night, and although I seemed able to start a story, I was usually at a loss as to how to end it. But it did not seem to matter. For a small boy, away from home, the telling itself was a reassuring ritual, maybe even a comfort. Endings were for grown people, or those struggling to grow, and if they were hard to find for stories, just think of their elusiveness in life.

A Quaker, she said, which was lovely and exotic sounding, and meant nothing to me other than my schoolboy remembrance of William Penn. It is curious how we learn words when young, with no understanding of their meaning, store them away as if in a wine cellar, and when later they are opened we have no sense of their savor. Who in Brooklyn knew a Quaker? Fortunately the movies came to the rescue, as I had recently seen Gary Cooper in *Friendly Persuasion,* an enchanting film that persuaded me I had met a friend just like one on that colored screen, charming, ingenuous, and absent all those neurotic tics that I instinctively associated with girls living east of the River. Actually, although a good line, that may not be fair or even accurate, and is likely a later view superimposed on a younger self, for at the time I had no sample of girls to stain with so broad a brush. Still, it is as if in my quest to get laid I had to travel far from the stones of the city, which sounds absurd even in the writing, but as I was living on the Island, took a long train to college, spent no time after school, how could I meet anyone and where would we go? Camp seemed the ideal opportunity, and Carolyn, from another place, charmed me from the start with the name she wore. We were thrown together, and made a natural fit, first year of college, done, first time counselors, in process. I chafe at all that I do not know, where she came from, what school she was at, and yet writing this surprises me, for I see her, clearer perhaps than at any time since those pristine days, her slight build, short, dark blonde hair, slender face, and skin so soft as to stir me even now. And the quiet manner matched those qualities, sweet, receptive, a disposition I had no experience with and was incapable of understanding. All I knew was *Jewish*, and I wanted something different, but it perplexed me when I found it. We crossed paths during the day, spent evenings relaxing with others, yet always together, and I began to take her for granted, and even wondered if I were with her only because she was the most promising girl to sleep with, and in the end what else was I there for?

Late in the season a stranger from a nearby farm or town rode into camp on horseback, sitting high, and I stood transfixed before this ramrod straight cowgirl, with her dark hair, working shirt, jeans and boots. I did not know her role, possibly giving riding lessons for the older campers, or tips about farm life, but she was *rural*, the real thing, casually riding in on a dirt trail, where everybody else, campers and counselors, knew only roads of concrete. It was as if an actor in a Western suddenly appeared live at your side, soft spoken, confident, and holding the reins of a tall horse as easily as if it were an ordinary leash. She never stayed overnight in camp, but we somehow met, talked at catch-as-catch-can times, and I remember being surprised at her sophistication, for she was alternately direct and nuanced in a way I would never have expected. Another revelation, sharpness was not the exclusive province of the city. The combination of skilled rider, clever conversationalist, and statuesque beauty was more than I could turn away from. But it was a lost cause, and although she was drawn herself, there was never any time when we could be alone, she learned about Carolyn, and her integrity was like her horsemanship, formal and correct. Even then, in her presence, however briefly, I was aware that her probity was of another order, and well beyond my shortened grasp. What I also discovered for the first time was that I could be with one girl, and shift my attention to another, a habit that years later led to painful confrontations, and a constant collapse into self-flagellation.

But this was an early day, I had no practice in self-criticism, and so I returned to the project at hand. That Carolyn was willing to be with me was clear, and it would be her first time as well. I remember going into Poughkeepsie alone, to buy condoms, a word never used, walking back and forth past the local drug store in the early evening, trying to muster the courage to enter and ask the pharmacist for a pack of *Trojans*, which were never displayed on the shelves, and the only name I knew. I have no idea how long I paced that small street, but in the end the sense of shame or embarrassment was too great, and I returned to camp empty handed. But I was determined to go ahead, and in my fevered mind I imagined I could concoct something similar to a Trojan by using a sock, never thinking about its thickness, or its being porous, or anything at all, because if I had for a single moment actually *thought*, I would have realized instantly how ludicrously ignorant I was, and how unprepared for raising a cock to enter a vulnerable girl's body. It is as if I were a living automaton, programmed for one task only, without the rudiments of a brain to oversee the performance. So we set out one night, Carolyn and I, into the woods, for there was no cabin in the camp where we could be alone, and we walked in the dark until we were far enough away, and then lay down on the ground, which was covered with needles and cones, and we struggled with each other, unwilling to get naked because of all the rough nature, but we finally felt skin, her stomach flat and lovely to the touch of my hand, but I was insistent on getting inside her, unwilling to linger and treasure her body, or fall into her beauty, for her face glistened, as if from the moon's light, yet it was all lost to me, as I fumbled with the sock, trying to get it over a thick cock and push it into her, small as she was, and in a moment it was all over, and I suddenly realized where we were, in the woods, under the pines, and I was spent. *Was it worth it?* she asked, quietly, a hint of expectation in her voice. *No,* I answered, much too quickly, as if I had never really heard the question.

These lines come after many a summer, as the old verse has it, the swan having long since died. The memoirist, whose lifeblood is retrospection, alternately controls the past and defies it, first by retrieving time through memory, and then by assigning meaning to that recovery. The latter process is the more problematic, because meaning comes filtered through years of experience. Whenever a writer looks back over a youthful moment when he behaved badly, there often follows an apologia for that early cruelty, one that mitigates the original act and makes him seem less callow, as if he had managed some kind of absolution. But however much the view has been altered by the passage of years, the act itself remains inalterable, and although it exists only in memory, the imposition of form after the fact is little more than a weak effort at atonement. If the bliss of gathered rosebuds is irrecoverable, it is equally the case that nothing can efface the wound of youthful cruelty. I have no way of knowing what effect our summer, and that night, had on Carolyn, or the memory she took away with her. Scott Fitzgerald nailed this in "The Rich Boy," when Anson Hunter tells Dolly Karger "I don't love you a bit," and the girl, who expected so much when he took her away for the weekend, could do nothing but lie awake and stare at the ceiling. Every time I read that scene I am reminded of Carolyn, and the one word I had not the sense to keep to myself. Fitzgerald could spin beauty out of sorrow, but for an ignorant boy wrapped in a cocoon of self-absorption, sorrow just stayed there, mixed with regret. You never forget the face of a woman you loved, a smart writer once said. True, but you may also carry with you the image of one you nearly loved, and left before ever you knew it, and

*her face returned to haunt you, not like Gene Tierney, that is way
too dramatic, but in your memory of a moment when life tested
you, and you failed the challenge, whether out of fear, or ignorance,
or ineptitude. But when Carolyn's face came back, after many a
summer, I saw in it more grace, and courage, than I could have
then known, let alone understood.*

And so my adventure was over. I returned to Long Island
different, if only in my head, and fortunately nothing showed,
for I would have been stumped if anyone asked me how I had
changed. But my homecoming was not glitch free, for my sister and I quarreled immediately, and I turned on my heels and
left the house like a character in a play. I called a high school
classmate, he told me to come to his parents' small apartment
in East New York, where he lived steps away from the overhead
train. I can still see the narrow, pinched space, hear the rumbling clatter of the el that entered the rooms, and yet I have no
memory at all of what Miriam and I fought about. It is strange
how simple physical movements survive as solid remembrances,
anchoring the past, while the insubstantial forces that spurred
them are nowhere to be found, as if they dissolved without a
trace into nothingness. After one or two nights I returned to
the Island, reconciled with my sister, and we both decided that
suburban living without a car was no life at all. At a used car
dealer in Bethpage I bought a 1953 Ford Crestline for $750, a
two door black and white hardtop, a deal Miriam never forgot,
because she and Harry picked up a Nash at the same time, their
car was a lemon, and mine kept going and going, like the little
red engine. *But where did the money come from?* I now wonder,
certainly my earnings from the camp job, and whatever else I
had, which could not have been anything more than pocket
change. It is odd how little I remember from that time in Massapequa, whether I left the car at the train station on my way to

school, or drove all the way to Brooklyn on the Island parkways, exiting in Flatbush and wending my way through the streets until I found parking near Avenue H for the day. What I retain is a dim picture of the house, ranch style, cedar shakes, small and comfortable, across from a trimmed golf course, all green from end to end, and the strange quiet at night. The noise of a block in Brooklyn was normal to me, and I was unnerved by the silence of the dark, broken only by the sounds of crickets and birds from the nearby Great South Bay. Although I knew I was in a nicer place, and told myself I should appreciate the natural beauty, I could not shake the feeling that there was something *un*natural about that quiet, as well as the eerie absence of people milling around day and night. City streets were deep in my bones, and in my head, in ways I never thought about, and could barely articulate.

3. *VERONA*, JERSEY STYLE

LONG ISLAND was the briefest of sojourns. Very early in the fall I received a call from an old friend from junior high, I must have run into him on the Brooklyn campus, asking if I was interested in a weekend job in New Jersey as a busboy. Strangely, I can see myself sitting at the table that held the telephone, the receiver in my hand, and my excitement at the possibility of work. The place was *The Goldman Hotel*, near Montclair, and I had to be there by Friday afternoon. Having a car made it possible, since the hotel was in a small town without easy access to public transportation. It was close enough to New York that people booked it for a weekend, Friday night through Sunday lunch, and it had a flourishing business in bar mitzvahs and weddings, events scheduled for Saturday nights, with guests often staying over for Sunday breakfast. I was assigned to an easygoing veteran waiter, who displayed no annoyance at being given a rookie to work with. A waiter's station time consisted of three round top tables that seated eight persons apiece, with each round top replaceable by one that seated ten. Any station with twenty-four people was full, and required skilled waiters to work them. But I would learn all that in time.

My first job was to clear the dishes as they were finished, a simple enough task until you realize you have no idea how to hold more than a single dish in your hand. If you take one in your left hand, and a second in the right, the silverware will invariably fall off the plates, and if you go back and forth with one or even two dishes you will never clear the tables fast enough. At dinner, as opposed to breakfast, everyone was eating together, and the dishes needed to be removed at the same time. So the first requirement was to learn how to carry more than one dish. That did not happen on Friday night. But what I remember as if it were yesterday was my first mistake. As I removed the remains of a man's gefilte fish appetizer, drawing it over his shoulder rather than taking it from the side, the plate tipped and horseradish dripped on the back of his suit jacket. I could see it sitting there, bright red on the dark cloth, and was sure I would be yelled at if not fired. I approached the waiter and quietly told him what I had done. *Did he say anything?* he asked. *He doesn't know*, I answered. *Well, then don't tell him.* Whether this was an unintended dining room lesson—*never volunteer anything that discredits you*—or simply the reflex of a veteran, I cannot say, but I was grateful not to be reprimanded, and so I continued on, clearing the dishes in a haphazard fashion, pouring coffee and serving it cup by cup, instead of three cups at a time, as I later mastered, even four when I was rushed, or wanted to show off a little.

But if the rest of the weekend was a blur, it ended with a bang. My tips topped out at thirty-two dollars. It seemed such an enormous sum for two days' work that I was stupefied. Not to mention that I was all thumbs all the time. I tried to imagine what it would be like if I actually *knew* how to bus tables. But I did not dwell on that thought. If I made thirty-two dollars that weekend, I could probably make it the next, and the next after that. It never occurred to me that incomes could fall as easily as they rose, but I was transfigured by the prospect of earning money, by the notion that I might make enough to support myself, maybe even to live by myself, and so I brushed aside all disquieting thoughts, and basked instead in the illusive dream of my future independence.

With my newfound wealth I rented a room in a private house very near the college. I *think* it was on East 21st Street, but I remember exactly what I paid—thirty-eight dollars a month. The modest house had a brick exterior, was neat and clean, my room one short flight up with a bathroom on the same level. I had no kitchen privileges and rarely saw the owner. The room fit a bed along one wall, its head under the adjoining window, a desk and a chair opposite, with a mirror, and a window on that wall as well. I clearly remember the window on that side because it was old and stuck, and one time I got sick, and thought beverages might be good for me, so I bought a bottle of juice and placed it outside on the slim stone sill to keep cold, only to discover in the morning that the juice froze when I forgot to take it in for the night. As for eating, I needed only four days to worry about since I would be spending long weekends at the hotel. Lunches I could manage at the college cafeteria, but dinners were a problem because I could not afford to eat in restaurants every night. It turns out I reverted to an early habit, found a luncheonette close by, and became a regular there, sitting on the last seat at the counter alongside the wall. It is odd to be a fixture in a small sandwich shop, eating egg salad, tuna, and BLT on toast, but it brought me back to my days in junior high school, and felt strangely familiar, even comforting in a way. And I persuaded myself that it did not matter what I ate during the week because I was getting serious dinners at *Goldman's,* which was not exactly true, but staff meals at hotels is another story altogether. In any case, my life took on an unvarying regularity that second year. From Monday to Thursday I would go to classes, eat at the luncheonette, sleep in my room, move my car to avoid being smacked with a ticket, and then on Friday I would drive to New Jersey. Brooklyn to Manhattan, the Lincoln Tunnel to Route 3 and Valley Road, through the stately streets of Upper Montclair, then Bloomfield Avenue and a narrow side road toward Verona. The hotel stood on one side of the road, low and deep, and on the other, a ramshackle structure that looked to be held together by tarpaper. This shaky caution—it later went up in flames—was where the busboys lived and slept, a tale reflective more of *Two Cities* than *Upstairs, Downstairs.* But these were long ago days, nobody knew the word *rights,* or even *workers* for that matter, and it was an article of faith that busboys were the most expendable hires in the dining room, just *a dime a dozen,* as the saying went.

Although *Goldman's* dining room was smaller than those in the major Catskill hotels, it covered at least ten waiter stations, two hundred forty people minimum, and on a busy night extra tables could be set up wherever there was floor space. It was an acrobatic feat to squeeze between people whose chairs nearly touched back to back at adjoining round tables, and, unlike a city restaurant, it was an unspoken rule never to pass a dish to a guest. The tightness all around just ratcheted up the pressure of serving and busing. One inerasable scene played out several years later, in another New Jersey hotel, where my friend Anna and I were working a dinner together, she waiting, I clearing. The room was so packed with people, the tables all cheek by jowl, that walking was like balancing on a narrow ledge. Anna came out with the last course, a tray of desserts on her shoulder, eight or ten apple pie dishes, she could not find a station to place the tray on, so she simply turned it upside down. The dishes crashed and broke and spread every which way in the narrow aisle and under the chairs, with guests moving their feet forward and backward and sideways to avoid getting the pie jam on their shoes. I knew exactly how she felt, we were working the same meal, but it was left to me to clean up the mess.

While dropping a load of plates on a dining room floor might seem berserk, we had never worked at that hotel before and had no intention of returning. What could they do? Fire us? The conditions that night were inexcusable, and waitresses and busboys were expected to bear it silently. Anna's upturned tray was an act of rebellion, figuring all the slights and furies we carried with us from hotel to hotel, and as I look back, the dirty plates have long vanished from memory, but I relish the picture of Anna in her white uniform, strands of blonde hair falling from her loosely tied bun, indifferent to the noise and the stares, the tray held fast by her side, slowly turning and walking out of the room. *A good story, he thinks to himself, but just a footnote to the saga of* Goldman's, *let alone that of the Catskills, which he has not even begun to compose, when suddenly the writer is struck with a revelation, unbidden and unwanted, that a whole memoir could be stitched together of the days lived in dining rooms and kitchens, of nights working hotel bars and coffee shops for extra money, and of the people never again met away from that world,* God's plenty, *as the poet called them, from Chinese kitchen crews to Cuban waitresses to Dominican busboys to Bowery dishwashers to Jewish waiters whose off the cuff commentary and scabrous wit rivaled the comics who highlighted the evening shows. God's plenty, indeed.*

But let us return to the dining room, and my apprenticeship, for it *was* a trade, although nobody thought to call it that, and like all trades it had its own work-related requirements.

Carrying two plates in one hand was essential. As each dish had a circular rim on the underside, by locking one plate under the rim of another, *voila!* you held both securely, and with that as your base you could add more given your facility. A good waiter could easily carry four appetizers, or three entrée dishes, to a table, and I quickly learned to clear away six and four of them at a time, since the plates were empty and flat. What next required mastery, and it came naturally to me, was balancing the long, oval aluminum tray, as basic to a waiter as a hammer to a carpenter. The tray fitted four large dishes, with stainless steel plate covers, four more atop those, also covered, so a waiter could carry out eight dishes for a table's main course. If there were ten guests, then two more covered dishes would go on top. I would like to estimate the weight, but it would be guessing beans in a jelly jar. Enough to say it was heavy, carried with one hand on the shoulder, while those who were less confident supported the load by buttressing the tray with their other hand, which I never did, even as a busboy, but after I became a waiter, I occasionally displayed a bit of one-upmanship, and carried a tray of eight completely off my shoulder, for it looked classier, and showed off my strength and skill.

Meanwhile, at *Goldman's,* to continue the thread of my story, once I was in control of the dishes in my hand and the tray in the air, all the rest was duck soup, learning the details of serving and, most importantly, the culture of the kitchen, where chefs were kings, and even cooks, princes. But I was glad to have a job, even though it was week-to-week, for at the end of the weekend, on Sunday afternoon, when we received our paltry paychecks, I have no idea how the sums were calculated since tips were all that mattered to us, Mel, the dining room captain, would tell us individually to come back the next weekend, or not. He was a gruff, heavy-set man, wore tortoise shell glasses, dark suits, and talked with a voice scraped from the streets. Later, he took to calling me *Gudderad,* which confused me until I finally unpacked it—*Gutter rat.* Since I was living on my own, distracted about the rent, the food, my car, I was a bit edgy those afternoons, waiting to hear Mel's verdict. For those he knew well, it was always thumbs up: *Next Friday!* Because I was not then one of the happy few, I had to wait until most had gotten their envelopes, but as I had not crashed a tray of dishes, and did nothing in the kitchen to catch the notice of the hawk-eyed steward, I was asked back, and in the course of that autumn became myself a seasoned regular.

Needless to say, my college courses slid away, although oddly enough the thought that work might affect my studies never occurred to me. I found it hard on Monday to get to class, but I did not make any connection between the two. It was just my life, work and school, and the option of choosing one over the other was not anything I thought about. I did take notice at the *end* of my sophomore year, when I saw the vertical drop in my English grades—*A, B, C, D.* But that came later. In the meantime, I was working and looking forward to the Christmas break, when I would be at the hotel for a complete week, possibly two, and anticipated making serious money. I drove to Verona on a Friday afternoon, parked the Ford on the lot, stowed my bag in the hazard shack, picked up my white uniform, a faux Nehru jacket with green trim that came down mid-thigh, and sauntered over to the dining room. I was early, hung around and wondered about the station I would get. Some waiters were more desirable because they were favored by the maître d' and their tables filled up first. If the hotel was full it made no difference, but if not, the others made do with smaller stations. As a busboy, you were in the same position, if your waiter scored, so did you. But none of that was in my mind that afternoon. Instead, visions of dollars danced in my head, and I was anxious for my assignment. Stanley, the busboy captain, came in shortly before the dining room opened, and assigned a number of us to waiters that evening, but I was not among them. And as I looked around I noticed that some who got stations were new, that is, I never saw them before, and I had been coming every weekend. They were probably veterans, chose not to work on the weekends, and came out just for the long holiday. I knew none of that, nor did I know that the first night was invariably slow, because people were likely to arrive on Saturday, and it did not matter whether you started work in the evening or the next day.

I could not see that. I had been working steadily for close to three months, and suddenly I was shunted aside and new guys were given priority. I told Stanley I wanted a station that night. He looked surprised. *Who is this crazy kid?* Thinking of it now, I am certain that he had no intention of screwing me, and I would have gotten a station the next day, and made the money that I had been counting in my head. But I felt it as a betrayal of some sort, although I never put it in those terms, and I was beside myself with anger. When he finally turned away, told me over his shoulder to come back the next morning, without thinking I instantly took off my jacket and flung it across one of the tables. If he had been puzzled before he now looked genuinely amazed. I bolted from the dining room, ran through the lobby, across the road to the shack, retrieved my bag, and began the long drive back to Brooklyn in a very dark night. Everything happened so quickly that I had no time to realize what I had done, for the next thing I knew I was barreling down the West Side Highway, off on Canal Street headed to the Manhattan Bridge, all as if on automatic pilot, when a cop car pulled me over. I did not see it on my tail or flashing its light, I simply remember being parked on the side of the street, and sitting behind the wheel in a daze. There was almost a complete absence of other cars, as if Canal Street was deserted except for my Ford and the police car. The cop walked over easily, without a hint of aggression, and seemed avuncular in his manner. *Where are you going, kid?* I can even now hear myself telling him, in my numbed state, that I was going home, I had just lost my job, and I had only five dollars in my pocket. I remember the precise amount because I kept repeating it over and over as I was passing through the Tunnel and on to the Highway, wondering what on earth I was going to do with five dollars. The cop leaned over and faced me through the open window: *Son, you can always get another job, but if you keep driving like that you sure as hell won't need one.* Strangely, his words calmed me down, brought me back to life in a way, and I continued on more slowly along Canal Street, crossed the Bridge, and returned safely home.

Back in my room I was in a quandary. *Goldman's* had become a home to me, I *may* have known of the Catskills, but it was far too distant a place for work. Yet when I reflected evenly instead of worrying over my five dollars, I realized that I had learned something these long weekends, like how to carry plates, take orders, and clear tables. Why not apply as a waiter to a restaurant? Brooklyn College had a classic place right on the edge of campus, *Wolfie's,* busy, bright, and with a menu that any Jewish boy could understand. It was not like *Junior's* in Downtown Brooklyn, an institutional icon for borough die-hards who insisted its cheesecake rivaled that of *Lindy's.* Only in New York could cheesecake create turf wars. But it was more accessible. My plan was simple enough: walk into *Wolfie's* and ask for a job. I went into the restaurant, had an interview that is a total blank, but apparently *Goldman's* was enough to get me hired. I would have to learn to make ice cream sodas and malteds, since I would be stationed at the counter, and I was to begin that weekend, working Friday and Saturday nights.

I was thrilled and nervous at the same time, excited to have a job a few blocks from my room and college, yet anxious because a restaurant was different from a hotel dining room, and there were few allowances for mistakes. Somewhere I picked up two or three cups and saucers, possibly from my landlady, and practiced holding and carrying them before the mirror in my room, an overabundance of caution, for I was more than able to handle the dishes. In any event, I went to work on Friday, managed the counter, received some advice from a waitress on the sodas, and all ended well. Saturday, ditto. Since I assumed that the two nights was a tryout, and I even *looked* like a waiter in my trim short jacket, as opposed to that Indian coat I wore for months, I was sure I passed the test and could look forward to a regular job. But nothing ever is as it seems. The manager told me not to come back. I was too astonished to say anything. It was not personal. I had not done anything wrong. They needed an extra hand for the weekend, and I turned up just in time. There is not much of *Wolfie's* that remains with me, but I see the glaring light that suffused the place, the long counter, the fountains, and can even revive that desperate feeling of wanting something badly, of having it in my grasp, only to find when I opened my hand that there was nothing there at all.

Done, the writer says, having compressed time and matter into a well-shaped section, and how good it is to be done. But I am not done at all, for one memory lingers still, suspended in air as a balloon, and I am loath to cut the string and let it float away. Why? Omission is not a sacrifice, and as a quality of great art it is equally of use in a common memoir. Yet I am unwilling to discard the lingering incident, as if tossing away a tactile memory were killing a part of recovered life that makes up the rationale for this book. If some memories are more equal than others, all share the same body, and are worthy of their own lines.

This last begins at the Jupiter Agency in Midtown, a clearing-house for hotel jobs. A large, open office, people milling about, busboys, pastry chefs, but there was no action, no postings. Two young guys, on break from college in the South, learning I had a car, proposed we drive to a resort in New Jersey and look for work on our own. The prospect of a job suppressed any qualms about a road trip with strangers. As we approached a turnpike entrance the next day, with its wide, open coin slot, one of the two jumped out of the car, ran around to the driver's side, and collected all the coins that missed the toss. Suddenly I doubted this enterprise. We arrived late in the morning at a large hotel, possibly in Lakewood, and located the kitchen as if we were familiars, grabbed cereal bowls, fruit and coffee. A burly man passing through spotted us. *What are you doing here?* he asked. *We're busboys, just arrived*, one of the two answered. The burly man nodded, said something about lunch, and left us to our meal. At that point I was reluctant to hang around with them any longer, and as we could not get jobs we separated. While I did not regret the chance exploit, I felt there was something of the con about the two of them, and I was an easy mark. But if I had little gold to be parted with, the lesson that a New Yorker can be taken in was not lost on me. Still, who would give over the picture of a college sharpie scrounging for silver at a turnpike entrance, or forget the chutzpah of three young men casually taking a meal in a random hotel kitchen, because, after all, we *were* busboys.

IRVING AND ME

STEPPING OFF the train at the Junius Street station in Brownsville I saw on the platform a familiar face from junior high, the boy who sang *Solamente Una Vez* with a bandana on his head, and who later walked through graduation in sneakers. He was taller now, maybe two or three inches below six feet, stocky build, dark curly hair, the cut of his jib broke easily into a wide smile, and he wore glasses with no pretense to fashion. We fell into conversation instantly, covering a hiatus of three years, Irving having gone to Stuyvesant while I was at Jefferson. We were both in college, each of us living alone in a single room, he at Judson House, the makeshift student residence that stood behind the Judson Memorial Church near Washington Square. These passing bits of information in a fleeting moment lit up like an incandescent filament. Brooklyn College was a commuter school. Nobody lived outside of home. When I was leaving Jeff an artist classmate talked with me about living together in the city, but his style was Low Bohemian, he eventually took a cold-water, railroad flat that I visited once, and regretted not at all. To find someone at school who wanted to say *sayonara* to his parents was almost impossible. Yet here were the two of us, meeting by chance on an elevated platform, in exactly the same situation. And while we had not been close friends, and knew little about the other except that our mothers were both dead, we never wondered if we could get along together. Necessity kept that thought at bay, for the prospect of an apartment, and its semblance of a normal life, shunted aside picky matters of compatibility. So we made the deal, took a flat at 769 St. Marks Avenue for $76.05 a month, as per the original lease, and I have no idea what the nickel was about. It was a neighborhood I recognized, several blocks above Eastern Parkway, one over from Nostrand Avenue, but whether it was still Crown Heights or the beginning of Bedford Stuyvesant was nothing I thought about, for we were glad to find a place we could manage. In two years we would move into a new building, at 639 Albany Avenue, paying thirty-two dollars more a month, and relish the luxury of *cleanness* and the absence of cockroaches. But that was in our senior year. For now, we had this one bedroom in an old prewar building, we flipped for the bed, I won, but Irving seemed so bent at the prospect of sleeping in the living room that I switched with him and took the couch. I cannot say if I was thoughtful, or simply trying to prevent our hasty compact from coming unglued. In any case, our new life had begun.

And here I find myself painted in a corner. The section title came to me in a blink, yet I have no idea how to fit the person I lived with into my narrative. We were not an odd couple, as Neil Simon would have it, but we had separate friends and different lives. Irving was a history major from the get-go, and immersed in New York's byzantine socialist politics. He idolized the éminence *grise* of that world, Max Schachtman, knew

Michael Harrington before he wrote *The Other America*, and co-founded the Eugene Debs Society at Brooklyn College. All this left me cold, for the fervor I had for politics in high school had gone out without my noticing, just as my passion for baseball vanished before I knew it was gone. And while I could not shake the feeling that the wars waged in Manhattan meeting rooms had more than a whiff of the 1930s, I grudgingly admired Irving's desire to change the world for the better, however quixotic I thought the enterprise. But even though he enjoyed provoking me about my politics, and was a formidable debater, it never seriously strained our relation. For beneath the gladiatorial discourse he was warm and generous, and our lives had more in common than we ever talked about. Our fathers were distant figures, we each had two sisters, and were completely on our own for money. These factors outweighed our different likings, Irving with his fondness for Odetta and folk music, forever tuned to Oscar Brand on WNYC, myself for Sarah Vaughan, who I caught in a rare appearance at the *Town Hill Supper Club* on Eastern Parkway. As I think of it now, I wonder that we never thought of taking separate apartments. All the while we lived together Irving worked at *Roseland*, checking hats and coats, and came home with pockets full of silver every weekend. And I had become a hotel regular, and made more than enough to be self-sufficient. But we had become our own family, strange as it seems, and although his hair-splitting manner might get on my nerves, it never got to the point where I could not stand living with him. He had a brilliant mind, and I marveled at his ability to skimp on class work and ace the course. What also kept us together was our sense that we were both thrown on our wits from very early, although I always felt that nothing in my background could match Irving's. Being left by your father for a new wife was chickenfeed next to being deposited with your sisters, lock stock and barrel, at an orphanage. But in an odd way our experiences overlapped, creating a bond that set us apart from our friends, all living with their original parents. So we were spliced, as the old word had it, for the rest of our college days.

4. REPRISE, *VERONA*

SOMETIME AFTER the start of the year I returned to *Goldman's*. My extravagant exit before the holidays, if anyone remembered it, was no block to a plain and simple homecoming. Hotel people were tough skinned. They had little time and less care for gestures, grand or small. The meal was always the thing, its preparation and delivery, and all else was consumed before it. So when I entered the dining room it was as if I had never left. All this was good, and I felt more like a veteran than ever before, the time away having somehow raised my status, transforming me from a run of the mill dish clearer to a hotel familiar, someone who sauntered through the lobby and around the tables as if he owned the place. But of course I was still just a busboy, and perplexed when told I would be working with Ida, a long-time waitress who had asked for me specifically. I could not figure it out, because in all the weekends I worked there I never had any contact with her. To my young eyes she was ancient, snow-white hair, cut short, with a small upturned wave around the bottom, lined visage, but nice looking, with plain glasses, I was sure she was the oldest person there, and I wondered if there was a story as to why she was still working. If this was a puzzle, it was open knowledge in the dining room that no busboy wanted her tables, even though they were certain to fill up, because she was a slave driver. But it was out of my hands, Ida spoke, and I was handed over. Looking back now, it seems almost quaint how cowed strong young men were by a lone woman in a white blouse and black skirt, but experience and seniority still counted then, and the dining room and kitchen was nothing if not a rigid hierarchy.

In a strange way I got along with Ida, even though the only name she called me was *Monkey*, which I could never understand, and she directed a litany of commands throughout the meal. But it was clear from the start that Ida was an exceptional waitress, and she ran an immaculate station. If the goblet did not sparkle, or a stain could be detected on a knife, *"Monkey"* could be heard blasted beyond all the neighboring stations. When the main course was done, and before dessert and coffee were served, she had me slowly crumb the table with a knife so hardly a speck showed on the white cloth. While this might be excellent practice in an expensive restaurant, it was over the top in a hotel dining room, where few waiters were so fastidious about their tables, and most were disdainful of the diners' ability to tell good service from bad. Still, *Goldman's* was a family hotel, and like its counterparts in the Catskills, aspired to *haute* dining if not quite *haute cuisine*, since what they were selling was the appearance of elegant service. Much later, when I worked at an outlier hotel that catered to singles, there was no such pretension, and the waiters complied, assumed their table guests were focused entirely on getting laid, and would not notice the food even if it was served on silver plates. But that is a different story, for another time.

Yet appearance can go a long way, and *Goldman's* swung for the bleachers. At dinner, the table was set with ornately decorative plates that I recoiled at, for my taste leaned toward the modern, and I was even then aware of *marimekko* design, which was all the rage. That was not New Jersey style. On the veneered and flowered platter we placed an *opener,* a shrimp concoction in a small glass dish, resting in an ice-filled cocktail bowl with a three to four inch stem. This *objet* was set out before the guests were let in, so when they entered they could see on their table eight cocktail bowls standing tall, with a touch of red in each one. After this, in rapid succession, came the appetizer, soup, entrée, dessert and coffee, all these courses with choices, except for the appetizer, and there was always the odd diner who turned away from the shrimp cocktail and insisted on a grapefruit or fruit cup, upsetting the rhythm of the serving before it even began. No waiter took orders with a pencil, there was no time, and on the rare occasion when I saw one scratching away I knew he would never survive, I felt disdainful that he could not hold the dishes in his head, and a little sorry for him. Back then I never thought much about it, concentrated as I was on my own small piece of the room, but as I rebuild the scene the entire spectacle opens out as if for the first time. Dinner started at seven o'clock and was over by eight-thirty, a quarter to nine at the latest. In process, ten waiters and ten busboys, give or take, running back and forth from the dining room to the kitchen, with trays of food and cleared dishes in the air, would unfailingly serve two hundred people a five course meal in under two hours. And some could even do it with panache.

Ida held fast the custom of the dining room by putting nothing on the table without a plate beneath it. A glass of orange juice was carried in a *monkey dish,* a small, shallow bowl that just fitted the slim glass, while a dish of prunes or a bowl of cereal was served atop a different one, called an *underliner.* A stack of dishes had to be stocked at the station to sustain this architecture of crockery, and if they were gone, and I tried to sneak a fruit compote to a guest instead of making a trek to the kitchen for a plate, at my back I would always hear, *Where's the underliner, Monkey? Get an underliner!* And to this day, when a server walks toward me with a naked glass of juice in her hand, I cannot help but recoil slightly, as if by reflex, and then I remind myself that this is another time, another place, and say nothing. *Yet thinking back to those frenetic days I wonder how I carried on while Ida carped away. For I stayed strangely unaffected, as if it was someone else she was berating, I happened to be there in the flesh, but really it had nothing to do with me. And as I write this now, and imagine myself then a visible spirit next to the material busboy, it comes to me like an unexpected shock, the memoir doing its underground work, that this is akin to a revelation, for in the way I shed or let slide Ida's fault finding, I recognize a habit that followed me through my working life. I can remember years later, after delivering a talk, someone tearing into whatever I said, and I appeared as if impassive, also, after a savage dismissal of my writing, I stayed quiet, and I see for the first time how that stance of seeming indifference, and the silent disavowal of criticism, had been acquired long ago, in far less studied surroundings.*

If the dining room was all display, the kitchen was raw power. It was small for the number of people they served, but remarkably efficient. What was singular about it was that all the chefs were Chinese, except for the pastry maker. While it was not uncommon to find Chinese working in Catskill kitchens, they never made up the entire cooking staff, as they did at *Goldman's.* I was a busboy, and had no occasion to face them in front of the counter. But imagine my surprise when I first went into the kitchen after the meal was over, and saw the entire crew seated around a common table, rice bowls and chopsticks in hand, and shared plates of food. I cannot say why it struck me so curiously, but I thought of all the food they cooked, steak, prime rib, gefilte fish, chopped liver, chicken soup, the din as they served and hassled with the waiters to get it on plates and trays, and when the show was over, and quiet fell upon the kitchen, they settled down to their own familiar cuisine. It made sense of course, but it was still an oddity to me, two worlds fused together, yet even now I can see them in their white coats, the top two or three buttons undone, relaxing the uniform, indifferent to the last minute tasks of the waiters running in and out, satisfied with the success of their work, and at ease with the rest of the evening.

But if the Chinese crew was tight and flawless, their work was overseen and buttressed by the steward of the kitchen. Mrs. Franklin was the one absolute power in that place, and her throne, a hard chair pushed back against the wall and flush with the stainless steel counter, gave her a clear view of the waiters as they picked up their entrée orders—*Don't forget the parsley! Put on some parsley, you schmuck!* A small nondescript looking woman, her hair in a flattened bun, she sat hunched over on the wood chair, legs together, a cigarette constantly between her fingers, with a glass tray close by, and I remember staring hard at the cigarette, for she let the ash grow forever, and I wondered how long she could wait before flicking it. When I first saw Picasso's portrait of Gertrude Stein, although no resemblance, the pose alone was enough to make me flash back to Mrs. Franklin. It might seem odd that so small a woman could instill such fear in the dining room staff, but the power was all in the position, and a steward guarded the costs of the food, which was a major expense. At the time I had no idea what exactly she did, apart from sitting in judgment on all who passed the swinging door that opened into her demesne, and she could get you fired with a tap of her cigarette, but later, in the Catskills, I saw stewards who were very active in the kitchen, moving around and screaming at the lower cooks for wasting food or ordering wrong, but *never* raising their voices to any head chef. Mrs. Franklin just sat in her chair. Even Dave, the maître d', deferred to her, a very tall man with a rough city accent, always dressed in a tuxedo that struck me as lounge lizard wear, matched with black shoes so glossy I wondered if you could comb your hair in their reflection. Gossip had it that the two of them were lovers, but I never believed it, because I could not picture them locked in an embrace, let alone having sex. But Dave was constantly in and out of the kitchen, while Mrs. Franklin never set foot in the dining room. *For that shining room, like the maître d', was all a show, open to an unending cavalcade of people who dressed for dinner, to be served by others hardened in the process, and who thought all that crafted food was wasted on swollen palates. Years later, when I first read George Orwell's* Down and Out in Paris and London, *I was drawn back, and recognized attitudes not so different from those Orwell described, except that nobody would have mistaken a dive bistro for a plated dining room.*

5. A MOUNTAIN RAT

How do you get to the Catskills? Unlike the lame joke about Carnegie Hall, it requires no practice, just keep driving past the auditorium and beyond the borough until you hit the Saw Mill River Parkway, I always loved the name of that road, then to Tarrytown, which triggered *Rockefeller* in my mind every time I saw the sign, across the Tappan Zee Bridge, holding my breath in case I should stall smack in the middle of the Hudson, and finally connecting to Route 17, the start of a long road to hotel heaven. As the spring term was ending, I thought about the summer, *Goldman's* being strictly a weekend operation, and I needed full time work. Since I now knew my way around the Jupiter agency, my rogue pickups from Christmas past still sharp in my mind, I went into New York one morning, climbed the stairs to their office, and returned home with a slip for a job at *The Pines,* location, South Fallsburg. I have to remind myself that despite having worked almost an entire year in New Jersey, I knew nothing of the Catskills other than the name. All I can surmise is that the crew at *Goldman's* did not work upstate. So even though I was seasoned, and knew the eccentricities of a single hotel, I would be a novice in an alien resort. The prospect did not trouble me, but it was clearly going to be different, and the first taste of that came when I went to pick up my uniform and linens, for the woman who ran that tucked away closet, white hair, stocky, mid to late 60s, had a mouth that shocked me, not that I appeared shocked, but I never heard anyone, let alone a woman, swear as she did. The chefs at *Goldman's* and *The Pines* were never foul, although they would scream and toss insults if a waiter was slow, or fumbled his orders, but it was mainly the dining room captains who poured out the occasional curse before or after the meal. And *fuck* was not a word that rolled off anyone's tongue casually or commonly. It is why even now I can see the scene, at the tail end of my last year in college, I had been working weekends in New Jersey, when the captain, sitting at his desk and barking assignments, told me to come back the following weekend. *Mel,* I said, *I can't work next week, I have graduation,* and before I could punctuate the sentence he shot back, *fuck your graduation, work a doubleheader.* So two years earlier, when a mature woman, in a snow-white uniform, passed me clean towels, along with a stream of obscenities, it was my entrance into another new world.

Words have an uncanny ability to pick up ancillary meanings that fix themselves like barnacles to the sound, cannot be peeled loose, and may even overwhelm the original. Catskills is one such, its geographic designation never the first thing that comes to mind, conjuring up instead for people who know nothing other than the word a picture of Patrick Swayze and Dirty Dancing, *and for those who know something it calls to mind comics who went on to greater fame, Red Buttons and Jack Carter, or even Jerry Lewis, who reportedly played at* Brown's *in Loch Sheldrake, or was he a busboy there? A bit of misremembered lore perhaps. And then there is the* idea *of the Catskills as a shorthand figure for an unsophisticated but aspiring Jewish middle class, escaping the heat of the outer boroughs, rarely from Manhattan, into the cool luxuriance of a chaise by day and cocktails and comedy at night. This was the reward for wives and mothers whose lives were still bound by city neighborhoods, and whose husbands made enough money for them to turn away from the* kuchalein, *those bungalow colonies with their dense units and poorer relations. But if* Catskills *came to define hotel culture in ordinary conversation, for me that word was* the mountains, *a specific and neutral phrase that put space between myself and all those paying guests who carried their habits from the city and checked them in for one or two weeks. A mountain rat was a tradesman whose skills resided in his head and his hands. He knew the hotels from inside, and had worked enough of them to be easy anywhere. He lived in the underbelly of towns like South Fallsburg and Monticello and Swan Lake. And his attitude was a variant of Oscar Levant's famous quip about Hollywood, 'take away the fake tinsel of the dining room, and you find the real tinsel.' For some, the phrase hinted at mild disdain. For myself, I always used it jocularly in public, yet silently considered it a badge of honor.*

As I think about *The Pines* I am struck by what a large part of my young life was passed there. It was a home away from home, bromide aside, for even though Irving and I put up with each other's peculiar habits, our apartment could hardly be called a home. We never ate the same meal, though we faced each other across a tiny table, opposite a standing sink, in a windowless kitchen that opened on the hallway. He was more of a cook than I, making pot roasts and meat loafs that I inwardly sneered at as a reversion to old Jewish culture. And there was little soul searching that went on between the two of us. But if our apartment was a roof and a secure place to sleep, *The Pines* was a world elsewhere, and took me in as one of its own. *Goldman's* was primarily a weekend gig, and in my last year in college often just a Saturday night affair. But living a hundred miles from the city, day in and day out, for two months straight, you were far from all you knew and everyone familiar. If you were lucky, it led to unexpected and unforgotten intimacies. Even friendship could be an intimacy, for it was at *The Pines* that I met Anna, a blonde, self-possessed German girl who always told the guests she was Swedish, because fifteen years after the war the word *German* was still enough to strike a raw nerve.

Miriam remembers my returning from the hotel with stories galore, imitating the comedians and keeping her in stitches as I acted out my tales from one of the mountains' "lost empires," a figure lifted from an old novel, and in this case a prophetic one. Yet I remember nothing of those stories or my performances. I did not go to the shows as a matter of course, and I usually saw a comic when I was working in the bar, after the dining room, for extra money. Early on I would hustle for bar and coffee shop gigs, starting about 10 pm and going until 1:30 or 2:00 in the morning. At some point I gave that up, as I was making enough money with my station, and it was a killer to get up at 7:00 am after only five hours of sleep. But I could never forget the bar scene, for the room was always dark, the small, round tables so tightly spaced that it was a wire act to edge between them with a tray of cocktail and highball glasses balanced on the fingers of one hand. And since women took up most of the seats at the tables, the drinks live on in name alone: Brandy Alexander, Whiskey Sour, Singapore Sling, Sloe Gin Fizz, Grasshopper, Daiquiri, and simplest of all, Cuba Libre, a ubiquitous mixture that accompanied the passion for Cuban music in all the hotels, where Tito Puente and Joe Cuba reigned supreme. These sweet and colorful concoctions were topped—I never heard anyone say *garnished*—with cherries and orange slices and pineapple, which the waiters added after picking them up from the bartender, who never failed to call out after us—*don't forget the garbage!* Years later, when I first sat in a bar in Honolulu, and saw the spectacular ornamentation of a Mai Tai, I reverted instantly to those old hotel drinks, and could never quite shake the feeling that this tropical wonder was secretly an island joke.

A swirl of memories leaves me feeling rich with reminiscences, yet stuck as to where or how to begin. The dining room at *The Pines* was far larger than *Goldman's,* holding at least twenty stations, which meant sixty tables and near five hundred people. The maître d' was Mr. Schreiber, medium height, conservative suits, and a mustache, the whole package reminding me of the movie actor Ronald Colman. His desk was at the front of the room, just inside the entrance, and he was there all the time. During the winter he worked in Miami, and the gossip I heard, and never confirmed, for there were always stories that moved as if in an air current through the hotel, was that he ran the dining room at *The Fontainebleau*, which just a couple of years after its opening was a legend among hotel staff. I credit the story because most of the waitresses at *The Pines* were professionals who worked in Florida during the winter and followed Schreiber up to the mountain resort for the summer. These women were tough, they worried about their legs, whose veins bore the visible signs of tray-years, the perennial movement between north and south, and how long they could keep it all going. Some took a protective interest in me, as if to help break me in, it might even have been maternal, though I never thought of it like that, but I *was* the youngest waiter on the floor, a baby really among all these veterans.

Here is how that happened. I got the job as a busboy from the Jupiter agency in New York, and settled in among eighteen or twenty other boys. It was the start of a very busy weekend, possibly Memorial Day, the hotel was booked solid, when Mr. Schreiber called the busboys to his desk. One waitress had failed to show up, he was on the spot for a replacement, and it was too late to call Jupiter, for even if they found someone she could not get up from the city in time. So he questioned whether any of us had ever worked as a waiter, none had, and then he asked if anyone would be willing to take on a station for the weekend. My hand shot up instantly. I am not sure if any others volunteered, but there could not have been more than one or two at most. It was not because they were indifferent to the benefit, waiters made more than busboys, but the leap between the two jobs was far steeper than it looked to an outsider, who saw nothing more than tables and dishes. The waiter controlled the flow of the meal, deciding when to take orders, holding them in his head, retrieving them from the kitchen, where on a whim the chef might get in your face, and all the while keeping personal contact with the guests. If your experience amounted to nothing more than removing plates, serving coffee, and fetching the odd dish, then you were wise to be cautious.

Writing this now makes me think of the movie cliché of the understudy who learned the star was ill and told she had to go on. And suddenly a star was born. That the image even passes through my head shows how saturated our minds are with melodrama, and it is better to state openly, where it can dissipate in plain ink and simple sentences. But when Schreiber confronted us the movie never entered my mind. I was confident I could switch jackets, had survived Ida for more weeks than I could count, and given the chance for my own station I jumped. And so Schreiber gave me the nod, I ditched my Nehru uniform, picked up a short waiter's vest, and bought myself a black bow tie rather than a cheap clip-on, which every waiter wore. I took an odd pride in learning to tie the bow, and when the meal was over I drew it open, unbuttoned my collar, and let the tie's black flaps lie flat on each side of my white shirt, and for some reason I felt all grown up, and very cool.

A small romance, or something like, in four very short letters. "Barb" was working at The Pines *that first summer, a lovely, lanky brunette, home state Iowa, student at Cornell College, who knew there was another Cornell? who knew anything of Iowa? I have no idea how she wound up in the Catskills, and no picture in my head of her on the floor of the dining room. Yet we spent time together, I must have been slightly smitten, is that an oxymoron? although I cannot recover any sense of that smitten-ness, the recollection of emotion lost to all but the* idea *of it, which exists only in memory, in four scribbled pages, and in a song that I attached to the romance, which ever after would bring back the memory of its existence, if not the existence itself.* Once in a While / Will you try to give one little thought to me / Though someone else may be / Nearer your heart … I know that I'll / Be contented with yesterday's memories / Knowing you'll think of me / Once in a while. *The song suited my romantic imagination, enabling me to create a scene of thwarted love that took on more meaning than the actuality. What remains of that actuality are the letters, and if unable to recreate our past they at least verify it, and in the process make it alive in a small way. The first was dated September 14, 1958.*

I started this letter before but what ever I write just doesn't sound right. What can I write Barry? – What can I say to you? I'd like to talk to you & see you but letters are so stupid – I probably won't write you again but I don't know. If I get terribly lonely & depressed I guess I will write – If I send a card you'll know I was thinking of you…. I'm here – I hate it – I wish I could see you – how I hated to

*leave – it's so frustrating to try & write to you – if you don't
write I'll understand completely Barry. We know – we are
so much alike – don't think I'll ever find such a friend as
you. Just remember, mon petit cher ami – 'July 4ᵗʰ isn't only
Independence Day.' I'll never forget the way you said that.*

This was an early gesture, it could not have been more than
two weeks after she left, the envelope, with the address "Dining
Room Staff, Pines Hotel, So. Fallsburg, N.Y." was forwarded to
me in Brooklyn. Barb did not even have a salutation, it was still
near enough in time to our closeness, and in the awkward struggle
for expression she revealed for just this once a depth of feeling that
surprised me. We had spent the July 4ᵗʰ weekend at her aunt's apartment in the Village, there was no sex, but it was two-three days by
ourselves, and if I remember near nothing of us at the hotel I can
still see that tiny apartment in the building, the elevator man who
saw us and knew the aunt, and those two young people who found
it such a charge to be alone together in the city.

But time had already begun its work. Three weeks later came
a Hallmark card, and the simple statement that she was seeing her
old boy friend again. I was more disappointed than hurt, it was
after all a small romance, and I had a kind of grudging admiration
for what seemed to me her unfiltered honesty, which she later made
even plainer: "Seems funny doesn't it? I hardly feel I know you anymore except as a friend in the East." She wanted information about
whom to write to at The Pines, she never had the correct names
or spelling of Mr. Schreiber or May Schweid, the owner, it was as
if everything Jewish was still a foreign country to her, yet she was
conflicted about going back the next summer: "N.Y. is too frustrating. Iowa is simple and middle class but it's such a happy, friendly
state." All this was new to me, for that entire place was a blank, and
I could conjure up no visual image of Mt. Vernon, the college town

and address on the envelopes. But in her last sheet, more than half a year after the first, she mentioned her boy friend, and of a sudden, opened up about me:

> I do love Gary and don't be sarcastic about it you snip –
> You're so hard & cold sometimes it would take a sharp, hot
> nail & a hammer to produce a bit of warmth within you.
> Life is wonderful, Barry. Sure – you've had it rough – but
> you're luckier than lots of people – you've, at least, got a
> good brain in that noggin of yours & if you'd only let it –
> I'll bet it would show you a lot of people who are genuinely
> good & kind.

What struck me then, and stays with me now, was something of myself, the first brief etching in script from someone who knew me closely, and made no effort to soften the sketch. Was she right? There is no question I had a tart tongue. Whether I was "hard and cold" I cannot say, certainly I never felt that way, and seeing it on the page jarred me. Although it was common for friends to call me "cynical," I always bristled at the term, for their cynicism was my realism. But I never held Barb's lines about me against her. It was the last time she wrote, she never again showed up at the hotel, but if once in a while I hear the old Dorsey-Sinatra recording, or maybe the Pied Pipers, I think of her, and our sharing cigarettes in my parked Ford, after the dining room was long closed, as we dreamed on all the world in the black night before us.

Was it heady to be nineteen years old and have your own tables on the floor of a major hotel? When I thought of it, in a quiet moment, I felt lucky, for it was mere chance that got me the job, but not privileged, for it was my own skill and diligence that kept it. But there were few moments for reflection, either you were working non-stop in the dining room, or recovering on your bunk bed between times. I am not sure if it was the nature or conditions of the work, but there was little care for status in the dining room. Clearly all jobs were not equal, but all who were doing them were. Many of the busboys were Dominicans, my first exposure to men who wore hairnets, which I acted blithely unaware of, and to bits of street Spanish, like *mariposa* as the slang term for *fag*. The busboy for my station was Cuban, one of the fastest at his trade, at times I even wondered if he was better than me, yet guests often short changed his tips because they *knew* he was "Puerto Rican," and did not need as much as a Jewish boy. What strikes me now as more strange than ironic is how the parsed and fabled *Borscht Belt* was oblivious to the tribes and colors that peopled the place. It is as if everybody knew by sight or from gossip that the hotels were filled with Chinese cooks and Central American and Irish busboys and Cuban and "Swedish" and Iowan waitresses, yet in some inexplicable way they thought of the "mountains" as altogether Jewish, their own place elsewhere, not the Poconos, or the Adirondacks, where the *goyim* went. The oral stories of the Catskills perpetuate this shallow picture, but it was not one that the staff ever saw.

Instead, there was the odd discovery that popped up when least expected. The kitchen at *The Pines* had a Rube Goldberg-like dishwasher tucked away and separated from the food service area. It had a long and wide conveyer belt, was operated by men who had been picked up from the Bowery, or were they shanghaied? so went the gossip, and who scraped and stacked the dishes with the expectation they would stay sober. When the machine was not working, or if there was a dramatic slowdown, you knew that paychecks had come and men had gone. But glassware was considered too fragile to be placed on this Chaplin-Ball lookalike. Just inside the kitchen, to the left and less than a foot away from the swinging doors, was a small sink, and a single Bowery man responsible for these glass dishes. Every time I pushed through the door I saw his back, hunched over, cautiously cleaning the glass under the running faucet. But one feature riveted me, apart from the care for his work: there was always a rolled up copy of a magazine sticking out of his right back pocket and reaching up to just above his lower back. I cannot remember if I asked him about it first, or if I saw the title in its rolled up form before talking with him, but it was the *Saturday Review,* and he was a regular reader. We could talk only in snatches, moments after I entered the kitchen, before I ordered my dishes, or hanging around near the end of the meal, when I had nothing on my tray, and I was always amazed at the range of his reading and his ease of conversation about writers. I can remember him chattering on about John O'Hara, as if he were just another author, even a familiar. I was a great fan of O'Hara's, and knew no other person in the hotel I could have talked with about his books. At one point I was emboldened enough to ask him how he wound up bent over a sink, but he took no offense, seasoned as he was to such questions, and if the details now escape me, I remember thinking that at one time he knotted a tie, folded a newspaper, and took the train to an office just like anyone on the street, or in a magazine. It seemed like a very normal story, one John Cheever might have written, and I later realized, without even knowing it, that the word *Bowery* had lost for me some of its deep and crusted meanings.

A letter dated November 21, 1958 from my aunt Irene, who had moved to Los Angeles, lists the sum of my earnings that summer at *The Pines.* "What's left of the $1,000 that you came home with. I hope you held on to enough to see you through the first semester." The figure is close enough to reality, for there was no reason to clip the truth in writing to Irene, whom I loved dearly, and who, like so many of the Goldman clan, had terrible luck, dying young, away from family, in a city as bright as it was distant from Bedford Stuyvesant. But she was right, the money certainly could not last the year, so during the winter I made a few weekend trips up to *The Concord,* one of two major hotels that stayed open beyond the summer. When *The Pines* built its own indoor swimming pool and flung open its doors for the winter holidays, I ditched *The Concord,* a place I never much liked. It was a behemoth, so huge that the distance from anywhere in the dining room to the kitchen was like running a football into the end zone. Yet there was one saving grace about the hotel. I met a kid from Queens there, Chick, whose last name was as Irish as a shamrock. We were both busboys, bunked and hung out together, and I liked getting to know someone my own age who was other than Jewish, and who did not go to Brooklyn or City but St. Johns, a school I knew of in name only, and for its basketball glory. Chick had a true gift of gab, a classic Irish charm, and he palmed that blarney on me every Sunday morning when he half-begged, half-cajoled me to pick up his tables so he could go to church and attend Mass, which I knew as much about as the internal combustion engine. And like Charlie Brown, I would invariably say yes, and bus his tables along with my own, although I never saw any indication of a halo upon his return to the dining room. Still, Chick was different enough from Jewish boys to make his sleight-of-hand tolerable, for while our own kind were quick and funny, none had that smooth affability that persuaded you of all they said, yet at the same time tantalized you with a hint that they were pulling your leg. Chick and I would occasionally talk of meeting in the city, but nothing ever came of it, in a way we were mountain rat buddies, and when I stopped working in our common hotel I never saw him again. But when Connie, a blonde, stocky Cuban waitress at *The Pines* insisted I drive her after work to *The Concord* so she could dance to Tito Puente's band, I half-hoped I might see Chick there, for I could never separate him in my mind from that monster of a resort, and I never after met an easy talking Irish guy who did not instantly remind me of him.

What follows is a very short story of two chefs, a young woman, and me. It was just before the start of summer, the hordes of guests had not yet arrived, and I was at the hotel early, puttering around my station. Suddenly there was the maître d', who rarely ambled over to anyone's tables, with a special assignment for me. A new girl would be working the floor, she had limited experience, and he wanted me to break her in, let her trail along for a week until she got the hang of the job. As I was trying to process what he told me, for this maître d' was the last person to hire anyone without serious skills, he revealed that the girl-in-training was a friend of the chef. While I was not sure exactly what that meant, I kicked myself for coming up to the hotel so soon. I would be dragging a novice behind me all week, made bearable only because my tables would be half-filled, and so a disaster was unlikely. All this flashed through my mind, and then Mr. Schreiber introduced the girl. She could not have been twenty years old, gorgeous eyes, porcelain skin, the whole set off by jet-black hair cut in a Louise Brooks style. It was as if someone had stepped out of an old movie magazine, and was standing next to me, head tilted up, for she was shorter, and waiting for me to say something. And all I could think was *what exactly does being a friend of the chef mean?*

She came from Hershey, Pennsylvania, which alone struck me as strange, a town named for candy, or made of candy, strange that people actually lived there, and she had worked in a local restaurant where one of the chefs cooked or knew the owner.

Either she wanted to venture out to a wider world, or earn more money, or the chef wanted her near him, any or all of these reasons might have explained her presence in so alien a setting. It was as if a sweet and lovely girl was suddenly transported to some big city, in the form of a mountain hotel. On some level I knew instinctively to keep my distance, whether out of regard for her innocence, or fear of the consequences. The head chef at *The Pines* was Polish, broad across the chest, well over six feet, with a toque that went higher, he wore rimless glasses that in the heat of the meal slid just below the ridge of his nose, and he looked over them at the waiter on the other side of the stainless steel counter, as if daring him to make a mistake. The second chef, younger, slimmer, less tall, was brought out to work with him as his protégé. And it was this young man, several years older than myself, who was Julie's presumed friend.

Both chefs were responsible for the entrées, so when I went into the kitchen it was a tossup as to whose line I would wind up on, as I wondered fitfully who might be harder on me, or if they would screw up my orders, but they never did, for the protocol of the meal was stronger than the covert private war that was waged among the three of us. When Julie was in the kitchen, and if I happened to be there, I noticed the courtesy, even delicacy that they adopted towards her, as if they could not do enough to ease her load. The seasoned waitresses on the floor all tried to talk me out of any relationship, but in truth there was no affair. Julie and I would drive around a bit at night, or sit in the car and talk, she was attracted to me, maybe even falling a little, but I resisted, despite her protestations that the chef was nothing to her. Perhaps I was afraid of what might happen if we pressed together, but she was so sweet and open that listening to her voice and being next to her in the car was its own tactility, its own kind of closeness. Why did it all have to be so complicated? Why was it impossible to make love to her with nobody else to care or bother? But it seemed it was always going to be like that, *every damn thing you do in life you have to pay for,* as Édith Piaf memorably said. And the price of being chaste was that the chefs never believed me, Julie was never mine to touch, nobody got what they wanted, and everyone was unhappy in their own way. There was no real ending to this story, except that the young chef went back to Pennsylvania for two-three weeks, and when he returned he took me aside in the kitchen, walked me into the night air, said simply that he had no claim on Julie, and all was fine. We shook hands, and I no longer had to gird myself when I pushed through the sliding door. But the summer was soon over, the nights emptied out, and there was no time left for the boy and girl. Julie proved the strongest, with the most courage, for she faced down two big men from her home state, and never flinched. She bit her lips at my own awkward distance, or was it cowardice? and walked away tall and upright. Looking back, I think to myself what would have happened if early on I had taken her in my arms, kissed her hard on the lips, and told her she was carved from ivory? It would have inflamed the chef, might have gotten me fired, and in the end I would be sitting here with another romantic memory. But none of that came to pass. Instead, a very long time ago there was an ordinary boy, twisted and torn inside, bound fast to his narrow picture of reality, nothing more than jungle law really, and with no idea how to make a dream in black and white come true.

All lunches were hard, but Saturday's was the toughest. If the hotels were not strictly Orthodox, they were mostly kosher, and the practice on Saturday mornings was to serve juice, boiled eggs, and cold plates—prunes, grapefruit, fruit dishes, etc. By midday guests had their toes on the floor edge of the dining room, as if they had been straggling across the Sahara and by a stroke of fortune had found the horn of plenty. And the choices were beyond counting, for besides the menu they could add their own dishes, *could you get me a bowl of cucumbers and sour cream instead of this melon?* or *I wasn't in for breakfast, would you please ask the chef to scramble a couple of eggs for me?* At lunch people arrived in scattershot fashion, and a table of eight would be asking for everything from juice to dessert at exactly the same time. You had to remember the dishes and keep track of the course, lest you ask for the entrée without first having served the soup. And triple all that for three tables. Saturday lunch was the supreme test, and even the best waiter was likely to get *buried,* the term for losing control of the meal. I write this by way of preface to an incident that seems comic in retrospect, but was anything so at the time. It was just before a long weekend, and the maître d' was shy one busboy. Without thinking, my mouth before my head, I suggested a friend of mine. *Call him,* he said. Jack had been in school with me at Jefferson, was living deep in East New York, and needed work. Although he was apprehensive at first, I persuaded him to take the first bus out of Manhattan. If I had paused for just a moment, I would have realized that he had never been in a hotel dining room, could not carry two dishes let alone a bus box, and was a classic babe in the woods. I had been doing the job for so long it was second nature to me, and I forgot that once I too knew nothing. When he arrived, and Mr. Schreiber said to me, *you wanted him, he's yours,* I was taken aback. It never occurred to me that he would be *my* busboy, just *a* busboy.

Jack was tall, broad shouldered and handsome, perfect for central casting, but not especially dexterous, and he moved with a bear-like gait, unlike the swift and nimble-footed apprentices I was used to. While these *dis*abilities were problematic, they paled before the problem of his intelligence: he was a philosophy major at Columbia. That was fine in the world, but the dining room was another place. If I told him to do something he would ask *why*, as if it were a question of logic, and we ought to discuss the *reason* for the action, like *why* should he serve coffee if nobody asked for it? Given that he could not keep the tables cleared, or would run into the kitchen every time anyone asked for something—a cardinal sin, that—he drove me to distraction. *Just get the coffee,* I blurted out, *this isn't a philosophy class.* But I was not angry with him, more upset at myself for being blind to the obvious, for in the guise of helping I succeeded only in making a jumble for the two of us. We could not even enjoy each other's company, he was bunked with the busboys, and we barely saw one another outside the dining room. By the third day I could not wait for it to be over, and I suspect he felt the same. But as I look back on that weekend, and think of Jack, and his disruptive-diverting queries, he shone a light without knowing it on an odd feature of hotel culture. Most guys working the floor were prepping for medical or law school, or dentistry or accounting. I knew no one carrying trays and studying history or philosophy. While the pre-meds were all smart, it was more text smart than intellectual, and they were never in knots over *why* anything was in that cacophony of trays and plates and silver. As for *meaning*, the Fifties' existential word, that would have to wait for a later day, after the hotel-sounds were stilled, and another voice, long silent, could be heard as if for the first time.

"Is that all there is?" Peggy Lee half-sung, as she pondered what it all meant, or if it meant anything at all. And after the paragraphs of prose, after the mountains have been stained in black ink, is that all there is? What am I missing? Something has eluded me, and I am not sure exactly what. All the recounted vignettes cannot revive

the days and nights spent in bunks and lounges and coffee shops, time spent with your fellows, rarely with guests, for even when you walked through the corridors of the hotel the last thing you wanted was an encounter with a guest. It was as if we shared a planet with another species, and wanted nothing to do with them. The people of the tables were your people. Friendships were close, and cherished. When Anna wanted to see her boyfriend in Brooklyn, I did not hesitate, even though it meant bolting right after dinner at 9:00 pm, barreling south for three hours, and turning around in less than five, in order to be back by 8:00 am. If desire drove her compulsion, we all shared the tedium of days without end, and relished any chance to get away, even for an hour or two. On one occasion, I was in the back seat of a Beetle, no memory of where we were going, the car flipped over, I instinctively wrapped my arms around the girl next to me, but by some miracle we all four walked away without a scratch. There are snapshots in my head that missed making it into sentences, like the anxiety of leaving the hotel just as the snow started falling, my car without a heater, a glass road for miles on end, and praying silently I would make it back without an accident and before freezing silly. Or the crap games and poker hands that began in the bunkhouse after Sunday lunch, when everybody was flush with tips. All that cash, nowhere to go. The bills on the floor and the table were staggering. Nathan Detroit would have been proud. I did not have the stomach to risk it all in an afternoon, but in truth I was a lousy card player, and I was clueless about the dice. Several years later I hung out with a waiter whose father was a professional gambler. In the afternoons he would cruise the lobby, pick up poker games with the guests, and always come back a winner. Since we were good friends I asked him if I could play, thinking I might learn something, but he dismissed it out of hand, "I don't want to take your money, Barry." I also carry a picture in my head of the waiter in New Jersey, where we worked catered affairs, and when it was a *wedding he came alive, peered at the ceremony almost greedily, but at a distance. We teased him, but no one wanted to know more.*

The mountains were so removed from the city that none of my friends in college had any idea what it was like. It was a different life altogether, and sometimes when I was driving up I felt as if I were going home. It might have been the freedom from Brooklyn, from school, from hard decisions. Up there I lived in a bubble, no care for food and housing, just show up for meals and take orders. How hard could that be? No wonder I had the bright idea of moving up there after graduation, renting a bungalow, working the hotels on weekends, and having weekdays free for myself. I would be a writer. It was probably a pipe dream, for I was convinced I lacked a gift for invention, and could not imagine writing anything beyond one autobiographical book. Still I thought the idea imaginative, and living alone in Monticello, while not exactly Paris, had a romantic touch of its own. On a deeper level I suspect I was simply afraid of the risk, much like the dice and poker. But I have strayed from my snapshots, and so I pass along one lasting picture. I was walking through the corridor of the hotel an hour or two after lunch, people were outdoors, and the feeling was that of a Sunday afternoon, quiet, the air resonant as if scented, but with no scent, I was glad to be there alone, with nobody to bother, nothing to think about, when I stopped before an open room, the doors flung wide, and a small combo rehearsing, piano, bass, drums, and a singer. Fly me to the moon / And let me play among the stars / Let me see what spring is like / On Jupiter and Mars....*I had never heard the song before, and stood there rapt, watching that young woman in slacks and a blouse finesse the tune as if it were a lover, slowly and rhythmically, so that I never forgot her and the afternoon, and never lost the picture of that boy in an empty hallway, transfixed by a song he only half-realized held the promise of love.*

6. A FIELD IN FLATBUSH 2

WHAT ARE YOU going to college for? A simple question and a fitting return of the narrative to my other life. In my ear it sounds like pure Brooklyn, *why are you wasting your time in school?* as well as *what do you plan to become?* Whether the line is Jewish or New York or both I leave for the linguists to squabble over. For myself, what I was in college *for* was a serious question, and one I had a hard time with. It was not as if I wanted to *be* something, but I was very conscious of having to pick a major that would enable me to work when I graduated. This was early on, and before I realized how well I was supporting myself from the hotels. For the first two to three years I chose majors that I imagined promised work, although in truth I had no visible idea as to what kind of work they promised. My brother-in-law told me about industrial psychology, though I doubt he had any real knowledge, but it was enough for me to take an auditorium-sized course, with a boring text, and nothing to interest. Next, I moved on to economics, and again, if I were asked what I expected I would have been dumb, except that the word *sounded* solid, even important, and gainful work was sure to be my reward. I took a course in labor relations, which was more like history, aced it and was excused from the final. At last, I thought, I found what I was after, marched straight ahead into money and banking, and went down as if in a bog. It was chemistry all over again. What was left? At this point I could no longer hold the lid on a prospect that kept pushing its way to the surface: teaching. My sister and her husband, my cousins the Nordells, all were public school teachers. Having exhausted the few hapless ideas of what I was in college *for*, I gave up and felt I had to follow suit. The only hitch was a single class required for entry into the education program. The title escapes me, but it had no content, and the girls I knew who took it dismissed it as an utter waste. So despite my willingness to swallow whatever stuck in my throat, certainly not pride, if I even knew what that was, I found myself in a dilemma: having persuaded myself to become a teacher, I could not bring my nose down to sit through a vacant course. And in the end, education, like chemistry, psychology and economics, went the way of all flesh, only this time without ever having been sampled.

It is a wonder to me that it took almost three years before I realized that the classes engaging me were the ones I was suited for. I just accepted that I was going to study what interested me, although *study* implies something systematic, in my own mind I was simply *reading*, not doing anybody harm, and indulging myself in a familiar and comfortable pastime. After ditching education, I declared for English, took Alfred E. Neumann's signature line and stopped worrying about what I would do with *the rest of my life*. And when I thought about it, I had been taking literature courses all along, even outside the English department. There was the wonderful course with Dr. Wolfe in Greek Tragedy, who I then took for Modern European Drama, the readings from both stayed with me for years, and bolstered my interest in theater, to the point that I reviewed a college production of Christopher Fry's *Tiger at the Gates,* giving it faint praise, and shortly after met the beautiful actress who played Helen, and who exhibited so much tact that I wanted to eat my printed words. Now, having declared a major, I needed a minor. Although one more class in either World Literature or Art would have done it, for some unaccountable reason I elected Philosophy. It is even stranger because I was always at sea in the classes. And the Philosophy majors struck me as weird, never animated, often abstracted when they talked, like disembodied figures in a comic strip, with words appearing alongside in a bubble. But friends of mine registered for Philosophy classes, including Irving, who had a far keener mind, and so I signed up as well.

Oddly, I can remember all my World Lit and Art classes, only two professors from my minor. John Hospers was down-home in manner, nondescript in dress, but formidable in intellect. In Aesthetics, a course I lifted from shamelessly for my English classes, he had the remarkable ability to make abstruse ideas clear, as if he were doing nothing more complicated than showing a tourist how to read *The New York Times* on the subway. It was later that I learned of his role in the founding of the Libertarian Party, that he was its first presidential candidate, and that it traced back to his meeting Ayn Rand when she lectured us in our freshman year. The other professor was an altogether different figure. Dr. Walter Cerf, short, dapper, with a barely detectable German accent, taught Modern Philosophy, where I lay buried in the dark caves of Edmund Husserl. Apparently Dr. Cerf never fully accommodated himself to American culture, disliked the idea that women were equal students, and began every class with *Good morning, gentlemen!* This grated on the women, but there was little they could do. One day the boys concocted an ingenious prank and skipped class. Dr. Cerf came into the room, looked around, and said, *Well, I see there's nobody here today,* and walked out. This story comes second-hand, I cannot point to its source, but it made the rounds among the philosophy grinds, and has stayed with me all these years, which is more than I can say for Husserl.

At long last, English, *I almost wrote* love, *for Sinatra's soaring rendition of Cole Porter's song long ago seared itself in my brain. Suddenly I find myself engaged in an interior dialogue, thinking this section could be done in italics, as an interlude, with the allusive three words spurring the form, but then I recoil and realize there were many teachers, and more books, and they require a strict narrative, when that thought gets parried by another, to omit is the greatest art, and so I come full circle, the first words triggering an old song, in turn stoking reflection and steering me pell-mell to assorted reminiscences. Dr. Claire Sacks, keen intelligence, commanding presence, prodded us to memorize a dozen or so lines from the* Canterbury Prologue (Whan that aprille with his shoures shoote / The drought of Marche hath perced to the roote), *and which years later I would toss out in fractured Middle English in my own class when we were reading T. S. Eliot. Dr. Miriam Heffernan, a senior professor with New York attitude and an Irish temper—smart, tough, and unforgiving—reamed me out in class for what, I had no idea. But it was there that I first learned of Henry James, a name that sounded to a Brownsville boy like a joke, along with a book title I thought ready-made for somnolence. What did I know? I found myself as riveted by* A Portrait of a Lady *as if I were Isabel Archer staring at the fire, trying to make sense of it all. As luck would have it, in my senior term I took a seminar in James, taught by Dr. Ulla Eder, a young professor recently out of Wisconsin, an engaging woman with a hip style, eager, exciting, and utterly audacious as well as singular in her display of cleavage. My connection with Henry James was solidified.*

Finally, Dr. Morton Seiden, the closest thing to an Esquire *model if* Esquire *thought to feature bookish-looking professors. Slender, brown hair, tortoise shell glasses, he wore gorgeous wool suits, usually with vests, colored shirts complemented by cloth ties, and it took almost two weeks for him to repeat an outfit. He entered the room, put a sheet of paper on the desk, glanced at it once or twice, and then proceeded to pace back and forth across the room, behind the desk, and lecture virtually nonstop for fifty minutes on the history of literary criticism, from the Greeks forward. Many Brooklyn College professors were adept at lecturing without notes, but he was in a class all his own. And he liked to appear provocative, saying there was no such thing as progress in art, in fact all art was in decline after the debacle that was the French Revolution. It was in that class I wrote an essay on a Keats sonnet, applying my new-found passion for New Criticism, and although the scribble has long since disappeared, for some reason the first lines of that poem never left me* (When I have fears that I may cease to be / Before my pen has gleaned my teeming brain), *and recur even now as I write afresh. Dr. Seiden encouraged me when I told him I was considering graduate school, said the Midwest was a good choice, they pushed people through, not like Columbia and NYU, and when I finished I could come back to the city. The department advisor, on the other hand, looked at my record as if she were peering down from the Pantheon, and said imperiously that she hoped the graduate schools were not lowering their standards. Not much I could say, so I left her office in silence.*

But we return to the class in Literary Criticism for our ending. The course was content rich, I still have the textbook, and as I pass my eyes over the pages I am astonished at the penciled notes throughout, so thick as to nearly qualify as Marginalia. On the

*morning of the final I was sitting in the college library, waiting
for the clock to turn, when I looked around and saw nobody from
class. That struck me as odd, and after a few moments I went to
the English department to confirm the time, discovered the exam
started an hour ago, rushed to the room, Dr. Seiden looked up and
said,* Mr. Menikoff, how good of you to join us, *and passed me
the exam. I wrote for the remaining hour, and when I handed
over the booklet he asked if I wanted more time, I could continue
writing in his office. I shook my head my head no. I was done.
When I saw the A soon after I could only attribute it to disgorging
all that Criticism in a single hour, which even now strikes me as a
bit of a tour de force.*

All these pages of school and work, of places and people
re-remembered and reassembled, and I suddenly stop and ask
myself, where was my family all this time? Was their absence
from the tale deliberate, or simply a lapse of memory amid the
compounding sentences and stories? But it was neither, I saw
nothing of my father, who after leaving the grocery on Belmont
Avenue retreated into his wife's world in Jamaica, and although
I surely visited my sister on Long Island, nothing sticks. But in
my last two years at Brooklyn College I kept up two connec-
tions with relatives. The deepest and most extensive was with
the Nordells, who lived in a house on Bedford Avenue, several
blocks from the college. Nat was my mother's first cousin, heavy
set, thinning hair combed straight back, rimless glasses, with a
genial temperament and welcoming smile. His wife Dora was
smaller, slenderer, less voluble, but with a disposition as even
and warm as her husband's. I visited their home with my mother when I was a boy, a year or two before her death. And I have
a distinct yet unfocused image of being in their house when
the *Andrea Doria* sank, two months before I entered college.
Although I have no idea how I reconnected with them in my

last year and a half, I could not have been gladder, as I would show up unannounced on a Friday evening for dinner, and there would always be a place for me. The dining room, facing the street, had a huge, squarish table that took up most of the space, with the parents at one end, close to the kitchen, and their four children, Susan and Larry, two years on either side of me, Charles and Maxine, all sitting in their selected places, with my seat at the far end. I loved going there because the house was always warm without ever being stuffy. Yet I could never shake the thought that they were a strange family, for nobody ever screamed, anyone could speak, and everyone was treated with respect. In my head the only place this shangri-la existed was on *Father Knows Best,* and even as a boy I knew that was fake, much as I watched it with wide eyes. But there was nothing false about the Nordells. Nat and Dora were unaffectedly kind, and their children never made me feel like an intruder. When Susan married I was invited to the reception, at the house on Bedford Avenue, and I relished a conversation at the dining room table with the groom's father, my first close encounter with a Sephardic Jew, who gave me a bit lesson in Ladino. After leaving New York I lost touch with the family, but years later I found my cousins again, bearing their graduate degrees lightly, and was pleased but unsurprised to learn they were all continuing their parents' practice.

What follows is a story within a story, both relate to family, with the inside tale more interesting than the frame. Around the time that I sat at table with my second cousins, I would also drop in for dinner at my aunt Anna's, always in the middle of the week. The wife of my father's brother Irving, she was a beautiful woman, dark hair, slender face, sweet smile, and as I write this I see her as if she were standing before me, the intervening decades buckling and falling away as if in an instant. She and her husband had a duplex on East 7th Street, in the same quiet, leafy, district as the Nordells, a world apart from my six-story building on Albany Avenue, edged with concrete, and mere blocks away from the sirens in and out of Kings County Hospital. Anna made simple dinners, which I ate with pleasure, but her warmth and affection were even more satisfying, although I could not drive away the thought that my mother was never far from her mind. At table, Irving was silent, so conversation had to be juggled between Anna and me, and with the help now and then of their older son. And here is where the second story comes in. Jackie Menikoff was about four years younger than me, but a boy who could barely be contained by high school. He wanted me to get him a job at *Goldman's*. At first I thought he was joking, he was underage, it was beyond me how he would get out to New Jersey, let alone manage school and work, and in truth I did not want the responsibility for him at the hotel. But Anna was unable to keep him in check, and to placate her I agreed to give him a chance.

What then? Jackie was a busboy for the briefest of moments. I saw little of him in the dining room, for he started cruising the hotel lobby, hawking portrait-sketches drawn on the spot, and next after he turned up as the boy friend of a daughter of the hotel. In just under two years he had gone from high school junior to hotel worker to itinerant portraitist to suitor of the rich. By the time I left the city I lost track of him, but we made contact a year or two after, and set a time for lunch in Midtown, as he was working in a nearby office. I see us at a two-seater, away from the walls, in an upscale but not lavish restaurant. Jackie was eager to talk, I was glad to listen, he had been in California, at the Disney studios, but even so august a workshop could not contain him. And then he said to me, as if in confidence, *You know who I want to be like, who I admire?*

Sammy Glick, he's somebody who knows what he wants and goes after it. Sitting across from him, an audience of one, I felt like Nick Carraway, privy to a shocking secret, and at the same time surprised that he even knew *What Makes Sammy Run.* But I said nothing. It was probably for the best. And that was the last time I saw him, for he dropped "Jackie Menikoff" and adopted a British moniker, replete with impeccable origins. Later, if his name ever came up, I reverted instantly to an image of his mother, soft, sweet, and always glad to see me at her table. Anna died young, and I could never rid myself of the visceral feeling that the women that meant most to me in those years, Mama, my aunt Irene, Anna, moved on far too early, leaving me with nothing but traces in my mind.

All things come to an end, Stevenson wrote as he finished a fantastic story, but my ending at Brooklyn College was the alternative to fantasy, a small and mean-spirited story despite its bright spring setting. It was the third day in May, and the city was conducting one of its periodic tests designed to shield us from a surprise atomic bomb attack. They were called "Civil Defense" drills, and they went as far back as elementary school, when we hunched over, kneeled down, and got under our desks. By the end of the Fifties the whole enterprise looked like nothing so much as a ludicrous charade. But they did not stop, and in response students at colleges throughout the city planned to protest the drill by refusing to take cover, although what kind of cover we would take confounds me, since nobody was descending into the subway, all we could have done was stayed in our classrooms. In any case, Brooklyn College students gathered on the steps of Boylan Hall, and as the sirens went off they stood their ground, and would not move. Now here is where the story takes its odd turn. Not only was I *not* protesting, I was vacant as to the entire affair, which is even stranger since my roommate was in the thick of it. On the morning of the action, I was clear across the square, in la-la land or my own brown study, when I saw the throng of students and started walking over to see what was happening. A college security guard and a patriotic chemistry professor were ordering students to turn in their identification cards, which many did eagerly. I passed my card over as well. It was an absurd gesture, I was merely a passerby, mainly because I tended towards apathy about politics, despite living with a theoretical revolutionist. I would like to say I acted out of solidarity with my fellow students, but it was probably peer pressure, and the idea gossiped around that the more cards that were collected the less likely the school would be to retaliate against anyone. And most of us knew next to nothing of our school's inglorious history. Just two days later, everyone received a letter from the dean of students, Herbert Stroup, demanding a "written disavowal … or face the consequences of your actions." We had six days to respond: "Failure on your part to do so will be taken by me, as the College's disciplinary officer, to be tantamount to an admission of your deliberate complicity and violation of the requirements of the College."

Stern words, and as I read his letter now I have to wonder what he thought we had done, other than mill around under the open sky, on a clear morning, while a screaming siren told us we would do well to go inside in case a more powerful bomb than the one dropped on Hiroshima should find its way to Brooklyn. The president of CCNY, Buell Gallagher, a champion of freedom, shrugged and let the episode slide away. But Harry Gideonse, Brooklyn's president, had made his reputation ferreting out Communists and sympathizers among the faculty ever since his appointment twenty years earlier. While I was ignorant of all this, and focused solely on the dean's letter, as I look at it now I am certain that Stroup was nothing more

BROOKLYN COLLEGE
BROOKLYN 10, NEW YORK

OFFICE OF THE DEAN OF STUDENTS

May 11, 1960

Mr. Barry Menikoff
639 Albany Ave.
Brooklyn, N.Y.

Dear Mr. Menikoff:

According to the information available to me, you took part in an unlawful "protest meeting" on May 3, 1960, on the steps of Boylan Hall, in connection with the Civil Defense air raid drill. Your response (or lack of response) to my letter to you of May 5, 1960, which sought to determine whether you were in fact present at the demonstration as a protestor convinces me that you are responsible for a breach of the College's requirements. This violation constitutes conduct unbecoming a student of the College.

Regretfully, therefore, it is necessary for me to suspend you from the College for a period of four days, from May 17 to May 20, inclusive. During this time you are prohibited from attending classes, making use of the College's facilities (such as the Library), participating in student activities, or trespassing upon the campus.

I trust that this action by the College will cause you to reflect deeply upon your obligations as a citizen both of the College and the community.

Sincerely yours,

Herbert Stroup
Dean of Students

HS:ef

than the president's stalking horse, although I credit him with the composition and its imperious tone of indignation. It was a letter that made you want to toss it on impulse, but it was not as simple as that. No one knew what "consequences" were being hatched in the dean's office, and I was a month away from graduation. Every grown-up offered the same advice: apologize, or admit to ignorance of the college's rules that were so grossly infracted. But the dean's letter stuck in my craw. I replied on May 10th, one day before deadline.

> *Dear Dean Stroup:*
> *It is not without regret that I am limiting the scope of this letter. My original intention was to present a considered discussion of Civil Defense air raid drills, and my reasons for deeming them hopelessly inadequate. But that is not what your letter seems to demand. It asks whether I was a "deliberate participant" or a "hapless bystander;" do I wish to disavow my action or suffer its consequences. It would be an insult to my intelligence and self-respect to state that I 'did not know what I was doing'. As a mature student, and citizen, I accept full responsibility for my action. Conscience dictates no alternative.*
>
> *Respectfully yours.*

It was a very young person who made that paragraph, as befits its style, but even now the argument seems defensible, and at the time he could not have imagined saying anything else. I walked the letter to Stroup's office, passed it to his secretary, who opened and scanned it quickly, dropping it on one of three piles. The first said *fuck you,* the second *I'm sorry,* and the third was inconclusive, for the dean to decide. Since the office claimed one hundred fifty students had participated, this was a neat way to sort through the responses. In the end fifty-three of us were suspended from college for four days: "During this time you are prohibited from attending classes … or trespassing upon the campus."

What to do? At first I thought of going to school despite the directive, how would anybody know? It is not as if our photographs were plastered across the campus. But that quickly passed, as there seemed no point to such a futile gesture, and then I thought about the real problem. None of us cared about the suspension itself, it might even have felt like a merit badge, except for the college's draconian policy on class attendance. A course that met three times a week allowed for no more than five absences, a sixth disqualified it for credit. As this was near the end of term, anyone graduating in a month was understandably bent and twisted at the prospect of the missed days pushing him or her over the top. Not knowing where to go or what to do, I drove to the Grand Army Plaza library, as if to a refuge. I passed in a kind of daze through the bronze doors, looked up and saw Professor John Hope Franklin standing by the card catalogue, going through a file drawer. I had sat in his class once after he arrived at Brooklyn College, for we all knew he was important, even if I could not say precisely why, and believed it had to do with his being Black and chair of the history department. But I can still see him in the classroom, sitting ramrod straight on a hard backed chair behind the desk, his large head and dark face framed by rimless spectacles, and with a piercing, serious look in his eyes. I stood in place in the library, my scrambled brain unable to sort itself, and as if by impulsion I slowly walked over to him. He was very tall, and even more magisterial close up. I told him of my anxiety about the absences, but I am sure my manner said more than my pleadings, and though I have no memory of his response, the mixture of words and presence had a calming effect. It is a strange thing about extraordinary people, they often go without notice when right before you, and only when gone are they seen fresh, and anew. John Hope Franklin left Brooklyn College as his fame rose, but ever after, when I read of him, I thought of those several minutes in the library, and the man who with few words, and none, put me at ease until term's end.

7. ENTER KRISTA

I'VE BEEN THROUGH the mill of love *runs the jaded lyric to an old song, but one not written for me. I was twenty-one years old, and knew little of sex, and less of love. That would all change soon. For it was at* Goldman's *that I first spied Krista, sometime in the early spring. A blonde with hair just above her neck, and a soft, full figure snug-fitted in a white uniform, she bobbed a long metal tray on her left hand as she sashayed through the dining room, looking for all the world as if she were a dancer from some exotic place, and I could see her dressed in bright clothes that swayed with her body, and here she was in little Verona, and came from the Bronx. When she turned, and I saw her face, and took in her gray-green eyes, something melted deep inside. The writer who said there was no explaining the mystery of a face that charms you was a bona fide romantic, but also spot on. And so it was with Krista, she shook and held me, like the poet's wind in the luff of a sail, and I knew I wanted her, even if I little understood the wanting. It was desire, to be sure, but what was that if not love made tactile? Of this too I was ignorant, but it did not matter. She knew it for me, and danced with me to the end of the music, as if for the first time.*

Where to begin? Chronology makes sense, but I have only the most distant recollections to rely upon, that and a sheaf of letters that Krista wrote during one long separation of three months. They recover desire, and at the same time revive pain, so they are a bittersweet treasure, but the summer of 1960 seeps through the lines. *Darling…If I could put the summer past out of my mind the ache wouldn't be so bad, but bits of it keep flashing through my mind, the time when I had the earache and you took me to the dr. at 4:00 A.M., the few times we spent at the bungalow and I told you of my love for you, the weeks we spent in Loch Sheldrake, the days, nights, and times we spent together keep haunting me Barry, the first time we went to the Beach together before summer I was so head over heals in love with you. It was like a first love. I don't think you realized how happy I was. The days are gone, perhaps forever. What remains is hope, desire, anticipation, and the knowledge that someday we'll be together again.*

Although we met at *Goldman's* doing weekend work, we were both dining room pros and expected to spend the summer in the mountains, though it took me awhile to discover we had two very different mountains in mind. We had not seen each other much in that tail end of spring, a movie date *(I saw "I'm All Right Jack" today and I thought of you so often during the picture. We went to see it on our first date. I love you Barry)*, a beach date *(Another thing that sticks in my mind … is how you looked that day at Jones Beach. I think I did a pretty good job to hide my feelings for you, but oh I loved you Barry. More than I thought possible for me)*, and strangely these both remain blanks to me.

But there was a memorable weekend at Lake Carmel, a hamlet in some no-name county, with four college friends, and our single excitement was to go horseback riding. If Krista was at a disadvantage by not having gone to college, she was the only one who knew how to sit in a saddle. My roommate Irving perched on his horse and was led by the animal to a slow moving stream, all the while insisting that the horse wanted to stay by the water and not leave. I was trotting easily behind Krista on a dirt road abutting the county highway, when she suddenly spurred her horse, mine flew instantly into a full gallop, I gripped the reins without the slightest idea of how to slow the animal down, and passed long minutes thinking I would be thrown forward or astride if I slipped the stirrups. But Krista reached a restaurant across the highway, brought her horse to a halt, and mine just slowed and followed suit. I remember wondering to myself if she had done that on purpose, or if she simply took off without realizing my horse was bound to do the same. I wanted to be angry with her, but since I was not thrown I felt I came out looking all the more like a rider, and walked straight. And as we were the only couple in the group that was sleeping together, I swallowed my quiet ire and let it go.

Although Krista later wrote of being *very much in love* well before the country weekend, we had not made plans together. A station awaited me at *The Pines,* but she had worked in the Adirondacks, at a place called *Green Mansions,* which she talked about as if it was some kind of paradise. I imagine I listened, but nothing sank in. I was simply besotted, as the old novels called it, and it made not a blade's worth of difference whether by love or sex, for in truth I could not tell them apart, nor even thought to. She was way more experienced, which embarrassed me at first, but I was a quick study. If I am unable to reconstruct what exactly was going through my head in late May-early June, I have a vivid picture of a single act that even now amazes me. Krista was working a long weekend at her ambrosial retreat up in Chestertown, I was beside myself at not being beside her, and

I got behind the wheel of my Ford and set out to drive up to Schroon Lake. Now one of my weaker subjects was geography. I could get my way around Brooklyn by car, I had the route to Verona down pat, and the trip up to the mountains was second nature. Beyond that, if I had not been there, like the Bronx and Queens, they were runes to me, and I had never been in the habit of reading maps. Yet I was going to trek up to New York State's great mountain range, which might as well have been the Rockies, with no paper guide, no provisions, and absolutely no conception of how far it was from Brooklyn. I drove through the day and beyond, the distance could not have been less than seven or eight hours, if I knew where I was going, and I arrived in the dark of the night. It is a puzzlement how I got there, but I remember the pounding in my brain all the way north—*Krista Krista Krista,* like the refrain in a popular song. When I saw Dustin Hoffman a few years later, in his little red sports car, dazed and hyped, running up the coast from Los Angeles to San Francisco in search of Katharine Ross, I was struck dumb, for in a flash I was transported back to that unending drive to the near end of New York. I surprised the girl, who with a little help secured a small cabin on the premises, the scent of pine and mountain air suffusing the space, where we stayed awake and burned alive all through the night, never stopping until the sun came up, and she had to go in for breakfast, and I started back to the city *(Honey, if the first night in New York will surpass the one in GM I won't mind a bit).*

The Pines made a place for Krista, and the summer began well. We decided to rent a bungalow in town instead of living separately in staff quarters. While that sentence might sound benign today, back then it had a touch of daringness. No one used the phrase *living together,* for the common throwaway was *shacked up,* which had a tincture of sexuality and a tint of opprobrium about it. Yet we never thought of it that way, having our own bungalow just seemed the natural thing to do, the wish for privacy driven by desire and our intense adhesion to each other *(Whenever I think of the days spent together at the bungalow this past summer I get a little shiver. I want so much to live with you and share everything with you).* And so we had love and work, or work and love, although I had never heard the great doctor's formula for being a grown-up, and it would not have meant anything to me at the time if I had. But the work was a necessity, because my next year in graduate school was going to be on my own dime, and I was determined not to labor outside of classes. My experience and reputation got me a prime location in the back of the dining room, where a fourth table could be set up if the house was full. I could not have designed a better plan if I had been carving out the stations myself. But as the wise poet said, even the most carefully crafted schemes can tumble and fall apart.

I could not have been on the floor more than two weeks when I came down with the flu, at first I thought it was a cold, tried powering through the meals, but finally had to give it up and retreated to the bungalow where I collapsed. I remember little of Krista during these days, but for the most part I was wiped out, and the only image I retained of our rental hideaway was from a supine position, scoping a wide, open room, with a narrow porch outside. Well, when young you recover quickly, and I expected to return to work shortly, as the stations in the dining room ran in weekly cycles. Krista came home, I was reclining in bed, but I can still see her, standing kitty-corner at the other end of the room, looking at me as if from a distance. *I called Green Mansions, they have a job for me and one for you, as my busboy.* As I write this now, how many long years since, the story sounds ridiculous, and my own actions preposterous.

But I was twenty-one then, Krista was all to me, and there was a pleading in her face that made it impossible for me to say *you have got to be out of your mind*. In truth *I* was the one who was crazy, unable simply to tell her *No,* and not knowing why. It would be easy to say I was getting so much sex that I could not think straight, or that I was afraid she would leave me if I refused to go. Neither was the reason. I was more conscious of not wanting to hurt her than of any wish to make her *happy,* since *happiness* was not a word in my vocabulary, as it was an alien concept in my family. Looking back, I can see that I was willing to absorb the pain so that Krista would be spared, although I never understood it at the time, and just went along as I was used to, acting before thinking, indeed acting without thinking.

Our Fallsburg idyll now was ended, while our journey to the northern lakes had just begun. There was no rush, we had a week before work started, and I could not help counting the lost earnings in my head, a week for the flu, now a week for travel, but I had enough sense to know that carping about it would do neither of us any good, and kept silent. I have little memory of the actual drive, and am perplexed by my odd resistance to picking up maps, for I was always attracted to place-names, and remembered what Hemingway called them, concrete things that never lied, in that clear book of his that never left me. On that straight shot into the Adirondacks on old route 9, signs for *Glens Falls* and *Warrensburg* and *Ticonderoga* spaced the miles, and I would imagine exiting and wandering the towns to see if they were as interesting as their names. If we never did anything quite so carefree, we did get off at Bolton Landing and rented a cabin on the water. Lake George was storied enough so that even a city boy knew of it, and although we had a sliver of a view, just being yards from that long lake, alone in our wooden shelter, was a pleasure and a wonder at the same time. We went to a nearby town one night to see a movie. It is curious how movies can work like popular songs, seeding themselves in memory as lasting reminders of where and when you saw them. That evening it was *The Apartment,* a black and white film that scrawled *New York* as a running title across every frame, from cast to dialogue to plot. As a habitual moviegoer, I had been mesmerized by the experimental new films that were all the rage, especially *L'Avventura* and *The Four Hundred Blows,* and I can savor the moment and the feeling as I stared in stunned astonishment at the final shot of the small French boy, frozen in time. But I was still an ardent fan of Billy Wilder, I knew that his long time writing partner was a hard-schooled Brooklyn boy, and the movie carried me back to the streets of the city, just as years later, whenever I heard those lovely romantic chords that opened the film, with their deep strain of bitter, I would be instantly transported to that cabin on the lake, and a lost love.

High in the Adirondacks, close to cold and limpid lakes, far from New York, *Green Mansions* was like nothing I had seen in the Catskills. Small, rustic, made of wood, and with a sloping, overhanging roof, it was more like a supersized country inn, the antithesis of the showy, glitzy structures that I was familiar with. And the eating space reminded me of a sedate restaurant rather than the pandemonium of a borscht belt resort. What is even stranger is that the entire period up there virtually erased itself from my memory, and there is not a single mention of that pit stop in paradise in all the letters. Yet here is where furiously rubbing the lamp paid off, for a small scene that had long floated in the shadows of my mind suddenly took shape. At *Green Mansions* Krista bunked with two or three waitresses, and I would go over after lunch to hang out until the evening meal. The girls stripped off their uniforms as soon as they were through the door, pulled their half-slips up above their bras, and *voila!* a short chemise that could be worn comfortably through the afternoon. It was a kind of dishabille that I might have read about, possibly saw in a backstage movie about show people, but no book or film could capture the excitement felt by a young man. The girls were unembarrassed, even a bit saucy, and it was hard to contain the charge in the air, as I would gaze at Krista, her slip tight over her breasts, dropping just above her knees, the silky white lingerie emitting sex with no smell except the scent of skin, and the taste of flesh imagined in the mind. All the erotic life in that room, reclining on bunk beds, sitting in a chair writing letters, leaning against a window, magazine and Coke in hand, and all a boy can think of is how easy it would be to slide that slip down, run his hands softly over that bare stomach, unhook a bra, take the girl in his arms and bury himself in her face. A fantasy that made no sense, really, but the air was almost too thick to breathe, and my girl friend loved me.

FAREWELL

AND HOW SHALL I END? How halt this long winding that is the making of a book, the unspooling of a life, and whose finale is another beginning? Memory is a compound of pleasure and pain, the clear handwritten lines that return a beautiful girl's voice to my head exists side-by-side with the hard knowing that the presence of the past implies its present absence. It is as if a memoir were a version of Keats' urn, with feelings frozen in time, never to live, and unable to die. But there is another view, reflected in that famous Highland warrior's shout, I've a grand memory for forgetting, a line I have reverted to often in this long struggle to balance remembering with its alter ego. For a memoirist is a bit of a tightrope walker, along the wire reminiscences are slowly gleaned, and on either side, a fall into oblivion. If he makes it across, his memories green and intact, he has both a book and a life, and the vast forgetfulness has done no harm, and no one is any the wiser. Krista and I returned to the city after the summer, and stayed with Irving on the Upper West Side. It was only two or three days before we were to leave for Wisconsin. The rear of the car was filled with just enough room to see through the window. I was a born New Yorker, but it never crossed my mind not to leave a packed car overnight on a city street. When we came down the next morning, the car had been broken into, but as there was little of value in a student's belongings, all looked fine. Except for the glove box, where I had placed Zeyde's gold watch, the only gift Bubbie had ever given me. I felt too embarrassed to say anything, fought hard not to brood, for I cherished that watch, and the hurt went deep. It would be another secret loss, I thought to myself, like my long gone mother, and one that would stay with me, forever hidden from the world.